Charting
the Sea
of
Darkness

*The Four Voyages of
Henry Hudson*

DONALD S. JOHNSON

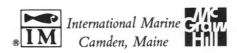

International Marine
Camden, Maine

To Nick Benton

Published by International Marine

10 9 8 7 6 5 4 3 2 1

Copyright © 1993 International Marine, an imprint of TAB Books. TAB Books is a division of McGraw-Hill, Inc.

Library of Congress Cataloging-in-Publication Data
Johnson, Donald S., 1932–
    Charting the sea of darkness : the four voyages of Henry
    Hudson /
Donald S. Johnson.
      p.   cm.
    Includes bibliographical references and index.
    ISBN 0-87742-321-0
    1. Hudson, Henry. d. 1611.   2. Explorers—America—
    Biography.
    3. Explorers—England—Biography.   4. America—Discovery
    and exploration—English.   I. Title.
    E129.H8J64   1992
    910'.92—dc20   92-32657
                                        CIP

Questions regarding the content of this book should be addressed to:
International Marine
P.O. Box 220
Camden, Maine 04843

Edited by James R. Babb, Dorathy Chocensky, C. Dale Nouse; Production by Janet Robbins; Design by Edith Allard; Typesetting by A & B Typesetters, Inc., Bow, NH; Printed by Arcata Graphics, Fairfield, PA

Illustrations on pages 83 and 136 reprinted with the permission of Rijksmuseum-Stichting, Amsterdam.

Contents

List of Illustrations

CHAPTER FIVE. *The Great Bay of Ice*

List of Illustrations

Preface

How did I come to write about Henry Hudson? Most people know little more about Hudson than that a bay and a river bear his name. That was all I knew, too—until I received a call from Nick Benton, a master rigger and longtime friend.

Nick did the rigging on *Nakomis*, my small schooner, many years ago. Since then he has worked on much larger vessels, including the *Western Union* and *Pride of Baltimore*. In 1989 he was in charge of creating an exact replica of Henry Hudson's ship, the *Halve Maen* (*Half Moon*), and he wanted me to come to Albany, New York, to act as construction director. I couldn't accept, but did agree to spend several weeks as part of a "visiting master craftsmen" program.

During my stay with Nick and his family we had long discussions about the ship and about Henry Hudson. Nick asked, "What was Hudson doing exploring the Chesapeake Bay and the Hudson River when his contract with the Dutch East India Company expressly stated that he was to search for the Northeast Passage to the East Indies, and take *no other route*?" No one came up with a satisfactory answer. I had my own belief, but no solid grounds to support it.

Out of these conversations grew an article on the *Half Moon* and the four voyages of Henry Hudson, which was published in *Maine Coastal News*. Subsequently I came across the evidence needed to back up my conjecture that Henry Hudson was obsessed with finding the Northwest Passage. It was part of his plan to sail in this direction even before he embarked on the 1609 voyage. Bolstered by this new information, the original article grew into the present book.

Just as every explorer is indebted to predecessors whose discoveries pointed the way, so too do I have thanks to pay. I wish to acknowledge John L. Allen for his insights on cartography and the search for the Northwest Passage, which he shared in a symposium on "The Land of Norumbega," sponsored by the Maine Humanities Council. Thanks also to Toby Mostel, who took the time and patience to read the manuscript and make countless suggestions, corrections, and criticisms. And finally, my gratitude to James Babb and Tom McCarthy, my editors. Undaunted by the size of the task, and with unfailing good humor, they took my rambling discourse and turned it into a book worthy of pride.

At this point it is customary for the author to absolve those who have worked with him from any responsibility for the errors and problems that may be found in the book, and to claim them solely as his own. I don't know when this practice started, but in 1627 Captain John Smith did it in the preface to his *Sea Grammar*. Since I have not seen it expressed better elsewhere, I will let Captain Smith speak for me:

Honest Readers,
If my desire to doe good hath transported mee beyond my selfe, I intreat you excuse me, and take for requitall this rude bundle of many ages observations; although they be not so punctually compiled as I could wish, and it may bee you expect. At this present I cannot much amend them; if any will bestow that paines, I shall thinke him my friend, and honour his endevuors. In the interim accept them as they are, and ponder errours in the balance of good will.

Your friend,
John Smith

Donald S. Johnson
Perry, Maine
August 1992

Introduction

Historians have not been kind to Henry Hudson, not through any enmity toward the man or his accomplishments, but evidently through indifference. In the period immediately following Hudson's expeditions (approximately 1611–1615), a flurry of publications on his voyages appeared in Holland. At about the same time, in England, historian Richard Hakluyt collected the manuscript journals of that country's maritime explorers, including Hudson. Hakluyt's *The Principal Navigations* covered a period of 1,500 years of "great traffiques and discoveries," and did much to awaken England's interest in her maritime heritage.

But the Reverend Samuel Purchas, a later compiler, gave us the most information about the life and ventures of Henry Hudson. Purchas took the Hakluyt records and added other relevant documents in his own book, *Hakluytus Posthumus, or Purchas His Pilgrimes*, printed in 1625. Unfortunately, in the few years between the voyages and the publication of the documents, some of Hudson's original writings were lost or destroyed. One of the most important of these was the logbook from his 1609 voyage, when he first visited America, discovered Delaware Bay, and explored the river that now bears his name.

We know less about Henry Hudson's background than we do about that of his great contemporary, William Shakespeare. There are no parish registers, diaries, town deeds, or local accounts to document his life. He was an Englishman who resided in London; he had a wife named Katherine and three sons named Oliver, John, and Richard. Other than that, we can only conjecture that he was the descendent of Henry Hudson the elder, alderman in the city of London in 1555, and that he may have had relatives among the officers of the Muscovy Company, an English merchant venture organized for the purpose of finding a northern sea route to China.

Everything we know about Hudson's career took place within a four-year period. On April 19, 1607, before departing on his first voyage in search of a northern passage to China, he took Holy Communion in the church of St. Ethelburge the Virgin, within Bishopsgate, along with ten men of his crew and a boy (presumably his young son, John). On or near June 21, 1611, he died, a victim of treachery and mutiny. During this short time he made four momentous voyages in search of a passage to Asia, journeys that greatly enlarged the geographical knowledge of the world.

It is not only biographical material that is lacking. Though some portraits appeared later, there are no contemporary portraits, paintings, or written descriptions of Hudson's appearance extant to give us an idea of his likeness. Not even in the decorative borders of the many maps that poured forth from the Netherlands during the seventeenth century can an image of Hudson be found.

After his death, nearly two centuries elapsed before further interest in Henry Hudson is documented. In 1809, the New York Historical Society commemorated the 200th anniversary of his 1609 voyage and the discovery of New York. Forty-five years later, the Historical Society of Delaware printed a rejoinder to New York's special claim to Henry Hudson. Its interest in Hudson is explained in the following quote from an address to its members:

People have been so long accustomed to regard Henry Hudson as the peculiar property of New York, that scarcely anyone dreams of associating his name with the history of Delaware, and very few are aware that in point of time the latter state has prior claim to him as her discoverer. On the 28th of August, 1609, he entered and explored this bay and river, revealing to the world this beautiful region to which your Commonwealth owes its name; whereas the Half Moon *(Hudson's ship) did not enter Sandy Hook until the evening of the 3rd of September. New York is accordingly Delaware's younger sister.*

Thereafter, with the exception of two books—one by G.M. Asher, published in 1860, and the other by Llewelyn Powys, published in 1927—interest in Hudson and his voyages appears to die out. Searching the history books on the European discovery of North America, we find the explorations of Henry Hudson largely ignored—a far cry from the admiration Hudson's accomplishments aroused during his time. Captain John Smith wrote, "the bounds of *America* doth stretch many thousand miles: into the frozen partes whereof one Master *Hutson* an English Mariner did make the greatest discoverie of any Christian I knowe of, where he unfortunately died."

If my only motive for writing this book had been to prevent the achievements of a remarkable man from falling into the brackish backwaters of obscurity, it would have been well worth the effort. But there is another compelling reason for further study of Henry Hudson: His 1609 voyage initiated the Dutch colonization of America and spawned many of our religious, philosophical, and governmental ideals.

Although we are accustomed to hearing about our English heritage and the part English and French colonists played in the struggle for control of New England, Dutch involvement generally is overlooked. However, it was the Union of Utrecht—a proclamation of independence from Spain made in 1579 by seven provinces in the Netherlands—that sparked both the French Revolution and the movement for American independence from England.

The English Bill of Rights, which circumscribed royal power and guaranteed limited freedom of religion, was signed under the reign of the Dutch Prince William III, who became king of England through marriage to Queen Mary II. The precepts of freedom of religion and separation of church and state were incorporated in the Massachusetts Constitution in 1780 and in the American Constitution seven years later. Other legacies of the

Dutch are our free public school system, legal equality of men and women, and a strong mercantile, entrepreneurial spirit.

Henry Hudson's exploits and great geographic discoveries were marked by sheer excitement, adventure, and intrigue. It is difficult to imagine the courage it took for those first voyagers to leave behind familiar lands and set out across the unknown seas in search of a distant, elusive goal. The ships that made these journeys were incredibly small. Hudson's *Half Moon*, only 65 feet long and 17 feet wide, had to contain all the stores, food, and drink to maintain the vessel and its twenty-man crew for a voyage of two months or longer. Conditions aboard were nearly intolerable. The cramped accommodations offered no privacy. The sailor rarely had time to change his clothes — even if he had a second set. The men quickly became infested with lice and infected with typhus, scurvy, and dysentery. Sir Walter Raleigh described the seaman's destiny as: "to endure and suffer . . . from a hard cabin, cold and salt meat (often crawling with maggots), mouldy biscuit, dead beer, wet clothes and want of fire for cooking or warmth." Cabins of privileged guests, or even the master, were "but sluttish dens that breed sickness."

If storms at sea or disease and poisoned food didn't claim the seaman's life, there was another enemy to confront — pirates. Piracy and privateering were rampant during Elizabethan and early Stuart times, and violence at sea, common in Western European waters, carried to North American waters as well. The second half of the sixteenth century and beginning of the seventeenth century were chaotic times in Europe, with most nations engaged in open hostilities. Any ship, be it French, English, Dutch, Spanish, or Portuguese, regardless of allegiances or treaties, was fair game for any other — every vessel was a predator, and every vessel was prey. Privateering was simply considered a form of commercial enterprise. Add to this the anxiety of potential confrontations with "savages" on the distant shore, and one might wonder why anyone would have considered crossing the uncharted sea. That they did is an eloquent testimony to their courage.

Fortunately, most of the source material about Henry Hudson is written in English, eliminating the need for translations. Journals of the voyages are reproduced here as they were written, except that I have taken the liberty of changing archaic phraseology and spelling to enhance readability. Unless there was a specific reason for retaining the original place names, they too have been changed to the present familiar ones. I have also converted distances, originally given in leagues, to their equivalent value in miles.

The use of side margin notes, a common practice in seventeenth century books, served as a form of running index. They appear in Samuel Purchas's books, *Purchas His Pilgrimes*. Many of these notes have been retained as Purchas wrote them—but not all. Some seemed redundant and have been deleted; others have been added where further explanation was necessary. All maps and charts, with the exception of the one drawn by Henry Hudson, have been redrawn from reproductions in various atlases of cartography. While this has the great advantage of stripping away all unnecessary detail, thus enabling one to focus attention on the relevant information, it prevents one from seeing the great beauty and full account of history contained in them. For further enjoyment and enlightenment, I urge the reader to seek out the original copies of these maps and charts.

Venient annis saecula seris
Quibus Oceanus vincula rerum
Laxet, et ingens pateat tellus,
Tethysque novos detegat orbes:
Nec sit terris ultima Thule.

In later years the age shall
  come
When the Ocean will unloose
  the bonds of nature
And the vast earth will stretch
  out,
And the sea will disclose new
  worlds:
Nor will the globe be utmost
  bound by Thule.
    Seneca: *Medea*, Act II, v.371.

CHAPTER ONE

Charting the Sea of Darkness

*T*he quest for the Northwest Passage would shape Henry Hudson's destiny. To explain why, and to understand the man, we must examine his times.

In the sixteenth century Spain and Portugal ruled the southern oceans, and the countries of northern Europe were compelled to search in other directions — north, northeast, and northwest — to partake of the treasures and profits to be gained from trade with the Far East.

The notion of a passage to the north of either Arctic Canada or Russia and Asia was based on philosophy and logic rather than on knowledge of distant regions gained from travel and discovery. The concept of a spherical earth and a geography of the general arrangement of land and water had been present since Greek and Roman antiquity. It was an ordered architecture in which masses of land were distributed over the surface of the earth in a balanced fashion, and all the world's waters were interconnected and in constant flow.

Plato, in the fourth century B.C., described in

Figure 1-1. *Fourth century cosmography of the earth, by Aurelius Macrobius in* Interpretatio in Somnium Scipionis, *published 1483. Obviously, knowledge of geography of the world at the time was more advanced than shown here, but philosophers of cosmography were more concerned with theoretical constructs of the earth than with practical details.*

Phaeda how all the waters pierced the earth to a sea called Tartarus at the center. All the rivers, lakes, and oceans were drawn into this "primary and original mass" of water. The constant oscillation and surging of this underground sea kept the rivers and lakes replenished, "but all of them pass round again in a circle to the original source from which they flowed."

Aristotle did not accept Plato's theory, and pointed out that according to the incline of the Sea of Tartarus, at times its surge would have to force water to flow uphill.

Aristotle placed the earth at the center of the universe, surrounded by spheres of the remaining three elements — water, air, and fire. These, in turn, were

Charting the Sea of Darkness

enclosed by the spheres of the planets—*Saturni* (Saturn), *Jovis* (Jupiter), *Martis* (Mars), *Solis* (Sun), *Veneris* (Venus), *Mercurii* (Mercury), and *Lunae* (Moon). Each planet was firmly attached to a rotating sphere whose equator inclined in a different plane to the others. Beyond this was a sphere containing the fixed stars. All these spheres were controlled by the outermost sphere, called *Primum mobile*—its own control imparted by "divine power."

Although elegant, this schema could not explain all the observed motions of the planets, and in the second century A.D. the geographer and astronomer Claudius Ptolemy tried to reconcile the discrepancies. He described a sphere rotating around a center, which itself moved in a circle around the earth. The planets moved in their own small circle, called the epicycle, at the circumference of the major orbit of the sphere, called the deferrent. This cosmic schema, with only small modifications, remained the accepted concept of the universe until the middle of the sixteenth century.

Then, in 1543, Copernicus made revolutionary changes to this established system. He described the motion of the planets as a circular orbit around a stationary sun, and accounted for the alternating pattern of night and day by the spinning of the earth on its axis. A year, he said, was one full orbit of the earth around the sun.

Great as these changes were, the basic structure of the cosmological pattern remained unchanged from the time of Aristotle. The universe was still conceived as a finite whole, constructed of a limited number of spheres moving in circles and bound by the outermost *Primum mobile*.

The Church, in its early years, rejected not only the paganism of the Romans but much of their scientific knowledge as well. Time spent investigating natural phenomena instead of contemplating the true faith was considered wasted. Many distinguished Church leaders condemned the notion, put forth in the sixth century by Pythagoras, that the earth is a globe. The corollary theory—that each country has its "antipodes" on the other side of the world, where there live people with "opposite facing feet" — was rejected as well. In his *Institutiones Devinae*, Lactantius (A.D. 260–340) exclaimed:

Is there anyone so foolish as to believe that there are men with the soles of their feet above their heads? Or plants and trees that grow downwards? Or, indeed, rain, snow and hail that falls to earth upwards?

I really do not know what to say about these matters except that, at times, I think people discuss them as a kind of philosophical joke. On occasions, it is possible that sensible and learned men maintain that these lies can be upheld as truth, as though to use their intelligence for wrongful purposes.[1]

Where is the wonder of the hanging gardens of Babylon, Lactantius asked, if one accepts such a thing as the antipodes? This question had been answered two centuries earlier by Pliny, who said, "In regard to the problem of why those on the opposite side of us do not fall, we must ask in return whether those on the opposite side do not wonder that we do not fall."

In medieval times, a rudimentary knowledge of the North Atlantic Ocean gleaned from early Celtic and Norse voyages was applied to the old Greco-Roman description of the physical character of the earth. Fourteenth-century references in the book *De Inventione Fortunata* echo Plato: Islands in the north are described as being separated by channels, or "indrawing seas," which pour into the polar ocean.

In 1360 Oxford friar and mathematician Nicholas de Linna, "Being a good Astronomer, . . . went in companie with others to the most Northern islands of the world, and there leaving his company together, he travelled alone, and purposely described all the Northern islands, with the indrawing seas: and the record thereof at his returne he delivered to the King of England [King Edward III]." Sixteenth-century cartographers showed these islands on their maps, and described the seas separating them as "dividing all the countries as they flow into the circle of the world from the outer oceans."

Philosophers of natural history and men of science

went beyond the learnings of Aristotle and Copernicus in their investigation of the structure of the universe. Giordano Bruno, a great thinker of the second half of the sixteenth century, took Copernicus's pattern and fashioned it into a completely new cosmological order. Central to his concept was the belief in an *infinite* universe embracing infinitely numerous worlds. All occurrences, spiritual and material, were interrelated in space and time. The whole universe was in ceaseless motion, "bounded in no direction of its ways." For such heresy Bruno was burned at the stake in 1600. His concepts,

---

Figure 1-2. *Johannes Ruysch map,* Universalior Cogniti Orbis Tabula. *Published in 1508 in* Geographia, *it incorporated the North American discoveries made by Columbus and Cabot into the old geography of Ptolemy. The northern portion of the New World is shown as continuous with Greenland, which merges in its western part with Cathay. A wide sea separates the islands of the Caribbean and South America from China. North of the Arctic Circle, nothing inhibits the flow of the ocean between widely spaced, unnamed islands. A legend inscribed there is from* De Inventione Fortunata, *from the tale brought back by Nicholas de Linna on his 1360 voyage.*

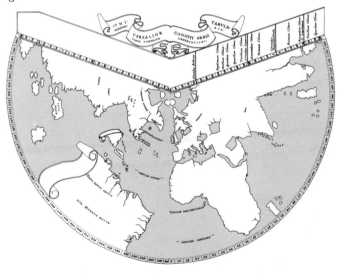

however, influenced other intellectuals—including Galileo (1564–1643). The Church allowed Galileo to express his thoughts on the Copernican model only if he treated it as a theory that facilitated his mathematical calculations. Even so, Galileo was eventually brought before the Inquisition.

Such was the intellectual climate of the world during the time of Henry Hudson—a time when men were attempting to understand the cosmography of the planet they inhabited, and its place in the universe. The notions of "indrawing seas" and a balance between land and water dominated all conceptual geography of the North Atlantic for more than three centuries after the voyages of Columbus, and were responsible for the continuing search for a Northeast or Northwest Passage to Cathay.[2]

Toward a New View of the World

At the beginning of the fifteenth century, when the greatest minds of Europe, the Byzantine world, and Arabia grappled with the cosmography of the earth, the limitless reaches of the Atlantic were "regarded with awe and wonder, seeming to bound the world as with a chaos, into which conjecture would not penetrate and enterprise feared to adventure."

Tempests beset the mariner; hidden rocks and uncharted reefs destroyed frail vessels with seeming malice; and, it was believed, grotesque monsters lay in wait—the giant squid to crush ships and men in its powerful tentacles, and the raging *Kraken* of Scandinavian tales to smash them with its thrashing spikes and shining horns. Arab geographers warned the navigator that along the coast of Africa he would enter an impenetrable green swamp filled with fiendish beasts, or encounter a sea of mud left from the sinking of the legendary continent of Atlantis. Sailors believed that if they came too close to the equator they would turn as black as the natives of that region, and remain that way. Notwithstanding the apparent contradiction, they also believed that the heat would become so unbearable that their blood would boil. At the other extreme, if they sailed too far north they would reach a frozen wasteland where blood would congeal like ice, and "where Judas lurked near the mouths of hell."

But tentative travels along the coasts gradually expanded into longer passages farther offshore, and mariners ventured into the Sea of Darkness. They were prompted less by intellectual curiosity or romantic deeds of glory in their sovereign's name than by their love of commerce: they sought new and faster routes to obtain the silks, spices, precious stones, perfumes, and other treasures of the Far East.

For centuries these goods traveled overland by caravan to Alexandria and Mecca, there to be bartered for Western goods and transported north. In the Mediterranean, the spice trade was monopolized by Venice, while the silk trade was handled largely by Genoa through its merchant colonies in Constantinople and Kaffa. When the Turks conquered Constantinople in 1453 and Alexandria shortly thereafter, this major trade route from the Levant was curtailed, leaving the nations of Europe to search for routes not controlled by the Turks — the sea.

Thrusting far out into the Atlantic, isolated from the rest of the world by the Pyrenees, lies the Iberian Peninsula, Europe's westernmost land. With Moslem trade in the Mediterranean monopolized by Venice and Genoa, Spain and Portugal took their only route — westward into the uncharted Atlantic — to expand their empires and seek riches. These voyages of discovery changed the known face of the earth.

The first voyagers brought back observations from unknown lands. New maps appeared, extensively embellished with scenes and people encountered — real and imaginary. Legends and myths collided with new perceptions.

Spanish explorations revealed the existence of an entire New World. Through the voyages of Christopher Columbus under the flag of Castile, the Spanish monarchy had created a vast Caribbean empire. As early as 1519 the Spanish conquistador Hernando Cortes had captured Tenochtitlan (Mexico City), the capital of the Aztec empire. Other explorers extended Spanish dominion from Florida in the north to the Yucatan in the south and Peru on the west coast of South America. That same year Magellan began the westward voyage in search of a passage to the Moluccas, where Spain hoped to gain a foothold in the profitable spice trade.

Under the direction of Prince Henry the Navigator, Portugal explored the Atlantic coast of Africa and its offshore islands, establishing colonies and trading posts. On each voyage they advanced a little farther, and in 1434 Gil Eanes made the then unprecedented journey as far south as Cape Bojador on the western bulge of Africa. Finding they could survive the hazards of the unknown sea, Portuguese mariners pressed on, passing Dakar, Guinea, and reaching as far south as Sierra Leone, only 10° above the equator. From her colonies along the African coast Portugal extracted wealth from gold, ivory, and slaves. Eventually, Portuguese ships doubled the Cape of Good Hope to reach India, opening a sea route to the East Indies. By the middle of the sixteenth century, Portugal had more than fifty forts and trading posts, ranging around Africa and Asia all the way to Macao on mainland China and Nagasaki, Japan.

Portuguese sailors also learned the workings of the wind and current systems in the waters off the African coast. Their caravels could sail no closer to the wind than five points (56°); to sail, they had to have the wind on their stern quarter or dead aft. Fortunately, the winds were favorable to Asia. On their return passage, faced with contrary prevailing winds and currents inshore, they were swept far out to sea, eventually reaching the northern latitudes of the prevailing westerly winds—a favorable wind for returning home to Lisbon or Lagos. This roundabout search for favorable winds led to the discovery of the Atlantic Archipelagos—Madeira, the Cape Verde Islands, and the Azores—to which Portugal laid claim.

Division of the New World

As a global sovereign power, Rome had the right to divide up the newly discovered world. Spain and Portugal justified requests for ownership on the grounds that "as crusaders, they were doing the Church's work and therefore entitled to some secular perquisites."

Romanus pontifex, issued by Pope Nicholas V in 1455, was the first of several papal bulls to back Portugal's aspiration for power. It gave Portugal exclusive rights to the conquest and possession of land along the African coast ranging "from the Capes of Bojador and

Figure 1-3. *Spanish and Portuguese holdings in the Far East by 1600. Regions under Portuguese control are denoted by a dotted line; those under Spanish control by a dashed line.*

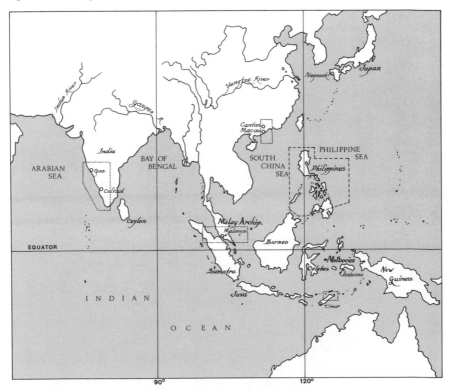

Nam as far as through all Guinea, and beyond toward that southern shore." This was confirmed the following year in the bull *Inter caetera*, issued by Pope Calixtus III. In 1479, in the treaty of Alcacovas, Spain and Portugal arranged a more comprehensive division of their possessions, with King Alfonso V of Portugal receiving Guinea, Madeiras, Azores, and the Cape Verdes, and Ferdinand and Isabella of Spain becoming owners of all the Canary Islands.

In 1481, Portugal again petitioned Rome for exclusive monopoly "in the Ocean Sea toward the regions lying southward and eastward." This was granted in the bull *Aeterni regis*, which produced a new demarcation: land north of a horizontal line extending eastward from the Canary Islands would be Spanish, and those to the south, Portuguese. As a result, Portugal lost both the Madeiras and the Azores, but gained everything south of the Bahamas.

Columbus's monumental discoveries in the New World left Spain concerned over her sovereign rights. In 1493, Ferdinand and Isabella inveighed upon Pope Alexander VI, a Spaniard, to issue a second bull of *Inter caetera*. This one furnished a *vertical* line, crossing the earlier horizontal line at "one hundred leagues toward the west and south from any of the islands commonly known as the Azores and Cape Verde." The location of this line was ambiguous, but it undoubtedly gave more territory to Spain than to Portugal.

This time, "for the sake of peace and accord," Spain and Portugal resolved their differences independent of the papacy. They reached a compromise in the 1494 Treaty of Tordesillas, with each power agreeing that:

. . . a boundary or straight line be determined and drawn north and south, from pole to pole, on the Ocean Sea, from the Arctic to the Antarctic Pole. This line shall be drawn straight . . . at a distance of 370 leagues west of the Cape Verde Islands. And all lands on the eastern side of the said bound . . . shall belong to the said King of Portugal and his successors. And all other lands shall belong to the said King and Queen of Castile.

...definitive line was located farther west, at
... ...ude, through Brazil on the western bulge
... ...nerica.

... while it seemed this would quiet the owner-
... ...utes. But when Vasco da Gama led Portugal to
I... ...nd the Far East in his epic voyage of 1497–1498,
the question arose whether the Ocean Sea (Atlantic
Ocean) extended to the opposite side of the earth, into
the Pacific. With Magellan's 1519–1522 voyage, a *south-west* passage to the Orient was finally achieved, making
the region accessible to Spain.[3]

Dividing the world into east-west regions with a
vertical line running from the Arctic to the Antarctic
poles no longer sufficed, and in 1522 the two powers entered into negotiations at the Congress of Badajoz and
Gelves. Among the doctors and lawyers representing
both sides at the conference were three cosmographers,
three pilots, and three mariners, including Hernando

Figure 1-4. *Division of the world between Spain and Portugal. Papal bulls
and treaties established a new world order between these two major powers.*

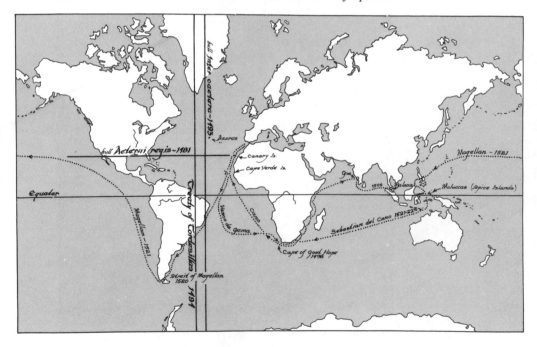

Colon (brother of Christopher Columbus), Esteban Gómez (Portuguese pilot in the service of Spain), and Juan Ribero (court geographer to Charles V).

Other than stipulating that neither Spain nor Portugal would send armadas to the Moluccas (Spice Islands) until property rights were decided, the Congress was a failure. To avoid war, the king of Spain, the Holy Roman Emperor Charles V, finally agreed to relinquish Castile's claims to the islands. Papers were signed in 1524, but Spain continued to insist that the new possessions were hers as part of the rights of conquest for Charles V.

The Pacific question was laid to rest with Spanish conquest and settlement of lands in Mexico and South America. Ports on Mexico's Pacific coast provided a more direct route to the Philippines, eliminating the need to make the long, perilous voyage around Cape Horn. Sugar produced in Hispaniola and other Caribbean islands and gold and other minerals plundered from Peru and Mexico brought great wealth to Spain.

Portugal had trade routes around the Cape of Good Hope to Mozambique and Zanzibar on the east coast of Africa, to Goa and India, to Malacca on the west coast of the Malay Peninsula, and to Macao.

Once Portugal and Spain had sealed off the seas south of the Canary Islands, the economic and political balance in Europe shifted, and their maritime supremacy remained unchallenged until the very end of the sixteenth century.

Search for a Northern Passage

The potential for wealth from Asian trade was so great that, despite papal bulls and treaties and the dominance of Spain and Portugal, France and England continued to try to reach the East Indies, concentrating efforts in northern latitudes, outside of Spain's domain.

Under the rule of King Henry VII, England began its search for the Northwest Passage. John Cabot was given ships, men, and the power to "saile to all parts, countrys and seas of the East, of the West and of the North, to seeke out, discover, and find whatsoever isles, countrys, regions or provinces . . . in what part of the world soever they be, which before this time had bene unknowen to all Christians." In 1497, Cabot left to find a short route to the Indies, arrived in Newfoundland, and took possession of this "newe founde ilande" for his sovereign. King Henry backed a second voyage in search of a northern route to Japan and Cathay, but of the five ships that left England, one of them returned shortly, and the other four, including the one with John Cabot aboard, disappeared.

The Northwest Passage to the riches of Asia proved elusive, but the world soon learned of equally great riches to be found off the banks of Newfoundland. Tales of "fish swarming so thick they impede the ship" spawned an extensive fishery off this new-found coast, and sparked England's claim to the entire North American continent.

In 1508 Sebastian Cabot, son of John Cabot, left England in search of a northwestern route to the Far East, exploring the coastline of North America from sixty miles north of the Arctic Circle south to Cape Hatteras or possibly even Florida. He, too, failed to find the passage.

Sebastian Cabot's accounts were filled with vagaries and discrepancies, but they did show that North America was a barrier between Western Europe and Asia. He returned to England to find its new ruler, Henry VIII, unwilling to spend money on such unprofitable ventures. England's interest in the Northwest Passage languished for the next sixty-five years.

By now, Spain and the rest of the world realized that the West Indies were not the islands of Japan, and that Central America was not China. To reach Asia by sailing west required a strait *through* the new continent of America. The explorations of the Cabots proved that no strait existed in Baccalaos, the name used for the general region of the cod fisheries off Newfoundland and Labrador. Spanish and Portuguese voyagers proved it did not lie anywhere from the tip of Patagonia to Florida.

This left the central part of North America as the only coastline not yet shown to be unbroken by channel or sea. Any passage from the Atlantic to the Pacific had to lie somewhere between 35°N and 45°N latitude. It was never a question of *whether* the passage to Asia existed, but always *where* it was to be found. Any river or strait penetrating the mainland was taken to confirm the linking of the two oceans.

In the second quarter of the sixteenth century, Florentine navigator Giovanni da Verrazano was convinced that the route to Cathay lay somewhere in the middle of the North American continent. A group of silk merchants and Florentine bankers from Lyons, France, formed a syndicate to finance Verrazano's expedition. Under the French flag, he set sail for America in 1524.

Verrazano closed with the coast at about 34°N, placing him near Cape Fear, southernmost of North Carolina's three capes. From there he headed south. Then, probably realizing he was as close to potentially hostile Spanish ships as he dared come, he turned north, following the shore, somehow missing the entrance both to Chesapeake Bay and Delaware Bay before dropping anchor in the outer harbor of New York. With the ship's boat Verrazano explored New York's Upper Bay, which he named Santa Margarita after the King's sister. The surrounding countryside he called Angouleme, the title of Francis I of France before he became king. Verrazano left without naming the river, and followed the coast to the northern end of Newfoundland before turning back to France. Upon his return, Verrazano gave a full account of the trip to Francis I:

My intention on this voyage was to reach Cathay and the extreme eastern coast of Asia, but I did not expect to find such an obstacle of new land as I have found . . . the ancients believed that our Western Ocean was joined to the Eastern Ocean of India without any land between . . . Land has been found by modern man which was unknown to the ancients, another world with respect to the one they knew, which ap-

pears to be larger than our Europe, than Africa, and almost larger than Asia, if we estimate its size correctly. . . .

When Verrazano reported, "We find that the land forms a much larger portion of our globe than the ancients supposed," he challenged the old belief that more of the planet was covered with water than with land. His findings also contradicted the notion that the whole continent of Africa and Europe was completely surrounded by two seas, one to the east and one to the west; the new continent he explored disproved it. He personally had sailed from the 34th parallel to 50°N latitude; 120° was accounted for by adding the 54° of south latitude others had explored, and the 66½°N latitude of the Arctic Circle the Portuguese had reached. He noted that this 7,200-mile distance embraced more land than the continent of Africa from the Cape of Good Hope to the North Cape of Norway in Europe. Nor did the land end at the Arctic Circle, for there "it turns east, and has no termination as high as the 70th parallel."

Now, the last unexplored section of the coastline of North and South America was closed. This new continent, extending from the southern tip of Patagonia to within 1,200 miles of the North Pole, was one long, continuous coastline, unbroken by any strait or passage leading to the Pacific Ocean. This did not end the search for the Northwest Passage; it merely shifted French and English explorations farther north.

Spain and Portugal still dominated the Atlantic, posing a major impediment to French exploration. Fortunately for King Francis I, Pope Clement VII was a Medici, and thus allied with France against Charles V of Spain. Also, the pope's niece, Catherine de' Medici, was betrothed to the future Henry II of France, one of the king's sons. When they met in Marseille for the marriage celebration, the king convinced the pope to change the *Inter caetera* bull issued by Alexander VI. Pope Clement subsequently proclaimed that the edict of Alexander "applied only to lands already discovered, not to those found by other sovereigns."

In the second quarter of the sixteenth century, Captain Jacques Cartier of France made three voyages to the New World. With royal support and Vatican approval, he sailed in 1534 to "the kingdom of Terres Neufves [Newfoundland], to discover certain isles and countries where there is said to be found a vast quantity of gold and other rich things." Like his predecessors, Cartier's primary goal was to find the Northwest Passage.

He entered the Gulf of St. Lawrence and made a complete circuit of its waters before the oncoming winter

Figure 1-5. *In 1580, William Bourne, in his* A Regiment for the Sea . . . Whereunto is added a Hidrographicall discourse to goe unto Cattay, five severall wayes, *lists the possible passages as: 1. Northern passage—directly over the North Pole. 2. Northeast Passage—through the Kara Sea, north of Russia and north of Asia. 3. Northwest Passage—by way of a strait in the Canadian Arctic. 4. Southeast Passage—around the Cape of Good Hope at the southern end of Africa. 5. Southwest Passage—through the Strait of Magellan at the southern tip of South America.*

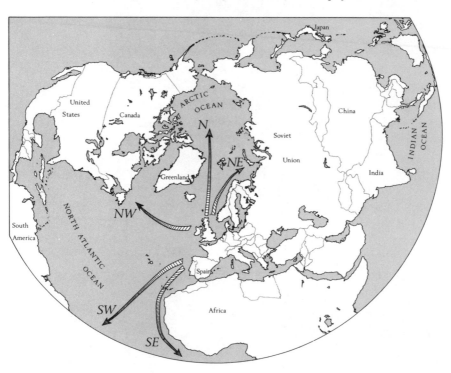

Charting the Sea of Darkness

Figure 1-6. *Frobisher Bay. From G. Hartwig,* The Tropical and Polar Worlds.

forced his return to France. Cartier did not find the route to China, but he did penetrate farther into the heartland of North America than any European before him.

In later journeys Cartier disproved his own theory that the "grand river of Hochelaga," as the St. Lawrence was called, might provide a passage through North America to the Far East. But in the minds of Henry Hudson and his contemporaries, Cartier's explorations reinforced the belief that the Northwest Passage existed in the arctic waters above Canada.

The closing decades of the sixteenth century were a time of rapid change. Elizabeth I of England warned Spain that "the pope had no right to partition the world and to give and take kingdoms to whomever he pleased." The writings of Robert Thorne urging explorations of polar routes, and those of William Bourne in *A Regiment for the Sea*, spurred renewed interest in the Northwest Passage. Discoveries in America were brought to the attention of the English-speaking world by the 1582 publication of Richard Hakluyt's *Diverse Voyages*. Not only would a northern route be far shorter, but, as Thorne said, "it could be a good opportunity to make a profit selling English woolens to the inhabitants of these cold regions."

Sir Humphry Gilbert's *Discourse of a Discoverie for a New Passage to Cataia* aroused in a group of merchant adventurers in London an interest in finding the Northwest Passage. They financed three expeditions led by Martin Frobisher in 1576, 1577, and 1578. Once again the strait to the Orient eluded the explorers, but they did greatly expand knowledge of North American Arctic geography.

They also found out how severe arctic weather could be. When Frobisher encountered snow at the end of July, he wrote: "In this storm, being the sixe and twentieth of July there fell so much snow, with such bitter cold air, that we could scarce see one another for the same, nor open our eyes to handle our ropes . . . everyman persuading himself, that the wynter there must needs be extreme, where they found so unseasonable a summer."

John Davis, too, sought the Northwest Passage in waters north of Labrador. He made three voyages between 1585 and 1587 — none of which led him into the Pacific. But he did push still farther north, exploring the southwestern shore of Greenland for the first time since the Norse had left. He sailed the strait that now bears his name north as far as pack ice in Baffin Bay would allow, to 72°46'N, and investigated many inlets and harbors on the eastern shore of Baffin Island. When Davis passed Frobisher Bay, he did not recognize it from his charts and gave it a new name — Lumley's Inlet. Frobisher was convinced that this bay, a deep penetration into Baffin Island, was going to take him all the way to the Orient.

At the entrance to Hudson Bay, Davis encountered a tidal overfall that sounded "lothsomly crying like the rage of the waters under the London bridge." It took him two days to pass the opening to the strait with "the water whirling and roaring as it were the meetings of tides." He named it the Furious Overfall; together with Lumley's Inlet it would figure later in the voyages of Henry Hudson. Even though he had not found the Northwest Passage, Davis wrote: "The passage is most probable, the execution easie."

CHAPTER TWO

Toward the North Pole: 1607

Prologue

O f all the nations seeking a northern passage to Cathay, England was the most persistent. Aside from the lure of honor and glory, England had more practical incentives: to circumnavigate the world at her high northern latitude required covering less distance than did a journey begun closer to the equator; and even more time would be saved because a ship would not have to sail south and back again to reach the traditional routes.

In 1515 Petrus Martyr d' Anghieva, a Spanish cartographer and humanist, popularized the idea of an Atlantic-Pacific passage. In his book *De Orbe Nova* (The New World), he described recent discoveries made in the western Atlantic by Sebastian Cabot. Martyr noted that Cabot "had discovered a new continent, lying where he had not expected to find another land but that of Cathay." As Cabot sailed along this coast he saw "a course of waters toward the west, but same running more soft and gently than the swift waters which the Spaniards found in their navigation southward."[1]

Both men believed that this course "betokened a

passage of water through the continent," but Martyr went a step further. He wrote:

It is not only more like to be true, but is also of necessity to be concluded that . . . there should be certain great open places, whereby the waters continually pass from the east to the west, which waters I suppose to be driven about the globe of the earth by the incessant motion and impulsion of the heavens.

Twelve years later Robert Thorne, an enterprising merchant committed to England's commercial success, promoted voyages in search of a northern passage and extolled the advantages its discovery would bring to English tradesmen. He believed it was possible to sail directly over the North Pole to Asia. Such a route would not only cut the distance of the voyage in half, but it would eliminate contact and potential battle with Spanish or Portuguese vessels. He even made a map "proving" how this would be possible, and asserted that the "perpetual clearness of the day without any darkness of the night" would make the polar route a safe one. Thorne, like other intellectuals and geographers of the day, believed that when explorers approached the North Pole they would find the weather warm.

Peter Plancius, the noted Dutch geographer, also believed in a warm polar climate. He explained that "near the Pole the sun shines five months continually; and although his rays are weak, yet on account of the long time they continue, they have sufficient strength to warm the ground, to render it temperate, to accommodate it for the habitation of men, and to produce grass for the nourishment of animals." He used the analogy, "If a small fire is kept lighted in a room all the time, the warmth of the room will be more easily maintained than by means of a large fire that is constantly allowed to go out."

Sebastian Cabot, unable to find English support for his proposed expeditions to find the Northwest Passage, went to Spain, where he was welcomed by Ferdinand I as a cartographer and nautical expert. Cabot rose to become pilot-major in the *Casa de Contratacion*, Seville's important school and center for maritime activities. In 1548 he returned to England, where by now he had a more receptive audience for his ideas on reaching the Indies.

Cabot believed that a sea route north of Russia to Cathay was not only possible, but that it actually had been navigated by the ancients. Appealing to their desire to obtain as much wealth as the Spaniards and Portuguese had from their discoveries, he convinced more than 100 London merchants to support his quest. They united in "The mystery and company of the Merchant Adventurers of the city of London . . . for the discovery of Cathay, and divers other regions, dominions and places unknown." Their charter named Sebastian Cabot governor.

Cabot was a sensible choice. In addition to his theoretical knowledge of the art and science of navigation, ship construction, and the economics of oceanic trading, he had practical experience in exploration. And he had contacts among the leading geographers of the day.

The Merchant Adventurers, better known as the Muscovy Company, prepared and furnished three ships "for the search and discovery of the northern part of the world, to open a way and passage to our men for travel to new and unknown kingdoms." Under the command of Sir Hugh Willoughby, the *Bona Esperanza*, *Bona Confidentia*, and *Edward Bonaventure*, set out in May 1553 to the Kara Sea in search of a route to Cathay.

They explored the northern coastline along the White Sea and the western shore of Nova Zembla, but none of the ships reached Cathay. Both the *Bona Esperanza* and the *Bona Confidentia* were frozen into the ice; Sir Hugh Willoughby and all the crew were lost. The *Edward Bonaventure*, under Stephen Burrough, fared better, reaching the town of Archangel on the Russian coast of the White Sea. Pilot-major Richard Chancellar then proceeded to Moscow, where negotiations with Ivan Vasilivitch (Ivan the Terrible), Duke of Muscovy, resulted in the establishment of trade with Russia.

Stephen Burrough was foiled again by the ice-

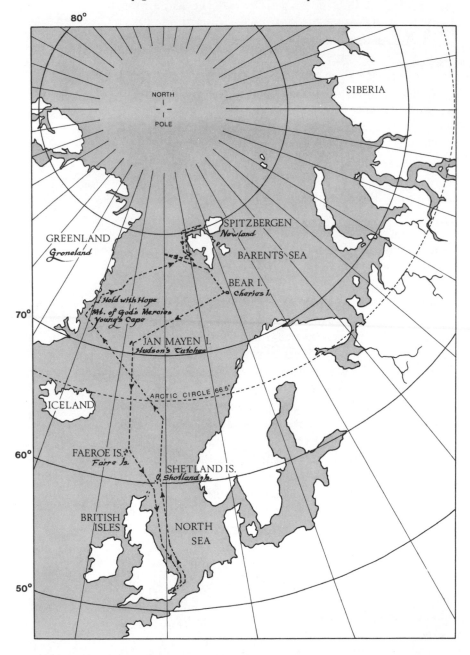

Figure 2-1. *Reconstruction of Hudson's route to Spitzbergen on his 1607 voyage. Labels in italic are names used by Hudson.*

Figure 2-2. *Detail of Spitzbergen portion of Hudson's 1607 passage.*

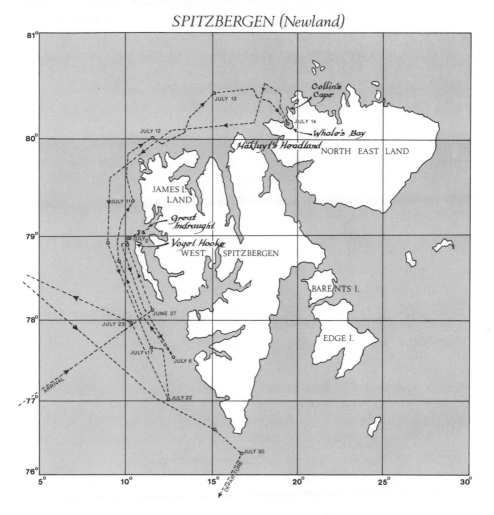

SPITZBERGEN (Newland)

choked Kara Sea in 1556, and more than fifty years passed
before the Muscovy Company decided to make another
attempt to find a northern route to the Indies. In 1607
they hired Henry Hudson, as master of the *Hope-well*, to
seek a route directly over the North Pole.

Hudson left Gravesend, England, on May 1, 1607, on the first of his four voyages. He sailed north to Spitzbergen, exploring its great bays and sounds, and ultimately came within 577 miles of the North Pole, to 80°23′N latitude—a navigational record that would not be exceeded for the next 100 years. However, he was thwarted by ice, thick fog, and severe storms, and with supplies dwindling and winter approaching he was forced to return to England. On his way south he sighted Bear Island (called Cherie's Island by the English), and discovered Jan Mayen Island, which he named Hudson's Tutches. After making a stop at the Faeroe Islands, Hudson returned to the Thames River on September 15, 1607.

The Journal

The following transcription is taken from Book III of *Purchas His Pilgrimes*, by Samuel Purchas, published in London in 1625. Note that the names and positions of crewmembers on this and on Hudson's subsequent voyages appear as they were written in the original.

DIVERS VOYAGES AND NORTHERNE DISCOVERIES OF THAT WORTHY IRRECOVERABLE DISCOVERER, MASTER HENRY HUDSON

His Discoverie Toward the North Pole, Set Forth at the Charge of Certaine Worshipfull Merchants of London, in May 1607. Written partly by John Playse, one of the Company and partly by Henry Hudson

1607—April 19 The following seamen, intending to go to sea in four days to discover a passage by the North Pole to Japan and China, took communion at Saint

Ethelburge, in Bishops Gate street with the rest of the parishioners.

Henry Hudson — master	*James Skrutton*
William Collin — his mate	*John Pleyce* (Playse)
James Young	*Thomas Baxter*
John Colman	*Richard Day*
John Cooke	*James Knight*
James Beubery	*John Hudson* — a boy

On *May 1st of 1607*, we weighed anchor at Gravesend.

Depart Thames River.

May 26 In the morning we arrived at the Shetland Islands, and by noon were 18 miles east of them in a latitude of 60°12′. The compass had no magnetic variation. Soundings showed we had 384 feet of depth, with a black, muddy, sandy bottom containing a few yellow shells. Our ship made more leeway than we had supposed.

May 30 By observation our latitude was 61°11′. Today I found the needle to incline 79° under the horizon.[2] For the next four days, contrary winds prevented us from making very much progress.

Magnetic dip.

June 4 Observation showed we were still at 61°14′ latitude, and 84 to 90 miles from the northern part of the Shetland Islands; their bearing, by our account, east by north of us. I found magnetic variation 5° westerly.[3]

June 7 We were at 63°25′ latitude.

June 8 All morning we had a fresh, southerly gale; we steered north by west. Observation placed us at 65°27′.

June 11 Today we saw six or seven whales near our ship; we were at 67°30′. About five o'clock the wind came up out of the northeast by east, and we steered north northwest all night with a fresh, east gale.

June 12 With a stiff gale[4] out of the east northeast, we steered away as before and by noon we had run 90 miles.[5] In the afternoon we steered north by west for 45 miles; throughout the night there was much wind and great fog.

June 13 Between one and two o'clock in the morn-

ing we saw land ahead of us, and some ice; but with
the fog being so thick, we steered away northerly.
With the wind strong we stood away south by east for
18 to 24 miles. Our sails and shrouds were frozen. At
eight in the morning it cleared up, and the wind was
out of the northeast by east, but it was so strong we
were hardly able to maintain any sail. This is a very
high land, for the most part covered with snow, the
remaining part bare. At the top it looked reddish with
a blackish clay underneath, and much ice lying about
it. The part which we saw when we came about
trended east and west, while the northern part trended
northeast by north and northeast. Of what we saw, its
total length was 27 miles. We saw many fowl, as well
as a whale close inshore. The headland we named
Young's Cape, and the high mound (like a round castle) which stood nearby, we called the Mount of God's
Mercy.[6] It rained all that afternoon and evening, and at
eight we came about and steered all that night north
by west and sometimes north northwest.[7]

June 14 Being near the land, we had snow. At four
in the morning the wind veered northerly, so we came
about and sailed southeast by south. Today we had
much wind and rain, and being near the land we shortened sail.

June 15 In the morning the wind was blowing so
hard out of the northeast that we weren't able to keep
any sail up, so we lay-a-hull and let the ship drift,
waiting for a better wind. Tonight there was very
much rain.

June 16 Much wind from the northeast.

June 17 We set sail at noon, steering east by south,
and east southeast.

June 18 In the afternoon there was a fine gale out of
the southeast, which toward evening increased, and we
steered northeast for three watches, a distance of 36
miles. At noon we had rain with fog. From 12 until four
we steered north northeast for 24 miles, and supposed
our position to be generally about 70°. We wanted to
determine whether the land we saw five days ago was an

Figure 2-3. *A large, northern sea bird, and member of the Alcidae Family, the Giant auk has been extinct since the last breeding pair in Iceland were killed in 1844. Its short wings were used only as paddles, not for flight.*

island or a part of Groneland[8], but with fog increasing very thick, and the wind strong out of the south, we had to alter our course, shorten sail, and steer away northeast. We believed we were still in the same latitude of the land as before, even though we have not been able to take any observations since the 11th, and had been lying-a-hull from the 15th until the 17th of June. We perceived a current setting toward the southwest. Today we saw three whales near our ship; having steered northeast almost one watch for a distance of 15 miles, we found the seas increasing every way. We supposed we were opposite the northeast part of the land we saw on the 13th, with the current setting to windward. The reason that caused us to think so was that after we had sailed 15 to 18 miles in this sea, with the wind neither increasing nor decreasing, we had a pleasant and smooth sea. All this night was foggy, with a good gale of wind, and we steered away northeast until the next day at noon, having sailed 60 miles.

June 20 Throughout the morning there was thick fog, with the wind out of the south; we steered northeast until noon. Then we changed our course to north northeast, hoping for a sea free of ice until we meet with

An island or a part of Greenland.

East Greenland Current.

Hopes for ice-free sea to Spitzbergen.

Newland.[9] Today, at two in the afternoon, it cleared up and we saw the sun, which we had not seen since the second day of this month. Having steered north northeast for two and a half watches, 45 or 48 miles, we saw land, trending northeast and southwest, on our port side about 12 miles from us. We steered away east northeast with the wind out of the south blowing a good gale, but

Great auk.

it was reasonably clear and we saw many birds with black backs and white bellies, in form much like a duck.

Much drift ice.

There was also much drift ice in the sea; one piece we avoided by keeping close to the wind, the other by running downwind. And this morning, about four, we saw a thick fog ahead of us.

June 21 In the morning we steered northeast and east northeast two watches, 15 or 18 miles. Then it became foggy and we came about, steering northeast and east northeast two watches, 18 miles, finding we were embayed. The wind changed to a small gale out of the east southeast; we tacked and headed south. All night there was thick fog and little wind, our ship's bow lay pointed east.

June 21[10] In the morning, while steering north northeast, we thought we had embayed ourselves, finding land with ice upon it to port, and a great many pieces of drift ice. We steered northeast, keeping careful lookout at every clear space for land; wishing to know whether it would leave us to the east, and also to know the breadth of the sea, as well as to shape a more northerly course. Since we knew of no other name given to

Land of Hold-with-Hope.

this land, lying in 73° of latitude, we thought it appropriate to name it Hold-with-Hope. The sun at its meridian passage was due south of us. Here it should be noted that when we made the Mount of God's Mercy and Young's Cape, the land for the most part was covered with snow, and when we approached, it was extremely

Very temperate climate.

cold, but this land was very temperate to our feelings.[11] This too should be noted, that even though we were not able to take any observations for two days, and had to lie-a-hull due to contrary winds, our dead-reckoning and observation were within 24 miles of each other. Our

Figure 2-4. *Closely related to the dolphin, the grampus, sometimes called Risso's dolphin, is widely distributed throughout the world. Its bulbous head, with a shallow, vertical groove, is a distinguishing characteristic.*

progress was greater than our estimate by the 24 miles. This night, there was very little wind.

June 22 In the morning it cleared up, but remained calm until about two or three o'clock, after which we had a pretty gale, and we steered east by north nine miles. Our observation placed us at 72°38'. Changing our course, we steered northeast, the wind a pretty gale out of the southeast. This morning when it cleared, we saw the land, its nearest part trending east northeast and west southwest, and estimated ourselves to be about 36 miles west of it. It was a main high-land, not at all covered with snow, even on the northern part which was very mountainous. According to observation, our bearing to the nearest part of land was 73°. However, the many fogs and calms, contrary winds, and much ice near the shore, prevented us from any further exploration. This might be held against us, being our fault for keeping such a westerly course. The chief reason for this course was our desire to see that part of Groneland, which for all we knew, was unknown to any Christian; we thought it could as well have been open sea as land, in which case our passage to the Pole would have been mostly completed. We also hoped to have a westerly wind, which if we were closer to the shore would have been an onshore [easterly] wind. Considering we found land which our charts made no mention of, we considered our labor so much more worthwhile. For what we

Land not covered with snow.

Desire to see the northern end of Greenland.

A newly discovered land.

could see, it appeared to be a good land, and worth exploring.

June 23 In the morning there was a hard gale on our head, with much rain that fell in very great drops, much like our thunder-showers in England, we tacked and stood east northerly under shortened sail; it was not as cold after the rain as before. From noon until three o'clock it was calm, with fog. Afterward, the wind came up out of the east and east southeast, we steered northeast with the fog and rain. About seven or eight o'clock the wind increased with extreme fog. We steered away under shortened sail east northeast. About midnight the wind came up out of the southwest, and we steered north with reasonably clear weather.

June 24 About two o'clock in the morning the master's mate thought he saw land on the port side. The longer we ran north, the more it fell away to the west, and we thought it to be a main high land. Today, the wind being westerly, we steered north, and by observation were at approximately 73°. At noon we changed our course, and steered north by east; at our last observation, and also at this, we found the meridian to be leeward of us south by west westerly part of the compass, when we had sailed two watches, 24 miles.

June 25 The wind scanted and came up north northwest; we lay northeast for two watches, 24 miles.[12] Then the wind became variable between the northeast and the north, and we steered east by north and sometimes east; we had thick fog. About noon three grampusses played about our ship.[13] This afternoon the wind veered to the east and southeast, and we sailed north by east. Tonight the weather was oppressive, but with little fog (we use the word night for distinction of time, but long before this the sky was always light); but as yet we could not see the north meridian of the sun. Tonight, in the latitude of 75°, we saw small flocks of birds with black backs, white bellies and long, sharp-pointed tails. We supposed that land was not far off; but no matter how diligently we looked, we could not see it, the weather

Greenland to port.

Sun's meridian.

Could not yet see the midnight sun.

Land not far off.

being so close that many times we could hardly see more than 18 to 21 miles off.

June 26 Weather was close in the morning, but we had our wind and held our course as before. Today our latitude by observation was 76°38'; and we had birds of the same sort as before, and various others of that color, having red heads, that we had seen before when we first made Mount of God's Mercy in Groneland; though this time there were not so many. After, we steered north by east two watches, 30 miles, with the intent of closing in with the southern part of Newland; by our account being 30 to 36 miles from the land. We then sailed northeast one watch, 15 miles.

Approach the southern part of Spitzbergen.

June 27 About one or two o'clock in the morning we made Newland; at sea there was no fog, but the land was covered with fog, and ice lay very thick all along the shore that we saw, for a distance of 45 to 48 miles. Having fair wind, we coasted along the shore in a very pleasing smooth sea, and although only 12 miles off, the depth exceeded 600 feet. Today, at noon, we were at 78°, and we continued along the shore. It was so foggy, that many times we could hardly see the land, but we figured we were near Vogel Hooke.[14] About eight o'clock this evening we proposed to shape our course northwest. Here should be noted that although we ran close along the coast we did not find it very cold; which made us think that if we had been on shore we would have found a temperate climate. We held this northwest course until about 10 o'clock at night, when we saw a great amount of ice ahead and west of us. We could not get clear of it maintaining this course, so we tacked, heading south and southeast, being as much desirous to see this land as we were to leave it.

Arrive at Spitzbergen.

Near Bird Cape.

Temperate airs.

June 28 There was a hard gale of wind all morning, between the south and southwest. We shaped our course [blank space in the journal] to be farther from the ice and the land. It pleased God that about midnight it cleared up, and we found ourselves between the land and the ice, the nearest part of Vogel Hooke bearing east of us. Then

---

we tacked and headed in toward shore, having sea-room between the ice and the land.

June 29 At four in the morning, with the wind a pretty gale from the northeast, we thought it best to shorten our course, so we tacked and headed north northwest, the wind increasing a little. About noon we saw ice ahead of us, and came about again toward the east southeast. There was very much wind and we reduced sail for the space of two watches. Then, about eight in the evening, with the hardest storm we had on this voyage, we lay-a-hull.

June 30 The morning was stormy, but about noon it ceased, and by seven in the evening it was almost calm.

July 1 All morning the wind was southwest; we headed northeast for the shore hoping to find an open sea between the shore and the ice. About noon we were embayed with ice, lying between the land and us. By our observation we were at 78°42', where we believed we were opposite the great Indraught. To free ourselves of the ice we steered between southeast and south, and to the westward, where we could have open sea. About six this evening it pleased God to give us clear weather; and

The Great Inlet.

we found we had been thrust far into the inlet, being almost a bay, and surrounded with very high mountains with low land lying between them; depth in the bay exceeded 600 feet. Then, being sure of where we were, we steered west, with the wind light out of the southeast, and found all the ice on the northern shore and a clear sea to the south.

July 2 It pleased God to give us clear weather, with a fair gale and a northeast wind; the ice being to the north of us on the weather shore, and an open sea to the south under our lee. We held our course northwest until 12 o'clock, having sailed on that course for 30 miles, and finding the ice to fall away from us to the [blank in journal] we gave thanks to God who so marvelously preserved us from so many dangers among huge quantities of ice and fog. We steered northwest, hoping to be free from ice; we were at 78°56' by observation. We met ice again, and followed along its general direction of west to south southeast.

July 3 Observation of 78°33'. Today our shrouds were frozen, and it was searching cold. We also followed along the ice, not knowing whether we were clear or not; wind was north.

July 4 It was very cold and our shrouds and sails were frozen; we found we were far into the inlet. The wind being north, we headed south southeast and south and southwest by west until 10 at night.

Shrouds and sails frozen.

July 5 At 12, with the wind very strong out of the northeast, and having brought ourselves near the mouth of the inlet, we lay-a-hull.

The mouth of the inlet.

July 6 In the morning the wind was as before and the seas had grown. This morning we came into a very green sea; our observation was 77°30'. This afternoon the wind and sea calmed a bit. About four o'clock we set sail and steered northwest by west, the wind being north northeast. Today proved the clearest day we have had for a long time.

Enter a green sea.

July 7 At four in the morning the weather was very clear, and the fairest morning that we have had in the past three weeks. We steered as before, by our account being roughly in 78° and out of the inlet's closed end. We found we were surrounded with land and ice, and again entered into a black sea, which we found proved to be an open passage. Now, having the wind north northeast, we steered south by east with the purpose of meeting with the southwest part of this land which we had first seen; hoping by this way either to defray the charge of the voyage, or else, if it pleased God in time to give us a fair wind to the northeast to satisfy expectation. All this day and night afterward proved calm.

A *black and green sea.*

July 8 All morning it was calm with very thick fog. This morning we saw many pieces of driftwood drive by us; we brought our boat to a standstill to stop a leak and mended our rigging. Today we saw many seals, and two fishes which we judged to be sea-horses, or morses.[15] At midnight we had an east by south wind and set our course northeast.

Much driftwood.

Many seals and morses.

July 9 All morning the wind was light out of the southeast and there was thick fog. Today we were in among islands of ice, where we saw many seals.

Figure 2-5. *Pen and ink drawing of a walrus by Albrecht Durer in 1521. The inscription reads: "This sleepy animal, whose head I sketched here was caught in the Netherlandish Sea. It measured twelve ells in length and moves on four legs." The European's reaction to first encounters with these creatures bordered on incredulity. Jacques Cartier described the walrus as "a beast big as an oxen, with two teeth in its mouth like an elephant, who lives in the sea."*

July 10 In the morning it was foggy; afterward it cleared and we found we were completely surrounded by ice; we tacked, heading south by west and south south-west, one watch, 15 miles, hoping to get more sea-room and to head northeast. We had a northwest wind.

[At this point, according to Purchas, John Playse leaves off writing, and Henry Hudson continues as author for the remainder of the journal.]

July 11 The weather was very clear, with a southeast south wind. Coming out of the blue sea into our green sea again, we saw whales. Now, having a fresh south southeast gale of wind, it was best to change my course and to sail northeast by the southern end of Newland. But having come into a green sea, praying God to direct me, I steered north 30 miles. After that we saw ice on

From blue to green sea.

our port side; we steered east by north for nine miles and left the ice behind us. Then we steered north until noon. Today, the sun at its meridian was south by west, westerly, with its greatest height 37°20'. By this observation we were at 79°17'; with the fresh gale of wind and a smooth sea, we had made more progress than we estimated. At 10 this evening the weather was clear, and then we had the company of our troublesome neighbors, ice with fog. The wind was south southwest. Here we saw plenty of seals, and assumed by the footprints and dung on the ice that bears had been here. Today many of my crew were sick from having eaten unsalted bear's meat from the day before.

July 12 For the most part there was thick fog and we steered between south by east and south southeast for seven and a half miles to clear us of the ice. Then we had a south wind and steered northeast for 15 miles until noon. This morning our shrouds were frozen. At noon we were in 80°; it was almost calm, with little wind from the southwest, and thick fog. This afternoon we steered north and sometimes northeast. Then we saw ice ahead of us; we came about, heading southeast with little wind and some fog. Before we had come about, the combination of thick fog, calm wind, and a sea setting us upon the ice had brought us close to danger. It pleased God at the very instant to give us a small gale, which was the means of our deliverance; to Him therefore we give praise. At midnight it cleared up and from the top of the mast our boatswain, William Collin, saw the land called Newland by the Hollanders, bearing south southwest 36 miles from us.

July 13 This morning, with a good gale, we came about and steered northeast by east; by observation we were at 80°23'. Today we saw many whales. This morning proved clear weather, and from aloft we could not see any sign of ice. Between noon and three o'clock we steered northeast by east, 15 miles, then we saw ice ahead of us; though we steered east two glasses, three miles, we could not clear the ice on that course. Then we steered southeast seven and a half miles; after, we sailed east by north and east 12 miles until eight the next morning.

July 14 The morning was calm, with fog. At nine, with an east wind, small gale and thick fog, we steered southeast by east, and by running this course found our green sea again, which proved to be the freest of ice, while the azure blue sea proved to be our icy sea. There were more birds than we usually saw. At noon, being a thick fog, we found ourselves near land bearing east of us; running farther we found a bay opening to the west by north northerly. Of what we saw, the sides and head of the bay were lined by a very high and ragged land. At the mouth of this bay is a small island, and the northern side of the bay is high land which we called Collin's Cape for the name of our boatswain who first saw it. We saw many whales in this bay, and while one of the crew had a hook and line overboard to try and catch fish, a whale came up under the keel of our ship and got caught; by God's mercy we were unharmed, our only loss being the hook and three-fourths of the line. In the afternoon a flood tide from northwest by north set into the bay. At the mouth of this bay the depth was 180 feet; after that it shallowed to 150 feet, yet farther in, the depth exceeded 600 feet; therefore we judged it to be a sound rather than a bay. In the swamps and valleys between the high, ragged peaks there was much snow. Here we found it hot. On the southern side of this bay there are three or four islands or rocks.

At the head of this bay, John Colman, my mate, and William Collin, my boatswain, with two others of the company went ashore. There they found a pair of morses teeth in a jaw; they likewise found whales bones, some dozen or more deers horns, footprints of beasts of other sorts, and rote-geese [barnacle geese]. Among other things they brought back aboard was the morses teeth and a stone off the land. They also saw much driftwood on the shore, and a stream or two of fresh water. Here they found it hot on shore, and drank water, which they commended, to cool their thirst. Here we felt the need for a good ship's boat. They assured me they were not on

Green sea freest of ice and the blue sea icy.

Collin's Cape.

Whale danger.

A sound is greater and deeper in draught than a bay.

Heat beyond 80 degrees latitude.

Figure 2-6. *Magdalena Bay, Spitzbergen. From G. Hartwig,* The Tropical and Polar Worlds.

shore for more than half an hour, and when they had left the boat the wind was calm. But almost immediately after, a northeast gale set in, coming with the flood tide and fog. We sailed back and forth, waiting for those on shore; but after they came aboard, the wind was east by south a fine gale. Keeping in mind the remainder of the voyage, and the time in which to perform it, we steered away northeast and north northeast. This night proved clear, and we had the sun at its meridian to the north and east of us.[16] With the cross-staff we found the sun's height to be 10°40′ from the upper edge of the horizon; this, without allowing anything for the semidiameter of the sun, or the distance off the end of the staff to the center of the eye. From a north sun [midnight] to an east sun [morning], we sailed between north and north northeast for 24 miles.

July 15 In the morning the weather was very clear, with the sun shining warm, but the wind was a light east southerly. By mid-morning we had brought Collin's Cape to bear southeast of us, and we saw the high land of Newland; that part discovered by us on our starboard, 24 or 30 miles from us, trending northeast by east and southwest by west. It is a very high, mountainous land,

Midnight sun.

like ragged rocks with snow between them. By my account, the northern part of this land we now saw continued into 81°. Throughout the day the weather was clear, with little wind, and reasonably warm.

Land at 81 degrees latitude.

July 16 In the morning the weather was clear and warm, with wind from the north. This morning we were completely surrounded by ice in abundance, lying to the north, to the northwest, the east and southeast. We headed toward the farthest point of land we saw, but found in drawing closer, and by means of the clearness of the weather, that it continued onward, trending north and stretching far into 82° latitude.[17] Perhaps it was even farther, judging by the bowing or showing of the sky.[18] Of what I first saw, I hoped to have a clear sea between the land and the ice, and be able to circle north of this land. But now, finding that proved impossible due to the ice surrounding us to the north and the joining of it to the land, and seeing that God did bless us with a fair wind to sail to the south of this land to the northeast, we returned. We brought the helm up toward the wind, for it was our plan to keep that land the Hollanders discovered in sight; if contrary winds should take us, we would anchor there, to find what we could to the charge of our voyage, and to proceed on our exploration as soon as God should bless us with wind.

Land stretching into 82 degrees latitude.

Return toward home.

This I am sure now, that between 78°30′ and 82° [81°], there is no passage by this way. But I think this land may be profitable to those that will adventure it. In this bay I spoke of before, and all about this coast, we saw a greater abundance of seals swimming in the water than we had seen any time before. At noon, with a stiff gale of wind from the north, we were opposite Collin's Cape, our position about 81°30′ [80°30′]; and by one o'clock the cape bore northeast of us. From there, I set our course west southwest, intending to keep in an open sea free of ice, and sailed that course for 48 miles. From 10 this night, until eight the next morning, we steered southwest for 54 miles, with a hard gale of wind from the north.

Chance for profit.

Opposite Collin's Cape.

Charting the Sea of Darkness

July 17 In the morning we had a good north gale; at eight we altered our course and steered south until eight in the evening, running 36 miles. Today proved reasonably clear and warm.

July 18 In the morning the wind increased, south by east, with thick fog. All this afternoon and night the weather was close, little fog and reasonably warm.

July 19 At eight in the morning, with the wind out of the south and thick fog, we steered southeast for 12 miles until noon; then the wind veered greatly and we steered southeast by east for 12 miles until four o'clock, then we veered our sheets [allowing the ship to fall off the wind] and steered east by southeast for 45 miles until eight the next morning.[19] The rest of the day was reasonably clear and warm.

July 20 This morning there was little wind, and at eight o'clock we saw land (being part of Newland) about 36 miles ahead under our lee, as well as land to weather of us. It is very mountainous land, the highest we have yet seen. As we sailed near it we saw a sound ahead of us lying east and west. The land closest to us, about 30 miles away, on the northern side of the sound's mouth, trends west northwest and east southeast for 36 miles, as far as we could see; while the land on the southern side, about 24 to 30 miles from us, trends south southeast and north northwest. From eight until noon it was calm. Today, by observation, we were at 77°26'. On the northern side of the mouth of this sound there are three islands set close together and all mountainous. The farthest of the three, to the northwest, has four very high peaks, like heaps of corn. The island next to the inlet's mouth has one very high peak on its southern end. Here, one of our company killed a red-billed bird. After the morning, for the rest of the day and night, it was calm, the temperature inclining more on the warm side than cold. Tonight we had warm rain.

Bell Sound.

July 21 All morning it was calm, until four in the afternoon, when we had a small gale with fog; we sailed east to close in with the land, and sailed nine miles until midnight. Then the wind changed to northeast and we came about, steering south for 30 miles until eight the next morning.

July 22 At eight in the morning the wind was strong and variable out of the east; with shortened sail we steered nine miles south by east, then the wind got very strong and we lay-a-hull. All afternoon and night the wind remained strong, with rain.

July 23 All morning the wind was out of the south, with rain and fog. At four this afternoon we saw land bearing northeast of us about 18 miles away. Then we had the wind from south southwest and we steered away southeast and southeast by east for 12 miles, the sea having grown considerably. We accounted that, in lying-a-hull, we had drifted northwest by north 66 miles, and north for 18 miles. Fearing the strong wind might set us on a lee shore, we tacked and made our way west by north for the entire night.

July 24 In the morning the wind was as strong as before, and the sea had grown. This morning we took down our main topmast to ease our ship, and from eight the evening before, until noon, we sailed 45 miles west and by north one. From 12 until eight we sailed as before for 18 miles, with the wind south by west; at eight we came about, and lay southeast by east with much wind and heightened seas.

July 25 It was a clear morning and we re-set our main topmast. We saw land north of us under our lee, our course being southeast by east. Then the wind headed us; we came about and lay southwest by west seven and a half miles until noon. Then it became overcast and the wind scanted again, so we came about to lay southeast by south. We sailed this course for nine miles until four in the afternoon. Then, once again the wind scanted, and we sailed nine miles south. Now, seeing how contrary the wind had become for us to maintain this course, I thought to improve our chances by sailing west again; and this evening at eight, being in the latitude of 78° or more, and 45 miles from land, which bears

Contrary winds.

Charting the Sea of Darkness

northeast to east from us, we steered away west with the wind southeast and clear weather.

July 26 Throughout the day we had rain with thick fog, and a hard gale of wind. Last evening, from eight until this noon, we ran 75 miles; from noon until midnight, 57 miles, with the wind east by south. From midnight until two the next morning we made six miles west.

July 27 Today, extreme thick fog, with rain, and little wind. Then it became calm, with the seas very lofty. We heard a great roar of the sound of waves breaking on the ice, which was the first ice we had seen or heard since we were at Collin's Cape. The sea was pushing us westward toward the ice. We lowered our ship's boat and rowed to try and tow us away from the danger, *Imminent destruction.* which was of little use because the seas were so high; but in this menace it pleased God to give us a small gale from the northwest by west, and we steered away southeast for 12 miles, until noon. Whether the wind that brought us to the ice continued, or if it remained calm, if not for the deliverance by God of a northwest by west wind — a wind not commonly found on this voyage — it would have been the end of us and our voyage. May God give us thankful hearts for so great deliverance. Here we *Escape from danger.* found the need of a good ship's boat, with half a dozen long oars to row, as we had found before at Whale's Bay. At noon it cleared up, and we could see by the sky there was ice bearing off us from west southwest through to the north and north northeast.[20]

Then we had a good westerly gale and steered south for 21 miles until four o'clock. From four until six, we sailed south 12 miles, and found by the icy sky, and our nearness to Groneland, that there is no passage that way; *No passage this way.* which, if there had been I meant to have made my return to England by way of north of Groneland and through the Davis Straits. Finding the benefit of a westerly wind, which all this voyage we had seldom found, we altered our course and steered eastward, running southeast for 12 miles. From eight this evening until noon the next day we made 90 miles east southeast. All this day and night it was very cold; I suppose it was due to the wind coming off so much ice.

July 28 It was very cold, with a west wind, but not foggy. At noon we steered southeast by east and our observation placed us at 76°36'. From noon until eight we made 30 miles. Then the wind changed to southeast by south, and we steered east by north for 54 miles, until noon the next day.

July 29 All morning it was wet with thick fog, and a raw wind from southeast by east. From noon until four we sailed nine miles. Then the wind veered to a quartering wind, filling our sails better, and we steered east by south for 24 miles until 12 at night. At this time we heard the roar of waves breaking on land to windward, which I also knew to be by the color of the sea. It was such an extremely thick fog that we could scarcely see a cable's length [608'] from our ship. We had ground at 150 feet, with the bottom being small, black pebble stones. We sounded again and had ground at 180 feet, with a bottom of small stones like beans; at the next cast [of the lead line] the depth exceeded 360 feet. I came about again and steered southwest 18 miles, and west by north six miles, until noon the next day. Throughout the day and night there was extremely thick fog.

July 30 All morning very thick fog. At noon it was almost calm, after which we had a little wind, and steered north northwest until two. Then it cleared up, with the wind northwest, and we could see for a distance of six miles. After it cleared, we steered east southeast. In the evening we were south of an island northwest of us, and about 15 miles away; we also saw land bearing 21 miles from us. We also had land, as near as we could judge, about 30 miles from us, east southeast to southeast. Then, having the wind west northwest, we steered south by east. It presently became calm until 10 this evening, at which time we had a little gale. We steered away south southeast until midnight and by our accounting were at 76°, and 30 miles from land. This is the most pleasant land we had seen on all parts of Newland; being plain ridges of medium height, and not ragged, or covered with snow, as all the rest that we had seen on this voyage. At midnight we saw two morses in the sea near us, swimming to land. From midnight to four it was calm.

July 31 At four this morning we had a southeast wind, and we steered south southwest. Then it became calm, and continued such all morning. In the afternoon we had an east southeast wind, and steered south for 24 miles. Then, having a strong wind against us, and finding the fog more thick and troublesome than before, as well as the lack of various other necessary things, and not having much time left to do further good this year; I commanded our return for England, and steered away south southwest. This night we had a hard gale of wind from the southeast by east. The next morning at four o'clock we were opposite Cherie's Island, to windward of us by 15 miles.[21] Knowing we were near, we kept a careful lookout for it, and the weather being clear, we saw it; a very ragged land on the water side, rising like haystacks.

Return for England.

Opposite Bear Island.

August 1 Being a very hard gale of wind from the east southeast, we shortened sail and steered away south southwest. This night was very foggy, with a hard gale of wind east by south, and by our account made 81 miles. From eight this evening until four the next morning we held the same course, making 30 miles. All this night was very foggy, wet, and raw cold.

August 2 In the morning it was calm, with a thick fog, cold and thick weather. About noon we had a little gale west by north, and steered away as before.

August 3 We had calm, clear weather in the morning, with a little gale; we sailed south southwest. Then we had the wind at southeast, and we sailed as before. All this day and night the weather was close, a little foggy at noon, but it did not continue for long. At 12 tonight the wind veered to the east by north, and we held our course south southwest as before.

August 15 We put into the Faeroe Islands, located at 52°.[22]

Faeroe Islands.

September 15 I arrived in Tilberie Hope in the Thames.

Epilogue: 1607

When Henry Hudson returned to England, the journal of his 1607 voyage was intact and available for anyone's perusal. In addition, there were two other very brief accounts of the passage, both by captains in the service of the Muscovy Company.

Captain Edge's *Brief Discoverie of the Muscovia Merchants* mentioned three additional place names given by Hudson: Whale's Bay, Hakluyt's Headland, and Hudson's Tutches. The July 27 journal entry refers to Whale's Bay, but gives no specific location; however, we can safely assume that it is the whale-filled bay located near Collin's Cape on the northern side of Spitzbergen. Hakluyt's Headland is not mentioned in the journal, but it does appear, along with Mount of God's Mercy, Hold-with-Hope, and Collin's Cape, on a map produced in 1611 by Jodocus Hondius to illustrate Willem Barents's third expedition to the north. Hondius may have gotten the headland's name and approximate position directly from Hudson. Although this map did not depict any new geography, it did show the ice field that prevented Hudson from sailing farther north.

Edge's account goes on to say, "being hindered with ice, [Hudson] returned home, without any further use made of the country, and in ranging homewards he discovered an island lying in 71°, which he named Hudson's Tutches." There is no reference to this in Hudson's journal, and we can only surmise it must have occurred sometime after his sighting of Cherie's Island (Bear Island) on July 31, and his arrival at the Faeroe Islands on August 15.

Hudson was considerably off course on his return to England. Hudson's Tutches is almost 400 miles west of a straight line between Cherie's Island and the Faeroe Islands, only 240 miles off the coast of Greenland, and—perhaps not coincidentally—at nearly the same latitude as Young's Cape. If this divergence had been caused by storms and contrary winds, it certainly would have been

Figure 2-7. *A glimpse of Jan Mayen Island. From G. Hartwig,* The Tropical and Polar Worlds.

mentioned in the journal. But currents in that region are weak, and if anything would have set him toward the northeast, not the west.

Why, then, was Hudson so far west of his course? The most likely explanation is that he intended to make an attempt to find the Northwest Passage. By wintering at Hold-with-Hope, that land "very temperate in feeling," he would have been in a good position to make another attempt to sail over the North Pole, hoping for an ice-free passage in the spring.

Alternatively, Hudson may have intended to sail up Davis Strait and continue his voyage to China by the west coast of Greenland. This was the route John Davis described as a "matter nothyne doubtfall, but almost at any tyme to be passed, the sea navigable." Ice had stopped Hudson from sailing farther north along the east coast of Greenland and north of Spitzbergen, thereby ruling out any chance of a North Polar Passage.

Instead of going ahead with either of these plans, Hudson returned to England that same year. He may have changed his mind, or it may have been changed for him by a crew unwilling to continue sailing in such a hostile climate.

Throughout the voyage, Hudson grasped for evidence in support of Thorne's Polar Theory. He went so far as to call the climate at Collin's Bay on Spitzbergen (at 79°N latitude, some 750 miles north of the Arctic Circle) "hot." Although it is true that the Gulf Stream (Spitzbergen Atlantic Current) moderates the temperature at the western shore of Spitzbergen, Hudson clearly was guilty of either hyperbole or self-delusion.

Henry Hudson's expedition did not reach Cathay, or even the North Pole. He brought back no precious cargo, and made no profit for his backers. But the voyage did establish, once and for all, that "an abundance of ice all around, and joyning to the land" prevented any passage by sea over the North Pole. The previously untested theories of Robert Thorne were finally laid to rest.

Ultimately, the Muscovy Company did benefit from Hudson's voyage. Just as Cabot's news about the great numbers of cod off the Newfoundland Banks spurred fishing efforts, Hudson's revelation of the abundance of whales off Spitzbergen set in motion a lucrative industry. Barely a decade later, its whales nearly decimated, Spitzbergen reverted to a forlorn, abandoned outpost. In 1920 the land was awarded by treaty to Norway and renamed Svalbard (Cold Coast).

Hudson's Tutches, too, eventually yielded wealth, primarily to walrus hunters, who killed the animals for their tusks. Like Spitzbergen, it is seldom visited now and remains unchanged from the time Henry Hudson first viewed it.

Origin of Hudson's Geographic Notions

In the years after the expedition by Sir Hugh Willoughby and Stephen Burrough, numerous other attempts were made to find the Northeast Passage. Most notable were those of the Dutch explorer Willem Barents, whose voyages convinced his contemporaries

Figure 2-8. *In the sixteenth century, the polar bear "big as a cow, and white as a swan," was greeted with the same amazement as was the walrus. When Willem Barents discovered a new land in 1596, he saw a great, white bear there. His men killed it, then "fleaced her and found her skinne to be twelve foote long; which done we eate some of her flesh, but we brookt it not well. Our island wee then called the Beare Island."*

Ibetson del.   Tookey Sc.

Published by W.Darton, J.Harvey, & W.Belch. London. May 1st.1797.

that China could be reached by sailing *north* of Nova Zembla.

Peter Plancius reasoned that Barents, on his 1595 expedition, had not sailed far enough north before turning east. Barents agreed, and on his third voyage to the Arctic he sailed to North Cape, Norway, then north to latitude 74°30'. There he discovered an unknown island, which he named Bear Island for the great white beasts he encountered.

Barents continued north until he reached another new land, which he could not circumnavigate. However, he did explore a large portion of its western shore, which he named Vogel Hoeck (Bird Cape), and a small portion of the northern shore, which he called Nieuland.

Unable to go farther, Barents returned to Bear Island and headed for the northeast corner of Nova Zembla. He intended to continue his voyage east, but was forced by the ice that blocked his path to overwinter on that desolate land. There he perished, a victim of the cruel climate.

Hudson was privy to all this geographical information. He possessed a map prepared by Baptista van Doetechum (or one almost identical to it) expressly intended to illustrate the third of Barents's three expeditions to the north (see page 79). In addition, Hudson had access to the logbooks and journals of the English explorers, which were held by the Muscovy Company, and to the journals of all the Dutch voyagers, which were available in the Hakluyt Society's publications.

When Hudson approached the Newland coast he knew precisely what to expect. Though it was foggy and he could not see land, he wrote: "By our account we were near Vogel Hooke. About eight o'clock this evening we planned to shape our course from there to northwest." Ice, fog, currents, and unreliable celestial observations made it impossible to determine the exact latitude of Vogel Hooke, but it appears to be close to 79°N latitude on the northwest point of Charles's Island (one of the islands of the Spitzbergen group).

Captain Fotherby, one of the passengers on the 1607

voyage, made the following statement about Hudson's journal:

Having perused Hudson's journall, writ by his own hands, in that voyage wherein he had sight of certayne land, which he named Hold-with-Hope, I found that by his owne reckoning it should not be more than 100 leagues [300 miles] from King James Newland, and in latitude 72°30 minutes.

Figure 2-9. *Jodocus Hondius map, 1602. The distinguished Flemish cartographer, Jodocus Hondius, was a contemporary and friend of Henry Hudson. In the cartouche, Hondius exclaims that his map of Europe is an improvement over those by the two best known cartographers of the time, Gerardus Mercator, and Abraham Ortelius. Hondius disconnects Greenland from its attachment to the mainland of Europe, but only cautiously.*

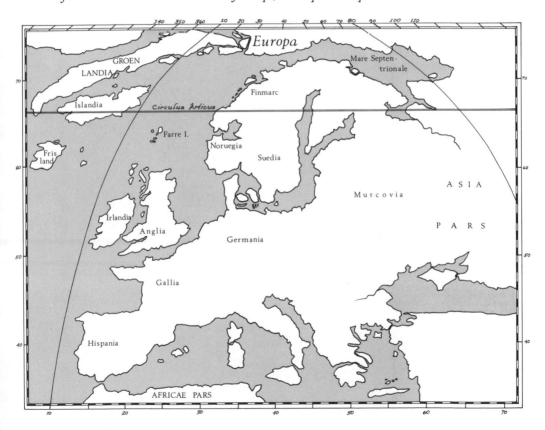

Actually, the distance between the two is 600 miles, not the 300 stated by Fotherby, but this discrepancy is easily accounted for: Even the most accomplished cartographers showed the east coast of Greenland trending northeast and southwest, but the direction is essentially north and south. Since Hudson used the van Doetechum map as a reference, Hold-with-Hope, Greenland, and the coast of Newland indeed appeared to be only 300 miles apart. This marked displacement can be traced back to earlier descriptions of Greenland's coast as a long peninsula extending from the north of Europe. It is also the reason Barents, when he first reached Spitzbergen, believed that it was Greenland, and called it by that name. Only that portion north of 80° latitude did he call Nieuland.

CHAPTER THREE

North of Russia and Siberia: 1608

Prologue

*I*n 1608 Henry Hudson, again under the auspices of the Muscovy Company, set out to explore the Arctic. In search of a Northeast Passage, he planned to investigate two routes to the Kara Sea: the sea north of Nova Zembla, and a strait or river through the main body of Nova Zembla. From there he intended to sail east along the coast of Siberia until he reached the entrance to the Pacific Ocean.

Explorers now believed that the great River Ob, which flows into the Kara Sea east of Nova Zembla at the known limits of the Russian northern shore, might lead them to Cathay. Interest was spurred by rumors that the sea beyond the River Ob was warm, and that on reaching it an easy passage east was at hand.

Any fragment of evidence, no matter how fantastical, was taken as proof that a passage existed. A six-foot narwhal tusk found on the shore of Vaigat Island and mistaken for the horn of a unicorn, for example, showed that "there must of necessity be a passage out of the said Oriental Ocean into our Septentrionall [northern] seas," because it was "known that unicorns are bred in the lands of Cathay, China and other Oriental Regions."

But it took more than fable, rumor, and half-truth to perpetuate the quest for the Northeast Passage. Besides the exhortations of Sebastian Cabot were the beliefs of more contemporary geographers, such as Gerardus Mercator, Abraham Ortelius, and Peter Plancius. Mercator, supporting his map showing an open-water passage, wrote: "The voyage to Cathaio by the East is doubtless very easy and short, and I have oftentimes marvelled that being so happily begun it hath been left off, and the course changed to the West, after more than half of the voyage was discovered."

The phrases "riches of the East" and "treasures of the Orient" were not inappropriate to describe the potential bounty of trade with the East. A single vessel could contain enormous quantities of exotic goods — as did the East Indian carrack *Madre de Dios*, captured in 1592 by Sir John Burrough. The ship was carrying, in addition to an unlisted number of jewels, 900 tons of

spices, drugges, silks, calicos, quilts, carpets, and colours, etc. The spices were peppers, cloves, maces, nutmegs, cinnamon, greene ginger: the drugs were benjamin, frankincense, galingale, mirablans, aloes, Zocotrina, camphire: the silks, damasks, taffatas, sarcenets, altobarsos, that is counterfeit cloth of gold, unwrought China silke, sheared silke, white twisted silke, curled cypresse. The calicos were book-calicos, calicolawnes, broad white calicos, fine starched calicos, course white calicos, browne broad calicos, browne course calicos. There were also canopies, and course diaper-dowels, quilts of course sarcenet and of calico, carpets like those of Turkey; whereunto are to be added the pearle, muske, civet and amber-griece. The rest of the wares were . . . eliphants teeth, porcellan vessels of China, coco-nuts, hides, eben-wood as blacke as jet, bedsteads of the same, cloth of the rindes of trees very strange for the matter, and artificiall in workemanship."

Their imaginations thus fired, it is small wonder that there were men willing to pursue a passage regardless of the uncertainties and dangers.

Figure 3-1. *Reconstruction of Hudson's route to Nova Zembla in 1608.*
Labels in italics are names used by Hudson.

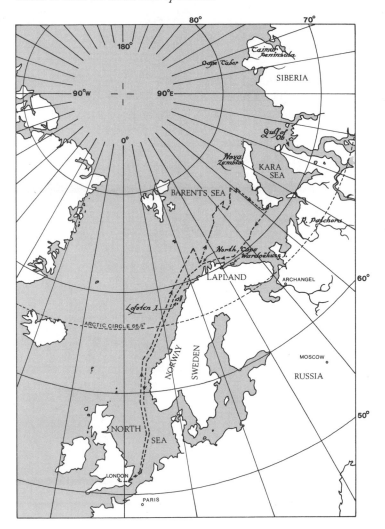

Henry Hudson left England on April 22, 1608 in the
Hope-well, the same ship he had sailed on his previous
voyage, and headed north, following the coast of Norway. He arrived at Nova Zembla during one of its rare
hospitable periods. Normally, "the Sea of Kara, bounded
on the west by Nova Zembla and on the east by the vast
peninsula of Tajmurland [Taymyr Peninsula in north-cen-

Figure 3-2. *Detail of Nova Zembla portion of Hudson's 1607 passage.*

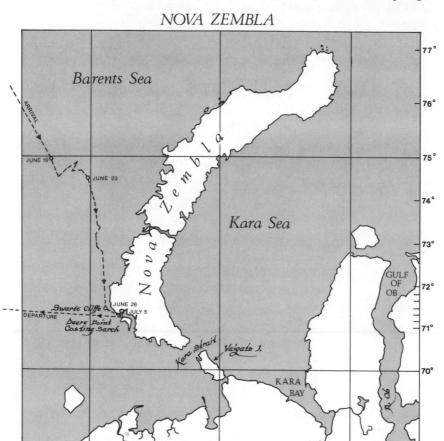

NOVA ZEMBLA

Barents Sea

Nova Zembla

Kara Sea

ARRIVAL

JUNE 19

JUNE 23

DEPARTURE

Swarte Cliffs

JUNE 26

JULY 5

Deere Point
Costing Sarch

Kara Strait

Vaigats I.

KARA
BAY

GULF
OF
OB

R. Ob

77°
76°
75°
74°
73°
72°
71°
70°

50°   60°   70°

tral Siberia] is one of the most inhospitable parts of the
inhospitable Polar Ocean. The absence of all trees or
shrubs, or even of all vigorous herbage, imparts a character of the deepest solitude to the Novaya Zemlya land-
scape, and inspires even the rough sailor with a kind of
religious awe; it is as if the dawn of creation had but just
begun, and life were still to be called into existence."

Hudson and his crew searched the bays and inlets
for a strait to the Kara Sea, but once again masses of ice
kept them from their goal. After they cleared North
Cape and descended as far as the Lofoten Islands, Hud-

son turned west. It wasn't until he had passed the North Sea that the crew realized he had no intention of returning to England. Henry Hudson had turned the bow of his vessel around to search for the Northwest Passage.

Any further attempt to continue sailing west was obviously thwarted by the crew. Although Hudson does not say so directly, we can infer from his August 7 logbook entry that mutiny had occurred: "I used all diligence to return to London, and therefore now I gave my companie a certificate under my hand, of my free and willing return, without persuasion or force of any one or more of them." This was the first mutiny under Hudson's command, but not the last.

The Journal

The following transcription is taken from Book III of *Purchas His Pilgrimes*, by Samuel Purchas.

A Second Voyage or Employment of Master Henry Hudson
For Finding a Passage to the East Indies by the Northeast:
Written by Himself

The names of the crew are as follows:

Henry Hudson — master and pilot
Robert Juet — master's mate
Ludlowe Arnall
John Cooke — boatswain
Philip Stacie — carpenter
John Barnes
John Braunch — cook
John Adrey

James Strutton
Michael Feirce
Thomas Hilles
Richard Tomson
Robert Raynor
John Hudson
Humfrey Gilby

The courses observed in this journal were by a compass, that the needle and the north of the Flye were directly one on the other.[1]

Set sail from docks in London.

Friday of *April the 22nd, 1608* we set sail at St. Katherines [docks], going with the tide down to Blackewall.

May 20 At noon we were at 64°52′, the observation being a good one due to smooth seas; at this time and place the needle inclined under the horizon by 81°

Inclination of the needle.

May 21 At night there was thick fog; we sailed north northeast. In the afternoon there was little wind, thick fog, and a smooth sea; by our account we were at 67°, with the needle inclining 82°. The night was calm and clear.

May 23 We had an easterly wind in the morning, and we steered northeast, and north by east. All morning it was foggy, but it cleared in the afternoon and although the wind decreased, we were able to hold our course north all night.

May 24 The wind was east northeast, and east by north; under full sail, we kept as close to the wind as we could. We estimated the Lofoten Islands to be east by north of us at a distance of 48 miles. From four o'clock this afternoon, and throughout the night, we kept our course as the night before [north].

Lofoten Islands, west of Norway.

May 25 The wind was from the east northeast; we steered as close to north as we could. Today the weather was clear, but searching cold; the cold began on the twenty-first, at which time my carpenter became sick, and still is. Three or four of my crew are also becoming sick, I suppose due to the cold. All night it was calm.

May 26 Cold, but clear weather today we sailed northeasterly until midnight; then we sailed southeast and east until noon the next day.

May 27 Cold and dry weather. At noon the wind was north and north northwest; we steered northeast and east northeast as best we could. With a smooth sea, our observation placed us at 69°40′, and the needle inclined 84°. All night we had wind and weather as before.

May 28 Dry, cold, clear weather, and with the wind between north northwest and north, we held our

Charting the Sea of Darkness

course east northeast. We saw the sun on the north meridian, 5°35′ above the horizon.

Midnight Sun.

May 29 Today, a hard gale from the north northwest. From midnight until noon, we had sailed east northeast for a distance of 63 miles. We had the sun on the meridian 5°, and our latitude was 73°13′, which placed the ship ahead of our estimated position.[2] At midnight the wind shifted to the southeast; we came about and steered east northeast. Today the weather was partly clear, with some snow.

A push from the Norwegian Current.

May 30 Cold, clear weather, with the wind between northeast and east by north. We steered east southeast, and by observation were at 73°50′.

May 31 Cold, clear weather; from yesterday until noon today we steered southeast by south, in the latitude of 72°45′.

June 1 A hard gale of wind from the east northeast, with snow; we made good progress southeast.

June 2 Wind still a hard gale from the northeast, and we maintained our course southeast all day, but towards night it became calm, with fog.

June 3 In the morning we sighted North Cape at 71°N; late at night it bore south-west and half a point southerly of us, at a distance of 24 miles. Having a smooth sea, I observed the needle inclined 84.5° under the horizon; also, I found the magnetic variation to be 11° westerly. We steered northeast by east. It was clear weather and we saw Norwegian fishermen at sea.

North Cape, Norway's most northern point.

June 4 Warm, clear sunshine, and we steered away northeast by east. Now, by God's help, our carpenter has recovered; he made a mast for our ship's boat, and the crew made a sail. We had the sun in sight on the north meridian, its height above the horizon being 5°40′. Inclination of the needle is 23°21′ [sic], and our latitude is 72°21′.

June 5 In the morning the weather was calm; we sounded and the depth was 140 fathoms, with a muddy, sand bottom.[3] Here, on the swells which set northeast by east and southwest by west, we saw lampreys. We also saw driftwood. Afterward, we had

---

wind, and were able to sail, making our way north northeast. Toward night we sounded and found a muddy, sand bottom at 150 fathoms. Today the weather was clear, and not cold.

June 6 From yesterday until noon today we had clear weather with the wind east northeast. By way of various headings our course was north by west, in the latitude of 73°24′. We found our ship had out-run us; soundings in 160 fathoms. Little wind in the afternoon.

June 7 In the morning the wind was out of the south. From yesterday until noon today, we figured that by various headings, we had made 45 miles in a general northeast direction. Today the weather was oppressive, but clear, and we had a good gale of wind. Three days before this, our cook and one other of the crew were very sick. In the morning we had ground at 150 fathoms, but by night, no ground at 180 fathoms, which increased our hope. Tonight we had some snow, which continued for four hours, then we had a storm, with the wind northeast by east. We steered north by west under shortened sail. Here the needle inclined 86°. By my account, our latitude was roughly 74.5°. Tonight we saw the sun on the north meridian; its height was 7°40′, which makes our latitude 74°23′.

June 8 From midnight last night, until noon today, we figured that by various headings our general course was north by east; our latitude was 74°38′, and there was no bottom at 200 fathoms. In the afternoon, the wind came out of the south southeast, and southeast by east. Throughout the day and night we had clear weather, and we are now entering into a black-blue sea.

Enter a dark blue sea.

June 9 Clear weather, with the wind southeast by east; from yesterday [noon] until noon today, we steered northeast with no trouble, then we encountered ice. It was the first ice we had seen on this voyage, and entered, hoping to pass through it. We held our course between northeast and east northeast, until four in the afternoon, heading up for one ice-floe and giving room to another. By this time we were so far in, 12 to 15

First encounter with ice.

miles, and the ice so thick and firm ahead, that we had endangered ourselves; we returned the way we had entered, suffering only a few rubs of our ship against the ice. By eight o'clock this evening we got free of it. Until noon the next day we steered southwest by south for 54 miles; soundings taken midway showed we had no ground at 180 fathoms.

June 10 The weather was hazy in the morning, but by noon it cleared up; then the wind being east southeast, we came about and steered north by east for two watches, 15 miles. Then we had an east wind; we came about and steered south southeast, making our way south for 18 miles.

June 11 In the morning, with a hard storm out of the east and east by south, we lay-a-hull.

June 12 In the morning there was fog, but after that we had clear weather for the rest of the day; with the wind south southwest, we steered east by north. At noon we were at 75°30′ of latitude. From noon until four o'clock we steered east by north for 15 miles, then we saw ice ahead of us and under our lee, trending from the northwest to the north and east of us. Soundings showed a bottom of greenish mud at 100 fathoms. Here we saw lampreys and various pieces of driftwood driving by us, lying south southwest and north northeast. Ever since the North Cape, we had seen this sort of thing many times.

Lampreys. Driftwood carried all the way from North America by the Gulf Stream.

June 13 With clear weather, and an east wind, we made our way south two watches, for 18 miles; then we came about, heading north one watch, for 10½ miles. At midnight there was much wind with fog, so we lay-a-hull with the ship's bow pointing south.

June 14 In the morning there was fog, and our shrouds were frozen, but we had clear sunshine in the afternoon and throughout the night.

June 15 All day and through the night there was clear sunshine, with the wind out of the east; latitude at noon is 75°07′. By our account we sailed westward 39 miles. In the afternoon the sea calmed, and with an east wind we set sail, heading south by east and south

southeast. This morning, one of our crew while looking overboard saw a mermaid calling the rest of the
crew to come see her. One more came up; by that time
she was close to the ship's side and looking earnestly at
the men; a little after, a sea came up and overturned
her. As they saw her, from the navel upward, her back
and breasts were like a woman's, her body as big as
ours, her skin very white, and she had long, black hair
hanging down behind. In her going down they saw
her tail, which was like the tail of a porpoise, and
speckled like a mackerel. Thomas Hiles and Robert
Rayner were the men who saw her.[4]

June 16 Clear weather with an east wind. From
yesterday noon until noon today, we headed south by
east 27 miles, and from noon until eight o'clock in the
evening, 18 miles. Then we came about and headed
northwards.

June 17 Clear weather, the wind southeast by east;
from last noon until noon today our heading was
northeast by east; at noon our latitude was 74°40′. In

White-green sea.

the afternoon the sea was whitish-green; we sounded
and found a bottom of green mud at 86 fathoms. Here
we saw whales, porpoises and a sea full of fowl. From
noon until midnight we had the sun at its lowest, on

*Latitude
observation from
the Midnight Sun.*

the north by east, easterly as shown by the compass;
our latitude is 74°54′. Taking soundings, we found 92
fathoms of water, with mud bottom as before.

June 18 Fair weather, with wind southeast by east.
From midnight until noon today we sailed northeast by
east, in the latitude of 75°24′. We had ground at 95
fathoms, with mud bottom as before. Here we sighted
ice to the north of us. In the afternoon, with but little
wind from the northeast, we came about and lay east
southeast, and at six o'clock had ground at 95½ fathoms; mud as before. From noon until midnight we
headed southeast and southeast by east, having the sun
at its meridian north by east, half a point eastward.
The sun's height was 8°40′. Soundings, 90 fathoms.
Throughout the day we had ice trending on our port
side; presently, it is northwest of us to the east south-

east. I have some reason to think there is a tide or current setting northward; comparing the course we held, to our actual course made good between this noon and midnight observations, makes me suspect it even more.

North Cape Current.

June 19 Fair and warm weather, with a smooth sea. Here the needle inclined 89.5°, our latitude at noon 75°22'; sounding, we had ground in 100 fathoms. From 12 o'clock last night until noon today, we calculated our progress to be east by north to southeast for 30 miles, always having sight of ice to our port. We had the wind between north and north northwest. We saw the sun on the north horizon at its lowest, north by east and half a point easterly; its height was 8°10', making our latitude 74°56'. Sounding, we had ground in 126 fathoms. From noon to this time we calculated our course east by south and east southeast, by a distance of 36 miles.

June 20 Fair, warm weather today, and at four o'clock this morning we had soundings at 125 fathoms. Here, we heard bears roaring on the ice, and there were an incredible number of seals. We had soundings in 115 fathoms, and later, 95 fathoms, with a bottom of sandy mud. We had the sun on the meridian north by east, and half a point easterly; its height was 7°20'. From 12 o'clock last night until 12 o'clock this night, we had made 36 miles to the southeast by south, and 10 1/2 miles southeast; the ice always being off to our port. The wind today was between north and northwest.

Roar of bears and a multitude of seals.

June 21 At four o'clock in the morning we sounded and had 120 fathoms, with a bottom of green mud; ice bore east of us. The wind was variable, but by various headings we made good a south southeast course; our latitude at noon was 74°9', and we found we were farther north than we had expected. Throughout the day the weather was fair, clear and warm, and after midnight we had ice on our port side. At this time the sun was at its lowest, his height 7°40', which makes our latitude 74°33'. From yesterday noon until 12 o'clock tonight, we had made 19 1/2 miles in an east northeast direction; it appears we were pushed northward. Here we had ground of green, sandy mud in 130 fathoms.

June 22 Fair, clear weather, with the wind west northwest. At eight o'clock this morning we had ground of green mud at 115 fathoms. From midnight until noon our course was northeast by east, being in the latitude of 74°35', and we found that our ship's position and our observed position were not [blank in original], but both were carefully taken.[6] All day yesterday we had ice on our port side, and now we have ice ahead of us. We steered southeast for 15 miles, then the ice trended south by west 18 miles; we sailed by, and got around it by eight o'clock in the evening. Having a smooth sea, we took note of the needle, which inclined 85°; from eight o'clock to 12 we steered north by east easterly. Then we had the sun at its north meridian, north by east and half a point easterly; its height was 7°45', which makes our latitude 74°43'.

June 23 In the morning, thick fog, with the wind north northwest. From midnight until four o'clock this morning, we sailed northeast for 15 miles, and then we were among the ice. We came about, and sailed southwest two hours, six miles; had no ground at 180 fathoms. Then we came about again and steered until eight o'clock, for six miles; it cleared up, and we had ice ahead of us. We changed course from north to southeast, and our shrouds were frozen. Then, until noon, we steered east by south for 12 miles, and we were near ice on our port side, in the latitude of 74°30'. In the afternoon the wind was out of the north; first we steered two and a half hours for 16½ miles, then three hours south southeast for 15 miles, then one hour southeast by south for four and a half miles, and finally one hour east for one and a half miles, which brought us to eight in the evening; always with ice on our port side. This afternoon we had some snow. From eight o'clock until midnight we steered south southwest for 12 miles, with ice as before. We saw the sun at its lowest, north northeast, its height 7°15', making our latitude 74°18'.

Surrounded by ice.

Day spent constantly avoiding ice.

Charting the Sea of Darkness

June 24 Clear but cold, with some snow. From midnight until four o'clock this morning we steered southward six miles, and southeast by east, six miles. And from four until noon we steered southeast southerly for 27 miles. Sounding, we had bottom at 140 fathoms. From noon until three o'clock we steered southeast by south for nine miles, then from three until four, southwest by south, three miles; had ice from the northeast to the southeast of us. From four o'clock until eight we steered southwest, seven and a half miles, then southward for one and a half miles, with ice near us.

June 25 Cold and clear, with the wind east southeast; from eight o'clock last night until four this morning, our course was south by east, 13¹/₂ miles; sounding, we had ground in 80 fathoms. The sun's meridian was southwest by south of us, at which time what little wind we had before began to fall; we were in latitude of 72°52'. Our nearness to Nova Zembla with its abundance of ice, and the ice to port of us, prevented any hope of passage this way. From noon until eight o'clock in the evening the wind was between north northeast and northeast; we steered southeast, 10¹/₂ miles, and had ice on our port, and shoaling of 68 fathoms.

June 26 Fair, sunshining weather, and wind out of the east northeast. From midnight until four o'clock this morning we steered southward six miles; sounding, we found 66 fathoms, with a mud bottom. From four o'clock until noon we steered southeast by south for 12 miles. We had the sun at its meridian southeast by south of us, in the latitude of 72°25', and Nova Zembla was in sight 12 to 15 miles from us. The place called Swart Cliff by the Hollanders bore southeast of us. In the afternoon we had a fine gale from the east northeast, and by eight o'clock we had brought it to bear off us east southerly, and sailed along the shore about three miles off.

Swart Cliff.

June 27 All morning it was almost calm; being only two miles from the shore, I sent my mate Robert Juet, and boatswain John Cooke, ashore with four others to see what the land would yield which might be profitable, and to fill two or three casks with water. They found and brought aboard some whales' fins, two deer's horns, and the dung of deer. They told me they saw grass from last year on shore, with young, new grass coming up among it a shaftman long. The ground was boggy in some places, with many streams of snow-water nearby; it was very hot on shore and the snow melted quickly. They also saw the footprints of many large bears, of deer, and foxes. They had left us at three o'clock in the morning, and returned in the late morning; on their return we saw two or three groups of walruses swimming near us, the sea being almost calm.

They go ashore.

I presently sent my mate [Juet], Ladlaw the carpenter, and six others ashore to a place where I thought the walrus might land; they found the place likely, but there was no sign of any walruses having been there. There was a cross standing on the shore, much driftwood, and sign of fires that had been made there. They saw footprints of very large deer and bears, many fowl, and a fox. They brought back with them whale fins, some moss, flowers and green things that grew there. They also brought two pieces of a cross which they found there. The sun was on the meridian north northeast and half a point easterly, before it began to fall.[7] The sun's height was 4°45', which makes the latitude 72°12'; inclination of the needle, 22°33'. There is disagreement between this observation and yesterday's, but much care was taken with it, and with the clearness of the sun, smoothness of the sea, and our nearness to land, we could not be deceived.

Goose Coast.

June 28 At four o'clock in the morning our ship's boat came aboard, bringing a whale's fin, two dozen fowl and some eggs, some of which were good. The sea was full of walruses, but there were no signs of their being ashore. And in this calm, from eight o'clock last evening until four this morning, a current or tide had set us back to the north as far as we had been last evening at four o'clock, and we decided to

Set to the north by a current.

pull the boat, rather than risk losing an anchor or spoiling the cable. Here, the ship's boat, which last year was inadequate, began to be of service, and an encouragement to the crew.

June 29 In the morning, being one and a half miles from the shore, and a calm sea, the needle inclined 84 degrees. There were many walruses in the sea near us, and desiring to find out where they came ashore, we used both sail and oars to tow our boat around a point of land which fell away toward the east. Indeed, the walruses did go that way. We had the sun at its meridian south by west and half a point west of us, in·the latitude of 71°15′. At two o'clock this afternoon we anchored in the mouth of a river which had an island in it 12 miles upstream; depth was 32 fathoms, and the bottom a black sand. The current swept much ice, on which many walruses were sleeping, out of this river or sound. It also caused us to drag anchor twice this night; though calm all day, it pleased God in our need, to give us a fine gale which freed us from the danger. Today was calm, clear and hot weather; the anchor holding all night.

June 30 Calm, hot and fair weather; we weighed anchor in the morning, and by rowing and towing, came to anchor at noon near the previously mentioned island in the mouth of the river. Very much ice was being driven out to sea about six miles from us; it was being driven toward the northwest so fast that by midnight we could not see it from the lookout. At the island where we were anchored lies a small rock, covered with 40 or 50 sleeping walruses; it being so small, this was all it could hold. I sent all the crew ashore to kill them, leaving no one aboard except my boy and myself; but they were so near the water, all got away, except one, which they killed and brought his head back.

Before they came back to the ship they went upon the island, which is reasonably high and steep, but flat on top. In an hour they came aboard, bringing with them a large fowl, of which there were many, and likewise some

Figure 3-3. *Chase of the walrus. From G. Hartwig,* The Tropical and Polar Worlds.

eggs. This island is two flight-shot long and one wide.[8] At midnight, due to the strength of current, our anchor broke free and we went aground; but by the help of God we pulled the ship off without any damage. We quickly moved our ship, and after, with little wind from the east and east southeast, rode quietly all night. At noon we took an observation, and are in the latitude of 71°15′.

July 1 We saw more ice to the seaward of us being driven to the northwest. At noon it was calm, and the sun at its meridian was south by west and a half point west of us, in the latitude of 71°24′. This morning I sent my mate Everet, and four of our crew, to row about the bay to find what rivers were in it, and where the walruses landed; also, to explore the sound or large river at the head of the bay which always sent a strong current to the northward against the tide coming from that direction. I found the same condition before, when coming in to a place north of this. It had been my hope to seek a passage north, between Newland [Spitzbergen] and Nova Zembla, but when this was eliminated on account

No passage between Newland and Nova Zembla.

of the great amount of ice, my plan was to pass south of Nova Zembla, by Vaigats, passing by the north of the river Ob; from there I would be able to round the North Cape of Tartaria [Cape Tabin or Taimur Peninsula].[9]

South toward the River Ob.

Failing this, I would at least be able to give good reason why it could not be accomplished. Judging from the evidence presented, the sound we are presently in might provide even a better passage to the east of Nova Zembla then the Vaigats route; for the current which runs in this sound or stream is so strong, that ice or anything else in it is carried away, even against the flood tide coming in from the north. In both the flood and ebb tide, the current holds a strong course; so that the flood tide flows from the north for three hours, and ebbs for nine hours.

Strong current.

July 2 The wind being east southeast, Friday and today was reasonably cold, and the walruses did not play within our sight as they did in warm weather. This morning at three o'clock, my mate and crew came aboard, bringing a large deer's horn, a lock of white deer's hair, and four dozen fowl. Their boat was half filled with driftwood, and some flowers and green things they found growing on shore. They had seen a herd of 10 deer, much driftwood lying on the shore, and many good bays. There was one fair river on the north shore for the walruses to land on, but they didn't see any there, though there were signs they had been in the bays. They declared that the river or sound was six to nine miles broad, its depth exceeded 20 fathoms, and that the water was the color of the sea, very salty, with a strong current setting out of it. At six o'clock this morning we had the fearful sight of much ice from southward being driven upon us; but by the mercy of God and His mighty help, we escaped the danger. We were moored with two anchors ahead, and by letting out one cable, and hauling in the other, we were able to fend off the ice with beams and spars; this labor continued until six o'clock in the evening, then it was past us and we rode quietly, having a restful night.

River, color of the sea.

July 3 A hard gale of wind from the north. At three

o'clock this morning we weighed anchor and set sail, intending to run into the river or sound we had spoken of before.

July 4 In the morning it cleared up, with the wind from the northwest; we weighed anchor, set sail, and stood to the eastward, passing over a reef on which we found five and a half, six, six and a half, and seven fathoms of water. Then we saw that the sound was full of ice, but there was a large river to the northeast which was free of ice, and had a strong current coming out of it. We were all hopeful of this northerly river or sound, and sailing in it we found a depth of 23 fathoms, with hard mud bottom, for a distance of 15 or 18 miles.

Then the wind veered more northerly, and the current became so strong that we could not make any progress; we anchored and had supper. Then I sent my mate Juet, with five or six more of our crew, in the ship's boat with sail and oars, to go up the river. Provided with food, and weapons for defense, they were to take soundings as they went; if the river still continued to be deep, they were to continue until it trended to the east or the south; meanwhile, we remained at anchor.

July 5 In the morning the wind was from the west; we weighed anchor, intending to set sail and run up the sound to meet our crew, but then the wind shifted northerly on us, and we stopped our efforts. At noon the crew came back, having had a difficult time, for they had been 18 or 24 miles up the river, taking soundings; at first the depth was 20 fathoms, then 23 fathoms, after which it became eight, six and one fathom; finally, no more than four feet at best. They then went ashore and found a good quantity of wild goose quills, a piece of an old oar, and some flowers and green things which they found growing.

They saw many deer, as did we later on. With the crew back aboard ship, we set sail with a north northwest wind and steered again to the southwest, sorry that our labor had been in vain; for had this sound, with its breadth, depth, safeness of harbor, and good anchoring ground, continued as it promised, it might have yielded

The river searched.

an excellent passage to a more easterly sea. Generally, all the land of Nova Zembla that we have seen is pleasant to look at; the main high land has no snow on it, and some places are green with deer feeding on it. The hills are partly covered with snow and partly bare. It is no wonder there is so much ice in the sea toward the Pole, what with so many sounds and rivers in Nova Zembla and Newland, in addition to the coasts of Pechora, Russia, Groenland and Lappia to generate it, which my travels in these parts has proved.

By means of all that ice, I suppose there will be no navigable passage this way. This evening we had a stormy sea, therefore we came to anchor under Deer Point, riding in 20 fathoms with a mud bottom. I sent my mate Ladle, with four more ashore, to see if there were any walruses there, also to kill some fowl. We have not seen any walrus since Saturday, the second day of this month, at which time we saw them leaving the ice. They found a good landing place for them, but no sign of their having been there; but they did find that fire had been made, though not recently. At 10 o'clock this evening they came aboard, bringing with them almost a hundred fowl called wellocks. At night it was wet, foggy and very thick and cold, with the wind west southwest.

July 6 In the morning it was stormy, with the wind shifting between west and southwest; it was against our making any progress, so we anchored, and had much ice driving by to the east of us. At nine o'clock this evening we had a north northwest wind; we weighed anchor and set sail, steering to the west, having lost hope of finding a passage by way of the northeast. I intend now to find out whether Willoughby's Land is located where it is shown on our charts. If it is, we might find walruses on it, for there aren't any here because of the ice. Our present location on Nova Zembla is called Costing Sarch by the Dutch, being discovered by Oliver Brunel, and later confirmed by Willem Barents's observation. It is plotted too far to the north by the Dutch; for what reason I do not know, unless it is to have it in keeping with a compass course, irrespective of magnetic variation. It is as broad as the Vaigats passage, and just as likely to yield a way; my hope was that the strength of current would have kept it cleared of ice, but it did not. It is so full of ice you would hardly believe it. All day it was foggy and cold.

Another potential passage denied.

July 7 Clear, but cold. From the evening before, to this morning, we kept our course west by south for 45 miles, the wind being out of the north; but from the morning until eight o'clock in the evening it was calm, then we had the wind again out of the north and we sailed until nine o'clock the next morning west southwest, 24 miles. Then we went north by west for nine miles, and we had the sun at its highest, south southwest, in the latitude of 71°02′.

July 8 Fair weather; at noon we had the wind east northeast, and we steered north for nine miles until four o'clock. Then we steered north by west until six o'clock in the evening, four and a half miles. Then the wind was a hard gale out of the northeast, and we steered west by north until noon the next day, making by our estimate 69 miles. We had the sun on the meridian south by west and half a point west, in the latitude of 70°41′.

July 9 Clear weather. From noon this day until noon the next day, we sailed southwest by west for 36 miles, and northward nine miles; in these courses had soundings of 41, 42, 46, 48, and 45 fathoms. We had the sun south by west and half a point west of us at its meridian. The sea was lofty; our latitude was 70°20′.

July 10 Clear, but close. From this noon until noon the next day we had little wind from the west northwest, and we made our way northeasterly 15 miles. We had the sun at its highest south by west, and a point and one-third westerly, in the latitude of 70°55′. I think we had a rustling tide under us, and during this time had soundings between 45 and 40 fathoms, with a white sand bottom.

Tidal overfalls.

July 11 Clear weather; from this [noon] until noon the next day there was little wind, and sometimes it was calm. By our account we had sailed west by north for 15 miles; and had the sun on the meridian south by west, and a point and one-third west, in the latitude of 70°26', and found a rustling under us. This morning we came into a green sea of the color of the main ocean, a color which we have not seen since June the eighth. This black-blue color sea which we have had in the meantime is a sea pestered with ice, according to last and this year's experience.

A green sea free of ice, but a dark blue sea pestered with ice.

July 12 Fair weather: from noon until midnight our course was between west northwest and south southwest. Then we had a south wind, and sailed west by north for 39 miles until noon the next day. By our calculations, we made 54 miles in a westerly direction between yesterday and today. This afternoon we saw more porpoises then during all the rest of the voyage.

July 13 Close weather: in the afternoon the wind was from the south and very strong; under shortened sail we steered west by north until eight o'clock this evening. Although the wind was southerly at eight o'clock, until noon the next day it was calm most of the time. We steered away as before for 12 miles, which made in all, 36 miles. We had the sun at its height, south by west, in the latitude of 70°22'.

July 14 We steered west northwest until midnight, for 51 miles; then the wind came from the west, and more on our bow, and we steered north northwest for four and a half miles. Then we sailed west northwest for 15 miles. From the last until this day at noon, by way of various headings we made 72 miles in a northwest by west direction. We had the sun just past its meridian at south by west, in the latitude of 70°54'.

July 15 Fair weather, but toward night it became stormy with thunder. From this, until noon on the 16th, our course was west by north, 81 miles. The sun began to fall at south, three-quarter of a point westward, in the latitude of 70°42'.

July 16 Fair; from this until next day at noon, by way of various courses we made 36 miles toward the northwest. We had a shifting wind; the latitude (by bad observation) was 71°44'.

July 17 Fair weather in the morning, the wind being west by north. At four o'clock in the morning we saw land bearing west and south southwest of us, which would be Ward-house. This afternoon we had a storm, and we lay-a-hull until eight o'clock in the evening, when we then set sail, the wind being between west northwest, and northwest. Our course until the next day at noon was southwest by south for 36 miles. Cape Hopewell bore south southwest of us, and we were about 12 to 15 miles from land.

Northwest of Vardoëhuss Island.

July 18 Gusty, with rain all morning; then the wind which was south southeast until noon the next day shifted to east and southeast. In general, our course was northwest for 72 miles. Then North Kene bore off us west, by one half point [5½°] south, at a distance of 12 miles from us. The North Cape remained in sight, bearing west by north.

Return of night after ten weeks.

July 27 Cold, with rain and storm; tonight we began to burn the candle in the betacle [bitticle] again, which we had not done since the 19th of May, since between then and now we always had light.[10]

July 30 We had the sun upon the meridian due south, in the latitude of 68°46'; whereby we found we were before the ship by 30 or 36 miles. Lofoten Islands bore east of us, but they were not in sight.

Norwegian Current against them.

August 7 I used all diligence to arrive at London, and therefore I now gave my crew a certificate under my hand, of my free and willing return, without persuasion or force by any one or more of them. For when we were at Nova Zembla on the 6th of July, void of hope of a Northeast Passage (except by way of Vaigats, for which I was not equipped to try or prove), I therefore resolved to use all means I could to sail to the northwest. Considering the time and means we had, if the wind should be favorable to us, as it had during the first part of our voyage, I would try for that place called Lumley's Inlet, and Captain John Davis's Furious Overfall, hoping to run there 300 miles into it, and to return as God should enable me. But now, having spent more than half the time I had, and only making a small amount of progress due

No Northeast Passage.

to contrary winds, I thought it my duty to save food, wages and ship's gear, and return speedily, instead of giving way to foolish rashness and wasted time, or expending more effort than was necessary—and arrived at Gravesend August 26th.

✳

Epilogue: 1608

Henry Hudson proved on this voyage that ice blockage made a Northeast Passage to Cathay as unobtainable as the Polar route. Reluctantly, "with sorrow that their labor was in vain," he ended his efforts.

Mindful that his previous voyage had proved unprofitable for his backers, Hudson made an effort to return with some marketable commodity. Whenever possible, his men tried to kill walruses for their valuable ivory tusks, their hides, which could be made into leather, and their blubber, which was used for lamp oil. Although his men were not very successful as hunters, the walruses on Nova Zembla's coast would soon face the same fate as the whales of Spitzbergen.

Having conscientiously tried to fulfill the requirements of the expedition as charged by the Muscovy Company, Hudson felt free to seek an alternative route— the Northwest Passage. But as we know, his crew did not feel the same way.

We can only speculate that Hudson attempted to seek the Northwest Passage in 1607 after the polar route proved unobtainable. But his intentions for the 1608 voyage are unequivocally stated in the journal: "Void of hope of a Northeast Pasage . . . I thereby resolved to use all means I could to sayle to the north-west." Both his goal and his route were precisely described. He would try to reach the Furious Overfall described by Captain John Davis, and to "run into it a hundred leagues, and to return as God should enable me." This opening on the north coast of Labrador, with its raging, whirling currents and thirty- to sixty-foot tides, is the entrance to Hudson Bay.

Origin of Hudson's Geographic Notions

Of all the regions visited by Henry Hudson throughout his career, the coast and straits of Nova Zembla were the best known. Explorers had long been convinced that the

Figure 3-4. *Routes of exploration for the Northeast Passage before Hudson's voyage. Voyages in which an explorer died in his attempts are marked by an encircled "x".*

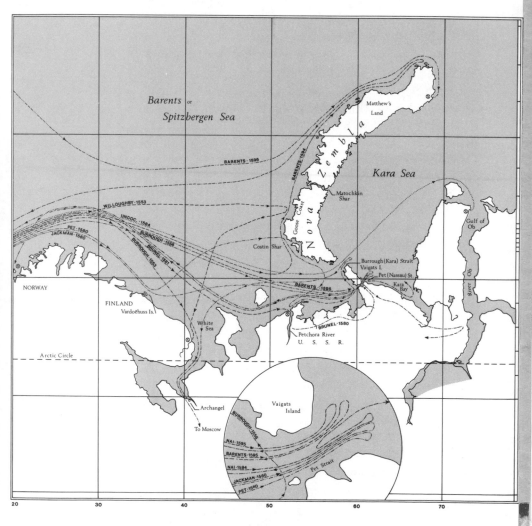

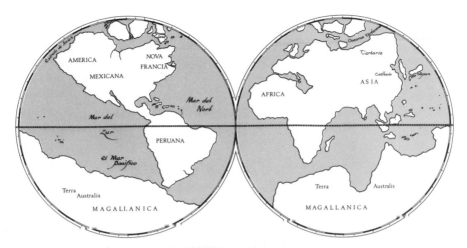

Figure 3-5. *Peter Plancius map, 1594. Based on the 1569 two-hemisphere world map by Gerardus Mercator, Plancius's map emphasized the relative ease with which a sea route to Asia could be made by sailing in Arctic waters. The narrow constrictions, which Mercator showed at the Strait of Anian, above Nova Zembla, and at the Tabin Promontory, were widened by Plancius to facilitate their use as a passage.*

Northeast Passage, like the Northwest Passage, had to exist—and, in line with the cosmographic dogma of the day, it was shown on the best maps. The same broad, unobstructed strait north of Russia and Asia leading to the Pacific appeared in the work of Ortelius and Peter Plancius, and on Mercator's equidistant-polar projection map.

On his 1569 polar map, Mercator made significant changes from the 1508 Ruysch Map. Like Ruysch, Mercator depicted the four islands with their indrawing seas (from the Nicholas Linna voyage in 1390) at the very center of the polar region. To accommodate the discovery of Spitzbergen, Mercator had to do away with the southwest coast of one of the islands; in its place is Barents's Newland (Spitzbergen). Only the western and a small part of the northern coast are shown, since that was the part that had been explored. Mercator also included Bear Island, discovered that same year.

The voyages of Martin Frobisher and John Davis created a major rethinking about the geography of

Greenland. It could no longer be attached to Asia, as on
the Ruysch map, or connected to the northern part of
Europe. Davis Strait now proclaimed Greenland to be a
separate, great island, surrounded by the *Mare Glaciale*
(Sea of Ice). Lumley's Inlet and the Furious Overfall — of
great importance in Henry Hudson's plans for the
Northwest Passage — appeared as a result of Davis's voyages.

*Figure 3-6. Polar projection map from 1569 edition of Mercator's Atlas.
The printing of Mercator's insert map to the main map of the world excited
more interest than the map in which Mercator first showed his new method
of projection for navigation. Its importance lay in clearly showing an open
sea passage in northern latitudes to the Far East. This particular edition obviously was made after the 1596 voyage of Willem Barents, for it displays
his discovery of t'Nieulant (Newland — Spitzbergen) and Bear Island.*

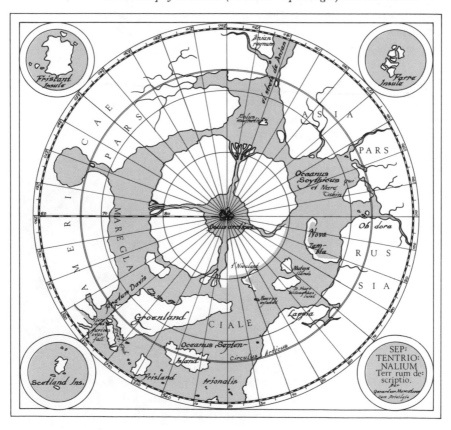

Before his death in 1553, Hugh Willoughby left a note aboard his ship describing an offshore island he had discovered, which "lyeth from Seynam east and by north 160 leagues, being in latitude 72 degrees." It turned out to be a phantom: not a new land at all, but a part of Goose Coast on the western shore of Nova Zembla—an error resulting from an incorrect determination of longitude. Dutch cartographers were unaware of the mistake. When Hudson gave up on finding a passage by the northeast, he set sail to the west to find out "whether Willoughbie's Land, were, as it is, layd in our cards [charts]." The land he investigated, however, was a large island immediately off the coast of Nova Zembla, in a deep bay called Costin Shar. On Dutch charts, the island was shown at 72°N latitude, the same latitude Willoughby gave for the new land. Its true latitude, however, is 71°N latitude, which is why Hudson exclaimed that it was placed too far north on Dutch charts. Subsequent charts placed the land much farther west.

This error created further confusion. Somewhere between 1608 and 1613, the Muscovy Company claimed exclusive fishing rights to the whales and walruses off the coast of Spitzbergen, based on the notion that Spitzbergen and the land discovered by Willoughby were one and the same.

The Matsyn Islands—the name is a corruption of the Russian *Mathuyshin*, for Matthew—represent another case of duplication. Located above 75°N latitude, their counterpart was Matthew's Land, the northern part of Nova Zembla above Matochihkin Shar. They appear on the Mercator map and on the chart created by Jodocus Hondius in 1611, published in Pontanus's *History of Amsterdam*.

The Hondius map is almost an exact copy of that created by Baptista van Doetechum twelve years earlier to show the third voyage of Willem Barents. The track of Barents's voyage north to Bear Island and Spitzbergen, then south and east to Nova Zembla, is preserved. But Hondius added to his map the new place names given by Henry Hudson in 1607. Hold-with-

Hope and Land of God's Mercy now appear on the Greenland coast. To Spitzbergen he added Collin's Cape and Hakluyt's Headland. Hondius also showed the limit of barrier ice Hudson encountered, which prevented travel farther north. He marked it as *Glacies ab H. Hudsono detecta anno 1608* — ice that Henry Hudson discovered in the year 1608. The date was wrong, possibly because Captain Edge had written in *Brief Discourse*: "In the year 1608, the said fellowship [Muscovy Company] set forth a ship called Hope-well, whereof Henry Hudson was master, to discover the pole." Sir Hugh Willoughby Land

Figure 3-7. *Jodocus Hondius chart of the polar region. Published in Pontanus's* History of Amsterdam, *1611, the Hondius Polar chart was derived from an earlier version by Baptista van Doetechum. The chart was produced to illustrate the third of Willem Barents's three expeditions to the north, but it also showed geographical information derived from Henry Hudson's 1607 voyage to the North Pole. Possibly, the knowledge was acquired through conversations with Hudson during his stay in Amsterdam. The error of depicting Greenland so close to Spitzbergen also can be attributed to an unadulterated copying of the van Doetechum chart (see Figure 3-8).*

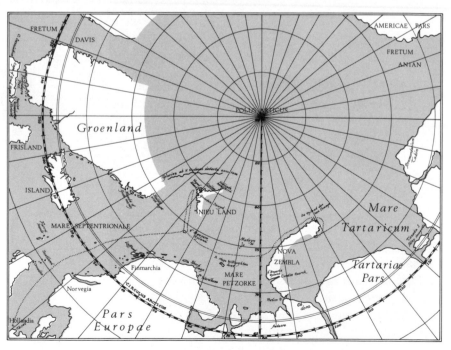

Charting the Sea of Darkness

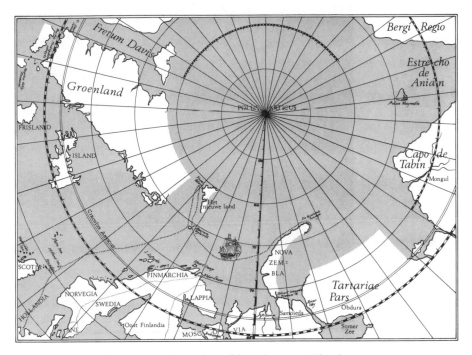

Figure 3-8. *Baptista van Doetechum Chart of the Polar region. This chart was produced to show the last voyage of Willem Barents, when he discovered Spitzbergen and Bear Island. It was published in Jan Huyghen van Linschoten's* Navigatio ac Itinerarium, *1599. The coastline of Greenland here, and on the Hondius version, is virtually unchanged from the map of the Zeno brothers's voyage in the fourteenth century.*

and Matsyn Island, shown by Mercator but left off van Doetechum's chart, are reinstated.

From these charts, we can see how thoroughly Hudson knew the northern parts of Scandinavia. His knowledge of the west coast of Nova Zembla is revealed in frequent references to English and Dutch explorations. Like Spitzbergen, the only part of the Nova Zembla coast displayed on charts was that which had been explored. Thus, Nova Zembla appeared as a single island, unbroken by the strait of Matochkin Shar, and without an eastern shore. Costin Shar was present, but whether it was a deep inlet or a strait connecting with the Kara Sea remained undefined.

Hudson's knowledge of this territory that covered

half a continent may have been imperfect, but he did have a framework he could expand through his own exploration. However, past the River Ob and the great sea north of Tabin Peninsula, Hudson's information was meager and often erroneous. For example, both van Doetechum and Hondius placed the River Ob almost directly south of Nova Zembla at the mouth of Kara Bay. They did not realize it was actually 360 miles farther west. This error left Hudson with a false conviction that if he could reach the Ob, just beyond the Vaigats Strait, he would have easy sailing in a calm, warm sea to complete the Northeast Passage. He had no notion just how far east he had to sail through the dense ice of the Kara Sea to reach his goal.

When Willem Barents explored Vaigats Strait in 1595, he talked to the Samoiedes, neighbors of the Laplanders, and asked them about the land and sea east of Vaigats.[11] These nomads inhabited the frozen tundra of Northern Russia and Siberia. With their herds of reindeer, they ranged from the eastern coast of the White Sea to the River Ob. They told Barents that after five days journey northeast, he would come to a great sea going southeast. "This sea to the east of Way-gats [Vaigats] they sayd was called Marmoria, that is to say, a calm sea." This was confirmed by the natives of Wardoehuss.

East of Nova Zembla, the coast of Siberia presents a series of promontories jutting into the icy waters of the Arctic toward the Pole. Its most northerly cape, at 78°N latitude, is the Taimur Peninsula, or Tabin Promontory, as labeled on the maps of Hudson's time. Doubling this was the final impediment to sailing through the Strait of Anian and out into the Pacific. When Henry Hudson's hopes of a passage between Nova Zembla and Spitzbergen ended, he turned his efforts toward the straits south of Nova Zembla—"my purpose was by way of Way-gats to pass by the mouth of the River Ob, and to double that way the North Cape of Tartaria."

It is uncertain whether Hudson was referring to Cape Tartaria or Cape Tabin. The van Doetechum map shows no coastline at all for the land labeled *Tartariae*

Pars—presumably because it had never been explored. Jodocus Hondius delineated it, but his map was produced three years *after* Hudson's voyage. Hudson may have had access to another map on which this shore was shown, or perhaps he learned about it directly from Hondius while he was in Amsterdam.

Hudson also was misinformed about the latitude of Cape Tabin. The promontory of Cape Tabin is shown at 73°N latitude, but Hondius qualified the location in the following inscription: "The real situation of Cape Tabin is unknown, and its very existence is improbable." He also wrote that it seems likely Asia "does not reach farther northward than to the 50th degree of latitude." The distance between 50° and 78° latitude is 1,680 miles, a sizable amount to be sailed in the high Arctic. The knowledge on which Henry Hudson planned his voyage east of Nova Zembla was based on the geography handed down from Pliny, a first-century AD Roman naturalist, and scraps of rumor from nomadic tribesmen.

It is just as well that Hudson never reached Cape Tabin, let alone Tartaria. He would have found a land so bleak, barren, and inhospitable, and experienced a climate so dreadful, that all his previous hardships would have paled by contrast.

CHAPTER FOUR

To *the Great River of the Mountains: 1609*

Prologue

*A*t the beginning of the sixteenth century, Spain and Portugal virtually ruled the world. By century's end, their authority was considerably diminished. Spain's rout at Gibraltar and the destruction of her "invincible" Armada by the English in 1588 greatly reduced her power. Both Spain and Portugal now lacked the ships and the men to back up the papal decrees, and neither could protect their established trade routes to the Orient.

Until the last half of the century, the Netherlands was a diverse group of provinces held together by geography and a common language but lacking national unity. Under Charles V and his successor, Philip II, these provinces were unable to consolidate—in part because of local and provincial selfishness and an aversion to centralized government.

William of Orange led the Netherlands in a rebellion against Spain's tyranny and religious intolerance, with the result that in 1579, at the Union of Utrecht, seven of the southern Belgian provinces united and proclaimed their political and religious freedom from Spain.[1]

Figure 4-1. *Ships in a roadstead. Engraving made in 1603 by Robert de Baudous, and reproduced from* Sailing Ships — Prints by the Dutch Masters from the Sixteenth to the Ninteenth Century. *The original print is in the Rijksmuseum in Amsterdam. The inscription at the bottom reads: "You can brag of horse-drawn carts, of elephants, You who carry heavy loads hither and thither; Carriers boast of wagons, but seamen trust their ships, The ships with which the Batavians voyage to the Antipodes."*

This Republic of the Seven United Provinces was to become the cornerstone of the Dutch Republic. The treaty wherein Spain formally recognized the independence of Holland was signed barely five days after Hudson departed on his 1609 voyage.

Emboldened by its recent triumph over Spain, Holland sought to press its advantage by attacking Spanish ships as they returned from their colonies in the New World. Such raids, the Dutch hoped, would cripple Spain by preventing her from importing significant resources such as silver and gold.[2] Opposing interests in Holland, however, prevented a concentrated effort in this direction.

At the close of the sixteenth century, Holland was a major sea power with a wide and complex trade network; her vessels carried Baltic grain, herring from the coasts of England, Scotland, and Greenland, and wine, silver, and salt from Spain and France.

Until 1580, Dutch ships were able to fill their holds with spices from the Far East by sailing to Lisbon, Portugal. From there they transported nutmeg, cloves, and pepper to the rest of Europe. But in 1580, with the death of Henry of Portugal and the seizure of the Portuguese crown by Philip II of Spain, Holland lost her access to the port of Lisbon. Her ships were forced to venture farther afield—to sail directly to the Spice Islands.

In 1595 the *Compagnie van Verre* (Company of Foreign Parts)[3] placed four ships under the command of Cornelis de Houtman, who reached Java by way of the Cape of Good Hope, thus inaugurating a new era in Dutch enterprise and colonial expansion. Holland was now able to trade goods directly from her settlements on the islands of the Malay archipelago.

De Houtman's success caused Dutch ships to flock to the Indies. The French ambassador in Amsterdam wrote to Francis I that after de Houtman's return on August 27, 1597, "all these countries [Zeeland, North and South Holland], which are full of ships and sailors, are running there like fire."

By 1601 there were no less than fifteen Dutch commercial ventures backing voyages to the Far East. But these expeditions faced two major problems. First, Dutch ships had to be prepared to battle with Portuguese and English vessels en route, and with Malay pirates once they reached their destination. Second, since these were private, independent ventures, they were in competition with one another, which reduced their profits.

Both problems were solved by the unification of many small, rival companies into a single corporate body—*De Verenigde Oost-Indische Compagnie* (United East India Company), or V.O.C.[4] In 1602, the States-General of Holland granted the V.O.C. a twenty-one-year charter, giving the company a monopoly on trade with the East via either of two routes: east, around the southern tip of Africa, or west, around South America by the

Figure 4-2. *V.O.C. Symbol of the United Dutch East India Company—De Verenigde Oost-Indische Compagnie. The letter "A" above, denotes the main, Amsterdam, branch of the company.*

De Verenigde Oost-Indische Compagnie

Strait of Magellan. Although these were the only routes specified, there was no mention of a prohibition against a northern passage. The charter also gave the V.O.C. far-reaching powers, including the right to wage war and conclude peace in that part of the world.

With its fleet of forty large and innumerable small ships, 5,000 sailors, and 600 cannons, the V.O.C. was far wealthier than its English counterpart, the Muscovy Company. This was no small matter: commercial rivalry between England and the United Provinces of Holland was extreme, and resulted in frequent battles. In the North Sea, the issue was herring; in the Molluccas, spices; and in the far north, whales.

After Henry Hudson's second voyage, English interest in the Northeast Passage waned. In Holland, however, a shorter, more profitable route, one not dominated by Spain, Portugal, or England, remained an attractive possibility. The V.O.C., fearing that another nation would discover the passage and usurp the monopoly's rights and profits, contacted Henry Hudson, whose explorations were well known.

Hudson was not the only explorer to sail under another country's flag. Sebastian Cabot was a Spanish captain in English service; Esteban Gomez a Portuguese captain in Spanish service; Giovanni da Verrazano an Italian in French service; and Christopher Columbus, an Italian in Spanish service.

Once Hudson was in Amsterdam, he found the directors of the East India Company hesitant to sign a contract, in part because of the recent failures of the Barents expeditions. Hudson was summarily dismissed with the claim that it was too late in the year to arrange an Arctic voyage. However, when members of the East India Company discovered that Hudson was negotiating secretly with Henry IV of France, they acted quickly. The signing took place on January 8, 1609.

Contract of the
DUTCH UNITED EAST INDIA COMPANY
with
HENRY HUDSON
January 8, 1609

On this eighth of January in the year of our Lord, One thousand, six hundred and nine, Directors of the East India Company of the Chamber of Amsterdam of the ten years reckoning of the one part, and Mr. Henry Hudson, Englishman, assisted by Jodocus Hondius, of the other part, have agreed in the manner following, to wit: That the said Directors shall in the first place equip a small vessel or jaght of about 30 lasts burden, with which well provided with men, provisions and other necessaries, the above named Hudson shall about the first of April, sail, in order to search for a passage by the north around the north side of Nova Zembla, and shall continue thus along that parallel until he shall be able to sail southward to the latitude of 60 degrees. He shall obtain as much knowledge of the lands as can be done without any considerable loss of time, and if it is possible, return immediately in order to make a faithful report and relation of the voyage to the Directors, and to deliver over his journals, log-books and charts, together with an account of everything whatsoever which shall happen to him during the voyage, without keeping anything back; for which said voyage the Directors shall pay to said Hudson as well for his outfit of the said voyage; as for the support of his wife and children, the sum of eight hundred guilders. And in case, which God prevent, he do not come back or arrive hereabouts within a year, the Directors shall further pay to his wife, two hundred Guilders in cash and thereupon they shall not be further lia-

ble to him or his heirs unless he shall, either afterwards or within the year arrive, and have found the passage good and suitable for the company to use. In which case, the Directors will reward the before named Hudson for his dangers, trouble and knowledge, in their discretion, with which the before mentioned Hudson is content. And in case the Directors think proper to prosecute and continue the same voyage, it is stipulated and agreed with the before named Hudson that he shall make his residence in this country, with his wife and children, and shall enter into employment of no other than the Company, and this at the discretion of the Directors who also promise to make him satisfied and content for such further service in all justice and equity, all without fraud or evil intent. In witness of the truth, two contracts are made hereof of the same tenor and are subscribed by both parties and also by Jodocus Hondius as interpretor and witness, dated as above. Signed: Dirk Van Os, J. Poppe, Henry Hudson and Jodocus Hondius.

Shortly before Hudson sailed, the contract was amended, and he received further instructions containing this specific prohibition:

To think of discovering no other route or passage, except the route around the north or northeast, above Nova Zembla. . . . If it could not be accomplished at that time, another route would be subject of consideration for another voyage.

In both the original contract and the amendment, Hudson's instructions were exact and unequivocal: he was to seek a Northeast Passage, and no other route. The directors of the East India Company must have become aware of their employee's proclivity to redirect his ship westward.

On March 25, 1609, Henry Hudson and his crew of sixteen[5] set out on the vessel *Half Moon* (see Appendix I) and proceeded north, generally following the coast of Norway. After clearing the North Cape they entered the White Sea, but were forced by stormy weather, "with much wind and snow and very cold," to double back. Hudson then gave up his attempt to complete the

Northeast Passage, but instead of upholding his contract and returning to Holland, he sailed west across the Atlantic to America, where he explored the coastline from Chesapeake Bay to Penobscot Bay.

On September 11, the *Half Moon* entered New York harbor. Taking advantage of the tides, Hudson navigated 150 miles from the ocean inland to a site near the present city of Albany. Determining that this was as far as he could go, he headed the *Half Moon* downriver. On October 4, Hudson departed the river that would come to bear his name, and set sail into the main sea.

Figure 4-3. *Rig and Sail Plan of the* Half Moon, *researched and drawn by Nick Benton for building the 1989 replica.*

Displacement: 122 long tons
Length on deck: 65 feet
Length of hull: 84.5 feet

Beam: 17 feet four inches
Draft: 8 feet
Depth of hold: 8 feet
Sail area: 2,757 sq. feet

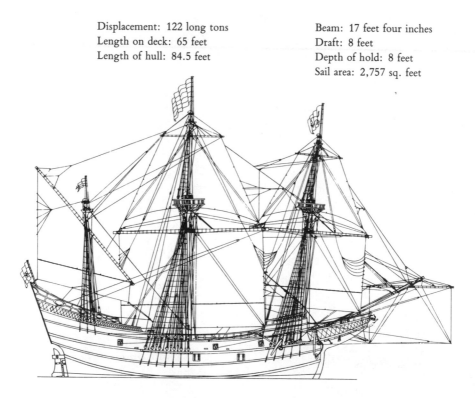

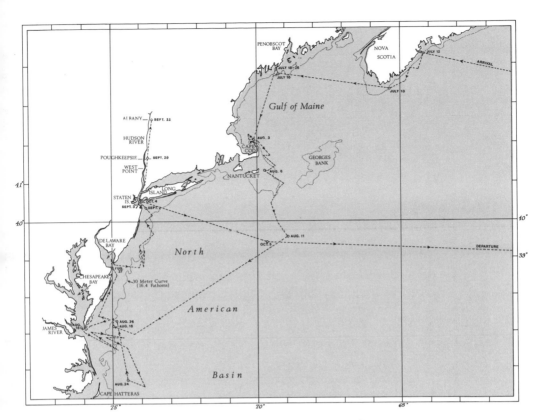

Figure 4-4. *Reconstruction of Hudson's route to Virginia on his 1609 voyage.*

The Journal

Most of the information about this voyage comes to us from a journal kept by one of Hudson's mates, Robert Juet of Lime-house. Unfortunately only a few fragments from Hudson's own journal have survived. These were published in 1625 in John De Laet's history *Nieuwe Werelt*[6], and have been inserted here in their proper order.

The following transcription is taken from Book III of *Purchas His Pilgrimes*, by Samuel Purchas.

THE THIRD VOYAGE OF
MASTER HENRY HUDSON

TOWARD NOVA ZEMBLA, AND AT HIS RETURNE, HIS
PASSING FROM FARRE ISLANDS TO NEW-FOUND LAND, AND
ALONG TO FORTIE-FOURE DEGREES AND TEN MINUTES, AND
THENCE TO CAPE COD, AND SO TO THIRTIE-THREE DE-
GREES; AND ALONG THE COAST TO THE NORTHWARD, TO
FORTIE-TWO DEGREES AND A HALFE, AND UP THE RIVER
NEERE TO FORTIE-THREE DEGREES.

Written by Robert Juet, of Lime-house

On Saturday, *March 25th of 1609* (after the old account)
we set sail from Amsterdam, arriving at the Texel two
days later.[7] At 12 o'clock the land lay six miles east of
us. Because it is a journey usually known, I omit re-
porting what passed until we came to the latitude of

Most northern point of Norway.

the North Cape of Finmarke, which we made by Tuesday, May 5th (*stilo novo*). On that day our latitude
observation placed us at 71° 46' and our compass variation was six degrees to the west. At 12 o'clock, with
the North Cape 30 miles off, we steered away east and
east by south.

May 19 Today (Tuesday) the weather was stormy
with much wind and snow, and very cold. The wind
was variable between north northwest and northeast.
We made our way west by north until noon, at which

A slake of the sun.

time we observed the sun having a slake.[8] Our latitude
was 70°30' and we were in sight of Vardoehuus Island,
which placed us 60 miles ahead of our estimated posi-

North Cape Current encountered.

tion due to the set of the stream of the White Sea. But
by two o'clock the wind was directly ahead of us and
we could not get about the North Cape, so we tacked
toward the east. By eight at night, on the 21st of May,

The North Cape doubled.

the North Cape lay southeast by south of us at a distance of 21 miles. And at midnight Assumption Point
[southwest of the North Cape] was 15 miles to the
south by east of us.

May 22 With gusting weather, hail and snow, we
continued our course west southwest along the land;
the sun breaking out occasionally. At 10 o'clock to-

night we were opposite Zenam [Senjen Island, west of Norway], of which the main body lay 15 miles east of us. The course from North Cape to Zenam is mostly west by south and west southwest for a distance of 162 miles.

Lofoten Islands.

May 23 From Zenam to Lofoten the course is southwest by west, with the distance between the two 150 miles. We steered along the land southwest and southwest by south, 24 miles a watch, in fair sunshining weather with an east by south and east southeast wind. These compass headings are with the needle of our compass set right to the north.[9]

May 24 Today we had fair, clear sunshining weather, with the wind variable; most often the wind was from the southeast. We continued our course west southwest as before, and at eight o'clock at night the southern part of Lofoten bore southeast of us by 30 miles.

May 25 Much wind from the northeast, with some snow and hail. At first watch the wind came to the east a fine gale, then it backed to the northeast; by the second watch, at four o'clock, it freshened, and by eight o'clock it had grown to a storm and continued at that strength.[10] Our noon observation placed our ship at 67°58', and we found our compass to have no variation. We continued our course southwest, making 36 miles a watch. At nine o'clock Lofoten bore east of us and 45 miles off. The wind increased to a storm.

May 26 A great storm from the north northeast and northeast, so we steered southwest before the wind with our foresail aboard. It blew so vehemently and the seas were so high, breaking all around, that we were unable to maintain any more sails without endangering a small ship by having the seas break over her. So for 24 hours we ran before the wind a distance of 210 miles. By four o'clock the storm began to abate.

Violent storm.

May 27 Had indifferent, fair weather, but a good stiff gale of wind from the north and north northeast; we held on our course as before. At noon we took observations and found our latitude to be 64°10'. It seems that in the last two days, a current had hindered us by 48 miles. Having fair weather, we set our mainsail, spritsail and our main topsail, and held our course all night.

May 28 With fair weather and little wind from the northeast we held our course southwest. At noon, by observation our latitude was 62° and 30′. In the afternoon there was a little wind from the north northwest, but by the second watch it fell calm. At four o'clock we sighted the Faeroe Islands and found them to be placed on the sea chart 42 miles too far to the west. In running southwest from Lofoten we took great care in our steering and observations; according to our course and celestial sightings we should have been 910 miles

off the Faeroes, yet we had them in sight only 48 to 54 miles off.

May 29 Fair weather, sometimes calm and sometimes a gale, with the wind varying from the southwest to the northeast. We got to the islands, but could not get in. With the ebb tide flowing we dared not put in, so we stood out along the islands.

May 30 Fair weather, the wind at southeast and east southeast. In the morning we turned toward a roadstead between Stromo and Muggenes of the Faeroe Islands, but did not get in until nine o'clock that evening on account of the strong tide that flowed there

that day. As soon as we arrived we rearranged the goods in the hold of the ship and sent our boat for water, filling the empty casks with fresh water. We finished organizing the hold by 10 o'clock at night.

May 31 Fair, sunshining weather, with wind from east southeast. In the morning our master, with most of his company, went ashore for a walk, returning aboard at one o'clock. Then we set sail.

June 1 (stilo novo) Fair, sunshining weather, with the wind from east southeast. We continued on our course southwest by west. At noon we took observations of the sun and found our latitude to be 60°58′;

and so, with fair weather, continued on our course all night. Tonight we lighted candles in the bittacle again.

June 2 Misty weather. At noon we headed west southwest to find Busse Island, discovered by one of the ships of Sir Martin Frobisher in 1578, to determine whether or not it was charted in its proper latitude.[11] We continued our course as before, all night with a fair gale of wind. Tonight we saw the first stars and the water had changed color to a white-green.[12] The compass had no variation.

Search for Busse Island.

June 3 Fair, sunshining weather, with wind from the northeast. With a stiff gale of wind we set our course southwest by west. At noon we took observations and found our latitude to be 58° and 48'. This was 48 miles behind our dead reckoning position on account of a strong current out of the southwest which held us back 24 miles a day. We believed ourselves to be near Busse Island; by midnight we looked out for it but could not see it.

North Atlantic Current.

June 4 In the morning there was much wind, with fog and rain. We steered southwest by west all morning; the increasing strength of wind forced us to take in our topsail. The wind continued this way all afternoon. We steered southwest all evening, and by 10 o'clock at night what little wind there was came from the south, and then south southeast.

June 5 Stormy weather, with much wind, so by four o'clock in the morning we took in our foresail and lay-a-trie[13] with our mainsail, and sailed away west northwest for 12 miles. But by noon the wind had lessened, the sun shone forth, and we were able to take observations. We found our latitude to be 56°21'. In the afternoon the wind changed to and fro between the southwest and southeast, with rain and fog, and continued this way all night. We found that our ship was to the west of our assumed position.

June 6 Thick, hazy weather, with gusts of wind and showers of rain. The wind varied between east southeast and southwest, making us change our heading many times in a general west southwest direction. During the afternoon the wind was a stiff gale east southeast, with mist and rain. We steered southwest by west for 24 miles. At noon the sun shone forth and we determined our latitude to be 56°08'.

June 7 Fair, sunshining weather all morning, and calm until 12 o'clock. In the afternoon the wind came around to the northwest a stiff gale, which continued all night. We steered southwest by west, making our way southwest. At noon our latitude was 56° and 01'.

June 8 Stormy weather, the wind strong, and variable between west and northwest, so that by eight o'clock we took off our bonnets.[14] At noon the sun shone forth, enabling us to take observations, and we placed our position at latitude 54°30'.

June 9 Fair, sunshining weather, but little wind until about 11 o'clock. Then the wind came to the south southeast and we steered west southwest. At noon our latitude was 53°45' and we had made our way south by west for 30 miles. In the afternoon the wind increased and continued all night from the northeast by east.

June 10 Fair weather, the wind variable between east northeast and southeast; we steered our course as before. At four o'clock in the afternoon the wind came up out of the southeast and we held our course as before. At noon, by observation, our latitude was 52°35'.

June 11 The morning was thick and foggy, with the wind varying. At four o'clock in the morning we tacked to the south and at 11 o'clock the wind came about to the northwest, and so to be north northwest. Today we saw a change in the color of water to a whitish-green, like the kind containing ice in the northwest. At noon it cleared up, so we put out our main topsail. Then we took observations of the sun and found our latitude to be 51°24'. We sailed many directions and found our ship was to the south of our course by about 30 miles by reason of a current from the north. The compass variation was 11° easterly.

A current from the north: Labrador Current.

June 12 Fair, sunshining weather, but much wind from the west. We sailed south all day, the wind shifting between the southwest and the west by north. We

made our way south by one half point west for 54
miles. Our latitude at noon was 50°09'. At eight
o'clock at night the wind increased and we took off the
bonnets.

June 13 Fair, sunshining weather, the wind variable. We made our way south southwest for 51 miles.
At noon we took observations and found our latitude
to be 48°45', but this calculation is not to be trusted
on account of the high seas. In the afternoon the wind
was calmer and we put the bonnets back on, sailing
southward all night in a stiff gale.

June 14 Fair, and clear sunshining weather, the
wind variable between the northwest and southwest by
west. At midnight I took observations of the North
Star with the guard star northwest by west.[15] It was a
good observation, placing our position at 49°30'. And
at noon we observed the sun, and determined our latitude to be 48°06'. By my calculations we sailed 36
miles between the two observations. At one o'clock in
the afternoon we tacked to the west, keeping that
course all night. The wind increased to a storm with
much wind and rain.

North Star observations.

June 15 We had a great storm which broke our
foremast. We lost it overboard, along with the foresail
which was set low.

Foremast broken in storm.

June 16 By reason of the unconstant weather we
were forced to lie-a-trie with our mainsail. So we sailed
this way for four watches southeast by south for 25^1/$_2$
miles, and two watches for 18 miles.

June 17 Reasonable, fair weather, with the wind
variable. It became a stiff gale of wind with a swelling
sea out of the west southwest, so great that we could
do nothing. For one and a half watches we pressed
north 13^1/$_2$ miles, and for four and a half watches south
by east and one half point east for 36 miles.

June 18 With the wind out of the northwest we
headed southward, making good a course south by
west for 15 miles. The afternoon proved little wind and
at night it was calm.

June 19 In the morning the weather was fair and calm, and we set a temporary mast with a foresail in place of the one that had been carried away.

June 21 Fair, sunshining weather, but much wind and a great sea. We split our foresail at 10 o'clock, then we lay-a-trie with our mainsail, and continued so all day. During the night the wind fell. Today our latitude was 45°48'.

June 22 Very fair, sunshining weather, and calm all the afternoon. At noon we took a very good observation and found our latitude to be 44°58'. At eight o'clock at night we had a small gale of wind from the southeast, and we steered away west for Newfoundland. The true compass variation was 11° easterly.

Head for Newfoundland.

June 23 Thick weather with much wind and some rain. At eight o'clock in the morning the wind came around to the west southwest in so stiff a gale that we were forced to take in our topsail, and we steered away north northwest until four o'clock in the afternoon. Then we tacked to the south. At eight o'clock at night, the wind being west, we took in our topsails and lay-a-trie with our mainsail.

June 24 A stiff gale of wind, varying between the west and north northwest; we sailed a-trie until six o'clock, at which time we set our foresail and steered west by south by our compass for 24 miles in four watches. Then we sailed a-trie to the south for one and a half watches.

June 25 Fair, sunshining weather, the wind north northwest and north; we steered west by compass until 12 o'clock, at which time we sighted a sail and gave her chase, but could not speak with her. She was sailing eastward, and we sailed after her until six o'clock in the afternoon.[16] Then we tacked to the westward again, remaining on our course. It was fair all night, with little wind at times.

Give chase to a sail.

June 26 All morning the weather was very fair and hot, but at four o'clock in the afternoon it became very windy and rainy. The wind was south southwest. At noon we took observations and found our latitude to be 44°33'. At eight o'clock at night the wind came around to the southwest and west southwest. We steered northwest for one watch, and at midnight west and west by south with much wind. We couldn't head any closer than north northwest.

June 27 Very much wind and a severe storm, with the wind westerly. At four in the morning we took in our foresail and lay-a-trie with our mainsail set low; continuing this way all day and night two watches to the north. At eight o'clock at night we tacked to the south.

June 28 Fair, sunshining weather, with the wind out of the west by south. We lay-a-trie to the south until eight o'clock in the morning. Then we set our foresail and sailed to the south in a stiff gale of wind, but the weather was fair with large seas out of the west. We maintained our course all night.

June 29 Fair, sunshining weather, the wind west by south. We sailed southward until six o'clock at night and made good a course south by east for 12 miles. Then the wind came around to the southwest and we tacked to the westward, making good a north-west course all night. At noon our latitude was 43°06'. Compass variation was 11° westerly.

June 30 Fair, sunshining weather. We steered northwest by west and made good the same course by reason of the variation of the compass.[17] At noon I found our latitude to be 43°18'. We continued our course all night and made our way northwest by west half a point west for 75 miles.

July 1 Close, misty and thick weather, but with a fair gale of wind. We steered northwest by west westerly and made our course so by reason of the variation of the compass. At eight o'clock at night we sounded for the Bank of Newfoundland, but did not find bottom.

Sounding for the Bank of Newfoundland.

July 2 Thick, misty weather, but little wind. At eight o'clock in the morning we tacked to the southward, and while our ship was in stays, sounded for the bank.[18] We found ground of white sand and shells in 30 fathoms. Presently, the weather cleared and we had sight of a sail but did not speak with her. In the night we had much rain, thunder and lightning, and shifting of wind.

July 3 Fair, sunshining weather, with a fair gale of wind. We steered west southwest by our compass which had 17° variation. This morning we were among a great fleet of French vessels which lay fishing on the bank, but we spoke with none of them. At noon our latitude was 43°41'. We sounded at 10 o'clock and found a gray sand bottom at 30 fathoms. At two o'clock we had gray sand at 35 fathoms. At eight o'clock at 38 fathoms had gray sand as before.

July 4 It was clear in the morning with a fair gale of wind, but variable. We held our course as before. The afternoon was misty, the wind shifting until four o'clock. Then we took in our topsail and spritsail and sounded, and had no bottom in 70 fathoms. The wind continued to shift until eight o'clock, then it came to the north northeast and northeast by north and we steered west northwest by our uncorrected compass, making good a course west by one half point north.[19] Compass variation was 15° westerly.

July 5 Fair, sunshining weather with the wind northeast by north. We steered west northwest, which was west half a point north. At noon our latitude was 44°10' and in sounding we had no ground at 100 fathoms. In the afternoon, until nine o'clock at night, it was either calm or there was very little wind. Then the wind came around to the east and we held our course. At midnight I took observations of the North Star and the Scorpion's Heart and found our latitude to be 44°10'.[20] Compass variation was 13 degrees.

July 6 In the morning there was fair weather with a stiff gale of wind; we steered west by north and west northwest. In the afternoon, from two o'clock onward, the weather was thick and foggy with a hard gale of wind varying between southwest by south and west by north. In four watches, by many headings, we made our way northwest by half a point north for 57

miles. At eight o'clock at night we sounded and had
no ground at 100 fathoms.

July 7 Fair, sunshining weather, the wind varying.
At four o'clock in the morning we tacked southward,
remaining on that heading until one in the afternoon.
At noon our latitude was 44°26'. At seven o'clock we
tacked to the northward. At eight at night we tacked
to the southward and in sounding had white sand in 59
fathoms.

July 8 Fair weather in the morning, but foggy
until seven o'clock. At four o'clock in the morning we
sounded and had fine white sand in 45 fathoms. We
had run 15 miles south by west. We held our heading
one glass and went three miles as before.[21] Then we
sailed one glass, sounded, and had 60 fathoms. We
tacked and sailed back toward the bank, where we had
25 fathoms. The wind fell calm and we tried fishing.
From eight o'clock until one o'clock we caught 118
great cods. After dinner we took 12 more and saw
many great schools of herring. Then we had a gale of
wind out of the south which shifted to the west northwest and we sailed for three glasses, whereupon we
sounded and had 60 fathoms. We sailed two more
glasses and the lead came up with red stones and shells
in 40 fathoms. So we sounded every glass and had
soundings of 35, 33, 30, 31, 32, 33 and 34 fathoms.

Many great cods taken.

July 9 Fair, calm weather. We lay becalmed all day
and caught some fish, but not too many, as our supply
of salt was low. By three o'clock in the afternoon there
was a gale and we steered by compass west by south
and one half point south. At four o'clock we sounded
and had only 15, 17 and 19 fathoms on a fishing bank,
so we sounded every glass. Then, in 25 fathoms, we
did not bring up any ground, and had sight of a sail
ahead of us. At noon our latitude was 44°27'. We
sailed westward all night, speaking with one French
vessel which lay fishing on Sablen Bank in 30 fathoms,
and seeing two or three more.

Sable Bank.

July 10 Very misty and thick weather with the
wind a fair gale out of the southwest. We sailed south-

ward, making our way southeast by east. At 12 o'clock
we sounded and had 48 fathoms, again at two we
sounded, and had 50 fathoms. And at six o'clock we
sounded and had 48 fathoms on the end of the bank.
Again, at eight o'clock at night, we sounded and had
no ground in 80 fathoms as we were beyond the bank.

Beyond the bank.

So we sailed along until midnight. The compass variation was 17° westerly.

July 11 Very thick and misty weather. At midnight
we came about to the west and kept that heading
all day, making good a course west northwest. We
sounded at 12 o'clock but had no ground, so we sailed
westward all evening and continued sounding, but got
no ground in 50 or 60 fathoms until midnight. Then I
sounded and had a white sand bottom at 15 fathoms.

July 12 Today was very foggy. We remained on
course all morning until 11 o'clock, at which time we

Sight of land.

had sight of a low, white sandy land right ahead, and
10 fathoms of water under us. Then we tacked to the
southward and sailed away from it for four glasses,
whereupon we tacked toward land again thinking we
had passed it. But the fog was so thick that we could
not see, so we tacked away from it again. From midnight until two o'clock we came to soundings in 12, 13
and 14 fathoms off the shore. At four o'clock we had
20 fathoms and at eight at night 30 fathoms. At midnight there was little wind and the water deepened a
while at 65 fathoms, though closer to the shore it
shoaled gently.

July 13 Fair, sunshining weather from eight o'clock
in the morning and for the remainder of the day. Then
at eight o'clock we tacked toward shore but could not
see it. The wind being south by our true compass, we
steered west by north. At noon we took observations
and found our latitude to be 43°25′, so we steered west
by north all afternoon. At four o'clock in the afternoon
we sounded and had 35 fathoms. And at six o'clock we
had sight of the land and saw two sails ahead of us.
The land by the water's side is low lying with white

sandy banks, rising full of little hills. Our soundings were 35, 33, 30, 28, 32, 37, 33, and 32 fathoms.

Cape Sable, Nova Scotia sighted.

July 14 Full of mists flying and fading, with the wind between south and southwest. We steered north northwest and northwest by west. Our soundings were 29, 25, 24, 25, 22, 25, 27, 30, 28, 30, 35, 43, 50, 70, 90, 70, 64, 86, 100 fathoms, and no ground.

Across the Gulf of Maine.

July 15 Very misty, the wind varying between south and southwest. We steered west by north and west northwest. In the morning we sounded and had 100 fathoms. At four o'clock in the afternoon we had 75 fathoms. Then, within the time of two glasses, having made a distance no greater than two English miles, we sounded and had 60 fathoms. It shoaled quickly until we came to 20 fathoms. Then according to our calculations we were near the islands that lie off the shore. At nine o'clock that night, with little wind, and a smooth sea, we anchored. After supper we tried fishing, and I caught 15 cods, some the greatest I have seen. We remained at anchor all night.

Approach to land again.

July 16 In the morning it cleared up and we had sight of five islands lying north and north by west from us at a distance of about six miles. We began to set sail, but the mist came so thick that we dared not enter among the islands.

Five islands sighted.

July 17 Today was all misty so we could not get into the harbor. At 10 o'clock two boats with six of the savages of the country came out to us, seeming glad of our coming. We gave them trifles and ate and drank with them. They told us there was gold, silver and copper mines close by and that the Frenchmen do trade with them. This is very likely for one of them spoke some words of French. The weather continuing misty, we remained at anchor all day and all night.

Six savages come aboard.

July 18 With the weather fair we went into a very good harbor and anchored close to the shore in four fathoms of water. The river runs up a great way, but close to us there is only two fathoms. We went on shore and cut us a foremast, then at noon we came

Anchor in George's Harbor.

St. George River.

aboard again and found our latitude to be 44°01′ with the sun falling south southwest. We mended our sails and eagerly began making our foremast. The harbor lies north and south a mile in where we rode to our anchor.

July 19 We had fair, sunshining weather and remained at anchor. In the afternoon we took the ship's boat to look for fresh water and found some. We also found a shoal with many lobsters on it and caught 31.

Mistrust of the savages.

The people coming aboard showed us great friendship, but we could not trust them.

July 20 Fair, sunshining weather, with the wind southwest. In the morning, half an hour before daybreak, our scout went out to catch fresh fish, and returned in two hours with 27 cod he had caught on two hooks and lines. In the afternoon we went for more lobsters, caught 40, and returned aboard. Then we saw two French shallops full of Indians come into the harbor, but seeing that we were on our guard they did not attempt to harm us. They brought many beaver skins and other fine furs which they would have

The trade of the French with the savages.

exchanged for red gowns, for the French trade with them for red tunics, knives, hatchets, copper, kettles, trivets, beads and other trifles.

July 21 Today was all misty with the wind easterly, so we remained at anchor and did nothing but work on our mast.

July 22 Fair, sunshining weather, the wind northerly, we rode to our anchor all day. In the afternoon our scout went to catch more lobsters and brought back 59. At night the weather was clear.

July 23 Fair, sunshining weather and very hot. At

Mast repaired.

11 o'clock our foremast was finished and we brought it aboard, set it into the mast-step, and in the afternoon we rigged it. This night we had a little mist and rain.

July 24 Very hot weather with the wind from the south, out of the sea. The early part of the day we worked on our sails. In the morning our scout went fishing and in two hours they [sic] brought back with them 20 great cods and a great halibut. The night was fair also. We kept a good watch for fear of being betrayed by the people, and noticed where they kept their shallops.

July 25 Very fair weather and hot. In the morning we manned our scout with four muskets and six men, took one of their [Indian] shallops and brought it aboard. Then we manned our scout and boat with 12 men and muskets, two stone pieces or murderers, and drew the savages from their houses and robbed them, as they would have done to us. Then we set sail and came down to the harbor's mouth and rode there all night, as the wind blew right in. The night grew misty until midnight, then it became calm and the wind came off the land at west northwest and it began to clear. Compass variation was 10° westerly.

July 26 Fair and clear sunshining weather. At five o'clock in the morning we set sail and put out to sea; by noon our ship had gone 42 miles southwest. In the afternoon the wind shifted variably between west southwest and northwest. At noon I found our latitude to be 43°56'. This evening being very fair weather, we observed the variation of our compass at sunset and found it to be 10° westerly.

July 27 Fair, sunshining weather, the wind a stiff gale. We sailed southward all day, and made good south by west 81 miles. At noon our latitude was 42°50'. At four o'clock in the afternoon we came about to the northward. At eight o'clock we took in our topsails, the bonnet off our foresail, and went under shortened sail all night.

July 28 Very thick and misty, with a stiff gale. We made our way northwest by west 81 miles, sounded many times, but could get no ground. At five o'clock, with the wind southwest by west, we tacked to the southward, at which time we sounded and had ground at 75 fathoms. At eight we had 60 fathoms. At 10, 60 fathoms. At midnight we had 56 fathoms with gray sand bottom. The compass variation was 6° westerly.

July 29 Fair weather, we sailed southward and made our way south by west a point south for 54 miles. At noon we found our latitude to be 42°56′. We took soundings often and had 60, 64, 65, 67, 65, 65, 70 and 75 fathoms. At night we tried checking the variation of our compass by the setting sun and found that it went down 37° to the north of west, though it should have gone down at only 31 degrees. Compass variation was 5½ degrees.

July 30 Very hot, with all the early part of the day calm; later we steered west southwest. We sounded many times and could find no ground at 170 fathoms. We found a great current and many over-falls. The current had deceived us, for it had headed us southward by 42 miles which we found when we took noon observations and determined our latitude to be 41°34′. At eight o'clock at night I sounded and had ground in 52 fathoms. At the end of the midnight watch we had 53 fathoms, but this last reading is not to be trusted.

July 31 Very thick and misty all day until 10 o'clock. At night the wind came to the south, and southwest and south. We made our way west northwest 57 miles. We sounded and got different readings of 56, 54, 48, 47, 44, 46 and 50 fathoms, with the bottom sometimes little stones, sometimes coarse gray sand. At eight o'clock at night it fell calm and we had 50 fathoms. At 10 o'clock we heard a great roar, like the roar of waves breaking on a shore. Then I sounded and found the former depths. Being there was so little wind that the ship made no movement, and mistrusting a current, I let the lead of our sounding line lie on the bottom and found a tide-set to be southwest and southwest by west so fast that I could hardly let out the line fast enough. Presently we came to a hurling current or tidal over-falls which turned our ship around. The lead was stuck so hard to the ground that I was afraid the line would break; and we had no more of that. At midnight I sounded again and we had 75 fathoms, and the strong stream had left us.

August 1 All the early part of the day was misty, clearing up at noon. We found that our latitude was 41°45′ and we had gone 57 miles. The afternoon was reasonably good. We found the rustling tide or current with many over-falls still continued, the water a changed color and the sea very deep, for we found no ground in 100 fathoms. The night was clear and we steered west.

August 2 Very fair and hot. Until noon, we had a gale of wind, but in the afternoon there was little wind. At noon I sounded and had 110 fathoms and our latitude was 41°56′. We had run 72¹/₂ miles. At sunset we observed the variation of the compass and found that it had come to its true place [no magnetic variation]. At eight o'clock the gale increased, so we ran with the wind 18 miles that watch in a very fair and clear night.

Zero degrees magnetic variation.

August 3 Very hot weather. In the morning we caught sight of land and steered in, thinking to go around to the north of it. So we sent our shallop with five men to take soundings close to the shore, and they found a depth of five fathoms within a bow-shot of the shore.²² They went ashore and found beautiful grapes and rose trees which they brought aboard with them at five o'clock in the evening. We had 27 fathoms within two miles of the shore. We found a flood tide from the southeast, and an ebb tide from the northwest, that came in a very strong stream with violent rushing and noises. At eight o'clock at night the wind began to blow a fresh gale which continued all night. Our soundings near the land were 100, 80, 74, 52, 46, 29, 27, 24, 19 and 17 fathoms, with a bottom sometimes of mud and sometimes gray sand.

They go on land at Cape Cod.

Strong stream with violent rushing.

August 4 Today was very hot. We sailed northwest two watches, and south for one watch, then headed in toward the land where we anchored at the northern end of the headland. We heard the voices of men call and sent our boat ashore thinking they had been some Christians left on the land; but we found them to be savages, which seemed very glad to see us coming. So we brought one of them aboard with us where he ate and drank with us and we gave him meat. Our master gave him three or four glass buttons, then sent him back to land again in our shallop. When our boat left the shore he leapt and danced, held up his hands and pointed us to a river on the other side, for we had made signs that we came to fish here. The body of this headland lies in 41°45′ latitude. We set sail again after dinner, thinking to get to the westward of this headland, but could not. So we went to the south of it, making our way southeast. Its southern point bore west at eight o'clock at night. Our soundings three miles from the shore around the eastern and northern part of this headland were: at the eastern side, 30, 27, 27, 24, 25 and 20 fathoms. The northeast point 17°18′ and so deeper [sic]. The northern end of this headland close to the shore had 30 fathoms, and nine miles off the north northwest there was 100 fathoms. Three miles off the southeast part there were 15, 16, and 17 fathoms. The people have green tobacco and pipes, the bowls of which are made of clay and the stems of red copper. The land is very sweet.

Southeast corner of Cape Cod.

August 5 At eight o'clock in the morning we tacked to the westward, keeping this heading until four o'clock in the afternoon, at which time the weather cleared and we saw the headland again 15 miles from us. The southern point of it bore west of us; we sounded many times and had no ground. At four o'clock we came about, and while in stays, sounded, and had 70 fathoms. We steered south south by east all night and could get no ground at 70 and 80 fathoms. We feared a great shoal that lies off the land, and steered south by east.

Fear of Georges Bank.

August 6 Fair weather, but misty. We steered south southeast until eight o'clock in the morning, then it cleared a little and we came about to the westward. Then we sounded and had 30 fathoms with a coarse sand, indicating the approach to the shoal. We continued sounding and had shoaling quickly from 30, 29, 27, 24, 22, 20, 20½, 19, 19, 19, 19, 18, 18, 17, then, as we steered south and southeast, it deepened again the same way it shallowed, until we came to 26 fathoms. Then we steered southwest, for that was the

Shoal approached.

direction the tide set. By and by, as it was calm, we sailed by the leadline, for here you can have 16 or 17 fathoms, and at the next cast only seven or six fathoms. And farther west you have only four and five feet of water, see rocks under you, and from the top of the mast see land.

Nantucket Shoals.

Upon this rise we took an observation and found that it lies in 40°10′ latitude. This is the headland which Captain Bartholomew Gosnold discovered in the year 1602 and called Cape Cod because of the great number of codfish he found about there. So we steered southwest nine miles, and had 20 and 24 fathoms. Then we steered west for one hour, 1½ miles, but could not get deep water on account of the strength of the ebb tide and the force of the current which brought us so close to the breaking of waves on the shoal that we were forced to anchor. So at seven o'clock at night we were at anchor in 10 fathoms, and I give God most hearty thanks that the least amount of water we had under us was 7½ fathoms. We remained there all night, and at slack water I sounded all around our ship as far as the light would allow, and we had no less than 8, 9, 10 and 11 fathoms. The mist continued being very thick.

Captain Bartholomew Gosnold.

August 7 Fair weather and hot, but misty. We remained at anchor hoping it would clear, but on the flood tide the wind became calm and the weather thick. So we rode to anchor all day and night. The flood tide comes from the southwest and does not rise any higher than 1½ fathoms at neap tide.[23] Toward night it cleared and I went out in the shallop to take soundings, and found no less water than eight fathoms to the southeast of us. But to the northwest of us we saw waves breaking on the shoals.

At anchor on the shoals.

August 8 Fair and clear weather. By six o'clock in the morning at slack water we weighed anchor. The wind was out of the northwest and we set our foresail and main topsail and got a mile over the flats. Then the ebb tide came, so we anchored again until the return of the flood. Then we set sail again, and by the

great mercy of God we got clear of the flats by one
o'clock in the afternoon. We were in sight of land
from the west northwest to the northwest, so we
steered away south southeast all night, and had ground
until the middle of the third watch, at which time we
had 45 fathoms, white sand and little stones. Approaching this, our soundings were 20, 20, 22, 27, 32,
43, 43 and 45 fathoms. Then, no ground in 70 fathoms.

August 9 Very fair and hot weather, the wind a
very stiff gale. At four o'clock in the morning our shallop came running up against our stern entirely splitting
her stem, so we gladly cut her away. Then we took in
our mainsail and lay-a-trie under our foresail until
noon. Then the wind lessened to a fair gale so we
headed southwest. Then we sailed close to the wind on
various courses in a general south by west direction 45
miles, and for three watches southeast by east 30 miles.
At eight o'clock at night we took in our topsails and
went with reduced sail because we were in an unknown sea. At noon we took observations and found
our latitude to be 38°39'.

August 10 Some rain and cloudy weather in the
morning, with the wind southwest. We made our way
southeast by east 30 miles. At noon we took observations and found our latitude to be 38°39' [sic]. At four
o'clock it fell calm and we had two dolphins and many
small fishes about our ship. At eight o'clock at night
we had a small lingering gale. All night we had a combination of large waves out of the southwest and the
northeast.

August 11 All morning fair weather and very hot.
Then the wind dropped and we could only sail southwest by south. At noon, contrary to expectations, we
found our latitude to be 39°11'. The current had set us
north by 32 miles. At four o'clock in the afternoon, it
became misty and lasted for two hours. But after that
it was fair and clear all night. Variation of the compass
was 11° westerly.

August 12 Fair weather, the wind light and variable. In the morning we killed an extraordinary fish and stood to the westward all day and night. Our observation of the previous day was not a good one, for at noon we found our latitude to be 38°15'. The compass variation was 10° westerly.

August 13 Fair weather and hot, with the wind northeast. We steered west by our compass for 66 miles. At noon we found our latitude to be 37°45' and that our course from noon to noon was west southwest half a point southerly. Compass variation was 7¹/₂° westerly.

Approaching Chesapeake Bay.

August 14 Fair weather, but cloudy with a stiff gale of wind. We steered west by south a point south all day until nine o'clock at night, then thunder and lightning began, whereupon we took in all our sails and lay-a-hull. We drifted north 4¹/₂ miles until midnight.

August 15 Very fair and hot, the wind north by east. At four o'clock in the morning we raised sail and set our course to the westward. At eight o'clock at night the wind came to the north and we steered west by north and west northwest, making good a course west. Compass variation was 7° westerly.

August 16 Fair, shining weather and very hot. We steered west by north. At noon we found our latitude to be 37°06'. This morning we sounded and had ground in 90 fathoms and within three hours it shoaled to 50 fathoms, and so to 28 fathoms by four o'clock in the afternoon. Then we anchored and rode there until eight o'clock at night. Since the wind was from the south, and there was good visibility by moonlight, we resolved to go northward to seek deeper water. So we weighed anchor and sailed northward, but found the water to shoal and deepen from 8 to 22 fathoms.

August 17 Fair and clear, the wind south by west. We steered northward until four o'clock in the morning, then we came to 18 fathoms. We judged that there must be land nearby, even though we couldn't see it. In order to be sure of our position, we anchored and waited for the sun to rise. Then we weighed anchor

and sailed westward until noon. At 11 o'clock we had
sight of a low land with a white sandy shore. By five
o'clock we had come into five fathoms and anchored.
The land was 12 miles from us, bearing west to the
northwest by north. Our latitude was 37°26'. Then
the wind blew such a stiff gale, creating heavy seas,
that we could not raise the anchor, so we remained
there all night in a difficult anchorage.

August 18 Fair weather in the morning and light
wind at north northeast and northeast. At four o'clock
in the morning we weighed anchor and headed toward
the shore to see if it deepened or shallowed. Finding it
to be deep, we sailed closer in order to anchor, for we
saw three islands. So we turned to the windward to
get into a bay which appeared to the west of an island;
the three islands bearing north of us. But toward noon
the wind blew northerly with gusts of wind and rain,
so we headed back out to sea again, remaining there all
night.

In going out we found a channel with no less than
8, 9, 10, 11 and 12 fathoms of water. In entering we
had gone over the Bar of Virginia, which lies 15 miles
from the shore and has only 4½ to 5 fathoms of water
over it. The bar lies north and south, with its northern
end 30 miles wide, but having deep water from 90
fathoms to 4½ fathoms. At the entrance to the bay
the land lies north and south. This is the entrance into
the King's River in Virginia where our Englishmen are
[Jamestown, Virginia]. The northern side of the entrance lies in 37°26' latitude, and you will know when
you are coming into shoal water or soundings, for the
water will look green or thick. You will have 98 fathoms, then it will quickly shoal until you come to 10,
11, 9, 8, 7, 10 and 9 fathoms, then to 5 and 4½ fathoms.

August 19 Fair weather, but a hard gale of wind
from the northeast. So we sailed away [from the en-
trance] until noon, and made good a course southeast
by east, 66 miles. At noon we tacked and sailed westward until six o'clock in the afternoon and went 61½

A *low land with
white, sandy shore.*

*Attempt to enter
Chesapeake Bay.*

*Proper channel
found.*

*The Bar of
Virginia.*

*Entrance to the
James River.*

*Sail away from the
entrance.*

Charting the Sea of Darkness

miles northwest by north. Then we tacked again to the eastward and sailed that way until four the next morning.

August 20 Fair and clear, the wind variable between east northeast and northeast. At four o'clock in the morning we tacked to the westward, keeping that heading until noon, at which time I sounded and had 32 fathoms. Then we tacked to the eastward again; we found our latitude to be 37°22'. We sailed eastward all night and had very strong wind. At eight o'clock at night we took off our bonnets and sailed under reduced sail.

August 21 Today we had a severe storm with much wind and rain all day and all night, causing us to sail eastward under reduced sail until one o'clock in the afternoon. Then a large wave broke upon our foresail and split it, so we were forced to take it from the yard and mend it. We lay a-trie with our mainsail all night. Tonight our cat ran crying from one side of the ship to the other, looking overboard. This made us wonder, but we saw nothing.[24]

August 22 Stormy weather, with gusts of wind and rain. At eight o'clock in the morning we set our foresail and sailed eastward under our foresail, mainsail and mizzen, and from noon to noon we made our way east southeast 51 miles. The night was reasonably dry but cloudy, and the wind variable all day and night. Compass variation was 4° westerly.

August 23 Very fair, but some thunder late in the evening, with the wind variable between the east and the north. At noon, with an east by north wind, we tacked to the northward. The afternoon was very fair, wind variable, and so it continued all night. We made our way east southeast until noon the next day.

August 24 Fair and hot, with the wind variable between the east and the north. At four o'clock the wind came around to the east and southeast, so we steered north by west and in three watches went 39 miles. At noon our latitude was 35°41' and we were far away from land.

Near Cape Hatteras, South Carolina.

August 25 Fair and very hot. All morning it was very calm until 11 o'clock, then the wind came to the southeast and south southeast, so we steered northwest by north two and a half watches, and northwest by west for one watch, altogether making 54 miles. At noon I found our latitude to be 36°20' and out of sight of land.

August 26 Fair and hot with the wind variable from all points of the compass. From two o'clock in the morning until noon we made our way north by east 21 miles. In the afternoon the wind came to the northeast, and veering to the east southeast. We steered northwest 45 miles from noon until 10 o'clock at night. At eight o'clock at night we sounded and had 18 fathoms, and had arrived at the Bank of Virginia but did not see the land. We kept sounding, and steered north until we came to eight fathoms. With the wind coming from the east southeast, and the coast lying south southwest and north northeast, we could not gain sea-way, so we anchored there. At noon our latitude was 37°15'. We found that we had returned to the same place we started from when we first saw land.

Back at the Bar of Virginia.

August 27 Fair and very hot, the wind east southeast. As soon as the sun was up we looked about and saw land. Then we weighed anchor and headed in toward the northwest for an hour, and found the land to be the same place we had left before. We kept the wind on our quarter, and sailed along the coast and the bank which lies parallel to it. Six miles offshore we had 5, 6, 7, 8, 9 and 10 fathoms. The coast lies south southwest and has a white sandy shore full of bays and points. The tide sets west southwest and east northeast. At six o'clock at night we were opposite a harbor or river, but saw a bar lying at its entrance. And to the northward, all along the land, there were many islands. At six o'clock we anchored and sent our boat to sound along the shore, where it was found there was no less than 4½, 5, 6, and 7 fathoms.

August 28 Fair and hot, the wind south southwest. At six o'clock in the morning we weighed anchor and

steered north 36 miles until noon, and came to a point
of land. We were close to the shore in five fathoms,
when suddenly we had only three fathoms, then we
brought the ship up into the wind and there was only
10 feet of water near the point. As soon as we were
over the bar we had 5, 6, 7, 8, 9, 10, 11, 12 and 13 fathoms. We found the land trends toward the northwest
with a great bay and rivers. But we found that the bay
shoaled and we soon had 10 fathoms and the sight of
dry sand between the channels. So we were forced to
go back, and sailed southeast by south nine miles.

Delaware Bay entered.

At seven o'clock we anchored in eight fathoms of
water and found a tide set to the northwest and north
northwest; it rises one fathom and flows south southeast. He that will thoroughly explore this great bay
must have a small pinnace that draws no more than
four or five feet of water and must take soundings
ahead of him.[25] The northern land is full of shoals, and
we were among them, for one time we struck. So at
five in the morning we weighed anchor, and by various
headings steered east and southeast until we had two,
three, four, five, six, seven fathoms, and deeper water.

A small pinnace needed.

Full of shoals.

August 29 Fair weather with some thunder and
showers, the wind shifting between the south southwest and north northwest. In the morning, at daybreak, we raised anchor and sailed toward the northern
land which we found to be many islands with extensive
shoals as far as nine miles off. As we passed them we
had only 7, 6, 5, 4, 3, and 2½ fathoms, and struck
ground with our rudder. We steered away southwest
for half an hour, and had five fathoms. Then we steered
southeast for one and a half hours, and found seven
fathoms, then northeast by east 12 miles, and came to
12 and 13 fathoms. At one o'clock I climbed to the
topmast head to take bearings of the land and found
the body of the islands to bear northwest by north.

Many islands and extensive shoals.

At four o'clock we had gone 12 miles east southeast, and northeast by east, and found only seven fathoms. It was calm, so we anchored. Then I went again
to the topmast head to see how far land was from us,

but could only see the islands. Bearing of the southernmost point of them was northwest by west and 24 miles away, so we rode to our anchor until midnight. Then the wind came to the north northwest, so we raised anchor and set sail.

August 30 Between 12 and one o'clock in the morning we weighed anchor and with a north northwest wind sailed to the eastward. From the time we raised anchor, until noon, we made our way east southeast 33 miles. Then we came to 18, 19, 20 and to 26 fathoms by noon. Then I observed the sun and found our latitude to be 39°05' and saw no land. In the afternoon the wind came north by west, so we lay closehauled with our foresail and mainsail. There was little wind until midnight, then for a while we had a gale. I sounded, and all night our soundings were 30 and 36 fathoms. We made little progress.

Off *Hereford Inlet, New Jersey.*

August 31 Fair weather and light wind. At six o'clock in the morning we tacked to the northward, the wind being light and from the northeast. At noon it fell calm and I found our latitude to be 38°39'. In the afternoon I sounded again, and had only 30 fathoms. Our observations and our depths showed that we had been thrown back and forth by the tide streams. From noon until four o'clock in the afternoon it was calm, but at six o'clock we had a little gale from the south. It was like this all night, sometimes calm, sometimes a gale. From noon to noon we went 24 miles north by east.

Back and forth by deceitful tidal streams.

September 1 Fair weather, the wind variable between east and south. We steered north northwest and at noon found our latitude to be 39°03'. As we went northward we had soundings of 30, 27, 24 and 22 fathoms. At six o'clock we had 21 fathoms. And all the third watch until midnight we had soundings of 21, 22, 18, 22, 21, 18 and 22 fathoms and had gone 18 miles north northwest.

September 2 Close weather in the morning, with the wind from the south. From 12 until two o'clock we steered north northwest and had a sounding of 21 fathoms. Within a half hour we had only 16 fathoms, and it became more and more shallow until we came to 12 fathoms. We saw a great fire, but could not see the land. Then we came to 10 fathoms, whereupon we brought in our tacks to be close hauled and sailed east southeast for two hours. When the sun rose we steered north again and saw the land, all like broken islands, and our soundings were 11 and 10 fathoms. Then we headed in toward the shore, which trends toward the northeast by north, where close by we had seven fathoms. It was a distance of 30 miles from the land we had first seen until we came to a great lake of water, which we judged to be a drowned land making it rise like islands. The mouth of the lake has many shoals upon which the waves break as they are cast out. From that lake or bay the land trends north by east.

Sandy Hook, New Jersey.

A drowned land.

We encountered a forceful current out of the bay, from which six miles out our sounding was 10 fathoms. At five o'clock, there being little wind, we anchored and rode in eight fathoms of water. The night was fair. Tonight I found that the land of high hills to the north of us changed our compass variation 8°, for the day before it was not more than 2° variation. This is a very good place for a landfall and pleasant land to look at.

Large change in compass variation.

September 3 Misty in the morning until 10 o'clock, then it cleared and the wind came to the south southeast, so we weighed anchor and sailed northward. The land is very pleasant, high and bold. At three o'clock in the afternoon we came to three great rivers. So we sailed along to the northernmost, thinking to enter, but a shallow bar prevented us. Then we tacked to the southward and found 2, 3 and 3$^{1}/4$ fathoms until we came to the southern side of them where we had five and six fathoms, and anchored. We sent our boat to take soundings and they returned an hour and a half later having found no less water than four, five, six and seven fathoms. So we weighed anchor, went in, and

The south coast of Staten Island.

Three great rivers.

anchored in five fathoms with a mud bottom. We saw many salmon, mullets and large rays. The latitude is 40°30'.

September 4 In the morning, as soon as it was light, we saw that there was a good anchorage farther up the river. So we sent our boat to take soundings, and found that it was a very good harbor with four and five fathoms within two cable's length [about 1,200 feet] from the shore. Then we raised anchor and went in with our ship. Then our boat went ashore with a net to fish and caught 10 large mullets, each a foot and a half long, and a ray so great that it took four men to haul it aboard the ship. We trimmed our boat and remained at anchor all day. At night the wind blew hard from the northwest, broke our anchor free, and drove us on shore. But thanks to God we were unharmed, for the ground is soft sand and mud.

Today the people of the country came around, seeming glad we had come. They are well dressed in loose deer skins, and brought green tobacco which they gave us in exchange for knives and beads. They have yellow copper. They desire clothes and are very civil. They have a great amount of maize, or Indian wheat, from which they make good bread. The country is full of large, tall oaks.

A very good harbor.

Driven on shore.

The people of the country come aboard.

Henry Hudson's journal reads:

When I came on shore, the swarthy natives all stood around and sung in their fashion; their clothing consisted of the skins of foxes and other animals, which they dress and make the skins into garments of various sorts. Their food is Turkish wheat [maize or Indian corn], whey they cook by baking, and it is excellent eating. They all came on board [around], one after another, in their canoes, which are made of a single hollowed tree; their weapons are bows and arrows, pointed with sharp stones, which they fasten with hard resin. They had no houses, but slept under the blue heavens, sometimes on mats of bulrushes interwoven, and sometimes on the leaves of trees. They always carry with them all their goods, such as their food and green tobacco, which is strong and good for use. They appear to be a friendly people, but have a great propensity to steal, and are exceedingly adroit in carrying away whatever they take a fancy to.

Charting the Sea of Darkness

September 5 In the morning, as soon as it was
light, the wind ceased and the flood tide came. So we
moved our ship again into five fathoms of water and
sent our boat to sound the bay, and found that there
was three fathoms close to the southern shore. Our
men went ashore there and saw many men, women
and children, who gave them tobacco upon their landing. They went into the woods and saw many splendid
oaks and some currants. One of them came aboard and
gave me some [currants] which were dried and very
sweet and good. Today, many of the people came
aboard, some dressed in cloaks of feathers, and others
in furs of various kinds. Some women also came to us
with hemp. They had tobacco pipes of red copper and
other things of copper which they wore about their
necks. At night they went back to shore, and though
we rode quietly at anchor we did not trust them.

September 6 It was fair weather in the morning,
and our master sent John Colman, with four other
men, in our boat over to the northern side to sound
the other river which was 12 miles from us. Along the
way the water shoaled to two fathoms, but north of
the river there was 18 and 20 fathoms in a good anchorage. There was also a narrow river between two
islands to the westward. They told us the land was as
pleasant with grass and flowers and handsome trees as
they have ever seen, and that very sweet smells came
from them. They went in six miles, saw an open sea,
and returned. On their return they were attacked by
two canoes, one containing 12, the other 14 men. The
night came and it began to rain, which extinguished
the wick of their lamp. One of our men, John Colman, was slain in the fight by an arrow shot into his
throat, and two others were hurt. It grew so dark they
could not find the ship that night, and had to row
back and forth. The current was so strong that their
grapnell would not hold them.[26]

September 7 Today was fair, and at 10 o'clock they
returned to the ship and brought our dead man with

*The great bay in
40°30': New
York Bay.*

*Cloaks of feathers
and furs.*

*Through the
Verrazzano
Narrows.*

*Colman slain and
two others hurt.*

them. We carried him to shore, buried him, and named the point after his name, Colman's Point. Then we hoisted aboard our boat and raised the side of our ship with waist-boards for defense of our men. We remained at anchor all night, keeping a careful watch.

September 8 Very fair weather, we remained at anchor and kept very quiet. The people came aboard and brought tobacco and Indian wheat to exchange for knives and beads. They offered us no violence, so we fit the boat up and watched them to see if they would show any sign of the death of our man—which they did not.

September 9 Fair weather. In the morning two great canoes full of men came aboard, one with their bows and arrows, the other, in an attempt to deceive us, pretended interest in buying knives. But we were aware of their intent and took two of them as prisoners, putting red coats on them and not allowing any others to come near us. They went back to land, and two others in a canoe came aboard. We took one and let the other go. But the one we had taken got up and leapt overboard. Then we hoisted anchor, and went off into the channel of the river where we re-anchored for the rest of the night.

September 10 Fair weather, we rode to our anchor until noon. Then we weighed anchor, left the channel, and found it to be shallow in all of the middle of the river, for we could find only 2¹/₂ and 3 fathoms in the length of three miles. Then we came to three and four fathoms and eventually seven fathoms, where we anchored in a bottom of soft mud, and remained there all night. The shore bank is sand.

September 11 Fair, very hot weather. At one o'clock in the afternoon there was a light wind out of the south southwest so we raised anchor and went into the river. Our soundings were 7, 6, 5, 6, 7, 8, 9, 10, 12, 13 and 14 fathoms. Then it became shallow again, and came to five fathoms. We anchored and saw it was a very good harbor for protection from all winds, and remained all night. The people of the country came

Treacherous savages.

East sandbank, in the Narrows.

aboard, showed signs of love, gave us tobacco and Indian wheat, and departed; but we dared not trust them.

September 12 Very fair and hot. At two o'clock in the afternoon, the wind being variable between the north and northwest, we weighed anchor, sailed six miles up the river (which flows southeast by south), and re-anchored. This morning, at our first anchorage in the river, 28 canoes full of men, women and children came to us, but we saw their intent of treachery and would not allow any of them to come aboard. They brought with them oysters and beans, some of which *Oysters and beans.* we bought. They have large tobacco pipes of yellow copper, and pots of clay to prepare their meat in. At 12 o'clock they departed.

Hudson's journal reads:

In latitude 40°48' — It is as pleasant a land as one need tread upon; very abundant in all kinds of timber suitable for shipbuilding, and for making large casks or vats. The people had copper tobacco pipes, from which I inferred that copper might naturally exist there; and iron likewise according to the testimony of the natives, who, however, do not understand preparing it for use.

September 13 Fair, the wind northerly. At seven o'clock in the morning, with the flood tide, we weighed anchor and went four miles up the river. At the end of the flood we anchored. Then four canoes came out to us but we did not allow any of the men aboard our ship. They brought a great many good oysters with them which we bought for trifles. At night I checked the compass variation and found it to be 13°. In the afternoon we weighed anchor, went 7^1/$_2$ miles farther up river with the flood tide, and anchored in five fathoms of water with a bottom of soft mud. We remained there all night, near a high point of land bearing north by east 15 miles from us.

September 14 In the morning, being very fair weather and the wind southeast, we sailed up the river 36 miles, with four and three quarters and five fathoms. We came to a strait between two points where

---

we had 8, 9 and 10 fathoms. It trended northeast by north for three miles, and we had 12, 13 and 14 fathoms. The river is a mile broad with very high land on both sides. We went upriver in deep water 4¹/₂ miles northwest, then five miles northeast by north, and six miles northwest by north, where we anchored. The land grew very high and mountainous and the river is full of fish.

In *the vicinity of West Point.*

September 15 The morning was misty until the sun rose, then it cleared. We weighed anchor, and with the wind from the south, ran 60 miles farther up river, passing by high mountains. We saw a great many salmon in the river, and had good depths of 6, 7, 8, 9, 10, 12 and 13 fathoms. This morning our two [captive] savages got out and swam away. After we were under sail they called to us in scorn. At night we came to other mountains which lie along the river's side. There we found a very loving people and very old men and we were well taken care of. Our boat went out to fish and caught a great many very good fish.

View of Catskill Mountains.

A *very loving people.*

September 16 Fair and very hot weather. In the morning our boat went out fishing again, but caught only very few on account of their canoes which had been there all night. This morning the people came and brought to us ears of Indian corn, pumpkins and tobacco, which we bought for trifles. We remained there all day and filled our casks with fresh water. At night we went six miles higher up the river where we had shallow water, so we anchored until day.

The latitude of Albany, New York.

September 17 Fair, sunshining weather, and very hot. In the morning, as soon as the sun was up, we set sail and ran 18 miles higher, where we found shoals in the middle of the channel, and small islands with only seven fathoms of water around them. Toward night we got so close to shore that we grounded, so we laid out our small anchor and hauled ourselves off. Then we got too close to the bank in the channel and went aground again. We were able to haul ourselves off with the high tide, then anchored for the night.

September 18 Fair weather in the morning and we

remained at anchor. In the afternoon our master's mate accompanied an old savage, a chief of the country, to his house where he was entertained.

Hudson's journal reads:

In latitude 42°18' — I sailed to the shore in one of their canoes, with an old man, who was the chief of a tribe consisting of 40 men and 17 women; these I saw there in a house well constructed of oak bark, and circular in shape, so that it had the appearance of being well built, with an arched roof. It contained a great quantity of maize or Indian corn, and beans of the last year's growth, and there lay near the house for the purpose of drying, enough to load three ships, besides what was growing in the fields. On our coming into the house, two mats were spread out to sit upon, and immediately some food was served in well made red wooden bowls; two men were also despatched at once with bows and arrows in quest of game, who soon after brought in a pair of pigeons which they had shot. They likewise killed a fat dog, and skinned it in great haste with shells which they had got out of the water. They supposed that I would remain with them for the night, but I returned after a short time on board the ship. The land is the finest for cultivation that I ever in my life set foot upon, and it also abounds in trees of every description. The natives are a very good people, for when they saw that I would not remain, they supposed that I was afraid of their bows, and taking the arrows, they broke them in pieces, and threw them into the fire.

September 19 Fair and hot weather. At the flood tide, near 11 o'clock, we weighed anchor, and with no less than five fathoms under us ran above the shoals six miles higher up the river. We anchored, and rode in eight fathoms. The people of the country came flocking around, and brought us grapes and pumpkins which we purchased for trifles. Many brought us beaver skins and otter skins which we bought for beads, knives and hatchets. We rode there all night.

September 20 Fair in the morning. Our master's mate and four other men took the boat to sound farther up the river, and found that six miles above us the channel was very narrow, with only two fathoms of water, but beyond, it became seven or eight fathoms. Toward night they returned, and we remained at anchor all night.

September 21 Fair weather, the wind southerly. We

decided to once again try and get farther up river to determine its depth and width, but so many people came around that we did not go today. Our carpenter went ashore and made a fore-yard. And our master and his mate decided to test some of the leading men of the country to see if they were treacherous. So they took them down into the cabin, and made them merry with much wine and Aqua Vitae. One of the men had his wife with him who sat as modestly as any of our women would have done in a strange place. In the end, one of them who had been aboard our ship since we arrived, became drunk. This was strange to them, and they didn't know what to make of it. The canoes, and everyone but the drunk man, went ashore, but some

Bands of wampum.

returned with bands of beads (some had six, seven, eight, nine and 10) which they gave him. So he quietly slept all night.

September 22 Fair weather. In the morning our master's mate and four others of the ship's company took our boat to sound the river higher up. The people of the country did not come until noon, but when they did come, and saw the savages aboard our ship were well, they were glad. So at three o'clock in the afternoon they came aboard, brought tobacco and more beads which they gave to our master, made a speech, and showed him all the country around us. Then they sent one of their men ashore who returned quickly with venison they had dressed, and bid our master to eat with them. They showed their respect of him and departed, all except the old man that lay aboard. To-night, at 10 o'clock, in a shower of rain, our boat re-turned from taking soundings of the river. They found

Could go no farther.

our ship could go no farther, for they had been up 24 to 27 miles in which there was only seven feet of water and unconstant soundings.

September 23 At noon we weighed anchor and

Return down river.

went down six miles to a shoal that had two channels, one on either side, but there was little wind and the current set us aground. And there we sat for an hour until the flood tide came. Then we had a little gale of wind from the west, so we got our ship into deep water, and rode all night very well.

September 24 Fair weather and a northwest wind. We weighed anchor and went 21 or 24 miles down the river until we ran aground on a bank of mud in the middle of the river, where we sat from half ebb until the flood. At 10 o'clock we got back into deep water and anchored.

Aground.

September 25 Fair weather, with a stiff gale from the south. We remained at anchor, and went ashore on the west side of the river to walk. There we found good land for growing wheat and garden herbs. Upon it were a great many handsome oak, walnut, chestnut, ewe and an abundance of other trees of pleasing wood. In addition, there was much slate and other good stones for houses.

An abundance of pleasing trees.

September 26 Fair weather, with a stiff gale, so we remained at anchor. In the morning our carpenter went ashore with the master's mate and four others of the ships crew to cut wood. This morning two canoes came up river from the place where we first found loving people, and in one of them was the old man who had been lying on our ship at the other place. Accompanying him was another old man who brought more bands of beads which he gave to our master and showed him all the country thereabout, as though it were at his command.

So he made the two old men and the old man's wife dine with him; for they brought two old women and two young maidens of 16 or 17 years, who behaved very modestly, with them. Our master gave one of the old men a knife, and they in turn, gave the master and us some tobacco. At one o'clock they departed down river, making signs that we should follow them down, for we were within six miles of the place where they lived.

September 27 Fair weather in the morning, but much wind. We weighed anchor, and set our fore topsail, but our ship would not take her heading and we ran onto the muddy bank at half ebb. We laid out our anchor to haul us off, but could not, so we sat there from half ebb until half flood. Then we set our foresail and main topsail and got down 18 miles. The old man came to us, and would have had us anchor and go ashore with him to eat. Since we had a fair wind we did not yield to his request, and he left, being very sorrowful of our departure.

The vicinity of Red Hook.

At five o'clock in the afternoon the wind came around to the south southwest, so we made a tack or two and anchored in 14 fathoms. The men fished in our boat right alongside the ship, while our master's mate and boatswain went on land to fish, but they could not find a good place. They returned in an hour with 24 or 25 mullets, breams, basses and catfish. We remained at anchor all night.

September 28 Being fair weather, as soon as it was light we weighed anchor and headed down river with the last quarter of the ebb tide. Then we anchored until high water. At three o'clock in the afternoon we hauled anchor and made another nine miles farther down river until it became dark, and then we anchored.

September 29 Dry, close weather, the wind south and south by west. We weighed anchor early in the morning, and headed down river nine miles until low water, whereupon we anchored at the lower end of an 18-mile-long reach. Some Indians in a canoe came over to us, but would not come aboard. After dinner, a canoe with other men came, and this time three of them came aboard. They brought Indian wheat [corn] which we bought for trifles. At three o'clock in the afternoon, as soon as ebb tide came, we weighed anchor and headed down to the edge, or northernmost, of the mountains. There we anchored, because the channel is narrow, the high land with its many points creates wind eddies. We rode quietly all night in seven fathoms of water.

Below Poughkeepsie.

September 30 Fair weather, with the wind blowing a stiff southeast gale between the mountains, so we remained at anchor that afternoon. The people of the country came around and brought some small skins with them which we bought for knives and trifles. This is a very pleasant place in which to build a town. There is a good spot where ships may conveniently lie at anchor near the shore, and it is protected from all winds except those out of the east northeast. The mountains look as though they contain some metal or mineral, for some of them are almost barren of trees, and what few trees do grow there are blighted. The people brought us a stone which like emery (a stone used by glaziers to cut glass) cuts iron or steel. Yet when powdered, and water added to it, made a color like glittering black lead. It is also good for painter's colors. At three o'clock they departed and we rode to anchor all night.

A *pleasant place to build a town (in the vicinity of Peekskill).*

October 1 Fair weather, the wind variable between the west and the north. We weighed anchor with the ebb tide at seven o'clock in the morning and got down below the mountains a distance of 21 miles. Then at noon it fell calm and the flood tide came, so we anchored. The people of the mountains, curious about our ship and weapons, came aboard. We bought some small skins from them for trifles. This afternoon a canoe with one man in it kept hanging about under our stern, and we could not keep him from it. He got up by our rudder to the cabin window and stole my pillow, two shirts, and two bandoliers. Our master's mate took a shot at him, which struck him in the breast and killed him. Whereupon all the rest fled, some in their canoes from which they leapt into the water. One of them who was swimming got hold of our boat thinking to overthrow it, but our cook took a sword and cut off one of his hands and he drowned. By this time the ebb had come, and we weighed anchor and got down river six miles. By this time it was dark, so we anchored in four fathoms of water and rode well.

Theft.

October 2 Fair weather. At daybreak we weighed anchor, and with a northwest wind got down 21 miles. Then the flood tide came in strong, and we anchored.

Then one of the savages who swam away from us when we were going upriver, came with others, thinking to betray us. But we were aware of their intent, and did not allow anyone to come upon the ship. Whereupon two canoes full of men came up behind our stern and shot at us with their bows and arrows. In return, we discharged six muskets and killed two or three of them. Then more than a hundred of them came to a point of land to shoot at us.

Treachery intended.

A skirmish and slaughter.

I shot a light cannon and killed two of them; the rest fled into the woods. Yet they sent off another canoe manned by nine or 10 which came to meet us. I set off another shot from the cannon and killed one of them. Then our men with their muskets killed three or four more. After a while they went their way, and we got down six miles, where we anchored in a bay on the other side of the river and clear of all danger from them. Here there was a very good piece of ground and a cliff close by of white-green color, as though it were a copper or silver mine. Judging from the trees that grow on it (which were all burnt) it must be either one of them, for other places are as green as grass. It is on the side of the river called *Manna-hata*. No people there came to trouble us and we rode quietly all night, although with much wind and rain.

Manhatten Island.

October 3 Very stormy. In a gust of wind and rain this morning our anchor broke free and we ran aground, but it was mud. As we were about to put out an anchor the wind came around to the north northwest and drove us off again. Then we put out an anchor while under way, letting it fall in four fathoms of water, and hauled in the other anchor. It was thick weather with much wind and rain, so we remained at anchor all night.

October 4 Fair weather. We weighed anchor and came out of the river into which we had run so far. After a while we came out of the great mouth of the great river that runs up to the northwest. We kept to the northern side, thinking we would have deep water, for when we entered we had sent the boat ahead to

The great mouth of the great river.

take soundings and found seven, six and five fathoms. We left the same way we had entered, but we were deceived, for there was only 8½ feet of water, which became 3, 5, 3, and 2½ fathoms. Then there were 3, 4, 5, 6, 7, 8, 9 and 10 fathoms. By 12 o'clock we were clear of the entire inlet. Then we brought in our boat, set our mainsail, spritsail and topsails, and steered east southeast and southeast by east into the main sea. At noon the land on the southern side of the bay or inlet bore west by south, and 12 miles from us.

They leave the coast of Virginia.

October 5 Fair weather, the wind variable between the north and the east. We held our course southeast by east. At noon I took observations, and found our latitude to be 39°30'. Our compass variation was 6° westerly. We continued our course toward England all the rest of this month of October without seeing any land along the way. And on Saturday, the seventh of November (*stilo novo*), by the grace of God we safely arrived in the range of Dartmouth, in Devonshire, in the year 1609.

Epilogue: 1609

Although Robert Juet wrote a detailed chronicle of the voyage, he left some gaps. The first occurs between March 27, two days after the *Half Moon* left Amsterdam, and May 5, when they sighted land at North Cape, Norway. Then Juet lapsed into silence again until May 19, from which time the course of the *Half Moon* was continuously southwest and west — the search for a Northeast Passage apparently ended.

Juet's only explanation for the missing dates is "because it is a journey virtually knowne, I omit to put down what passed." He did not comment on why no further efforts were made to hold to the intended passage. It couldn't have been the weather, for at most times they had "faire sun-shining weather," with winds east by south. Nor was Hudson unable or unwilling to navigate in far northern latitudes; he had encountered far more severe conditions on previous voyages and yet approached to within 577 miles of the North Pole. Yet on this voyage, Henry Hudson sailed 3,000 miles in the wrong direction, against prevailing winds and currents, and in direct contradiction to the orders of his employers. Why?

Emmanuel Van Meteren's *Historie der Nederlanden*, published in 1614, provides a partial answer to this question, and an explanation of what took place during the periods missing from Juet's journal. English authorities prohibited Hudson from traveling to Amsterdam to give his report to the directors of the V.O.C., so Hudson sought out Van Meteren, the Dutch Counsel in London. Thus, Van Meteren had access to Henry Hudson's journal, logbook, and charts, and presumably read them before they were passed on to the officials of the Dutch East India Company.

Unlike other Dutch historians, who imaginatively interpreted Hudson's explorations to the greater benefit of Holland, Van Meteren conscientiously and accurately reproduced the facts. He may even have had the journal in hand when he wrote his history, for in his account of the voyage there are frequent shifts from the use of "they" to "we." This kind of error is common when journals are copied. Van Meteren's knowledge of the events may also have been derived from direct conversation with Hudson.

Van Meteren writes that a mutiny took place, originating in quarrels between Dutch and English members of Hudson's crew. The Dutch crew, accustomed to sailing in the torrid heat of the Indies, were profoundly discouraged by the snow, ice, and bitter cold, and refused to sail a single league farther in so inauspicious a climate.

Robert Juet preserves a suspicious silence in these matters, which strongly suggests his complicity in the mutiny. If he had been an innocent bystander, he certainly would have mentioned it in the journal. While it is true that the early part of the journey covered territory that was well known and charted, Juet's omission of any reference to the voyage along this part of the coast—even daily position fixes—seems like an attempt to mask his own involvement in the rebellion.

When mutiny occurred, Hudson did not attempt to suppress it. His natural inclination was always toward peaceful compromise. Since his convictions about the Northeast Passage were not strong to begin with, he needed little excuse to change direction and head west to find the Northwest Passage—the route he wanted to follow all along. Hudson was well prepared, having all the necessary charts with him. He could justify his actions to the V.O.C. on the grounds that, as before, ice and fog made the original route impossible; and as a last resort, he could blame the mutinous crew for his change of course.

Hudson had two choices: he could sail directly to Davis Strait and investigate the Furious Overfall and Lumley's Inlet (Frobisher Bay)—a passage he had attempted to make at the end of his 1608 voyage; or he could seek a route north of the Virginia Colony—a route his friend Captain John Smith thought promising. Hudson put these choices to the crew, who chose the latter option, because it was warmer; but it hardly mattered, for Hudson planned to cover both by starting at the most southerly point and working his way north.

Juet ended his journal as vaguely as he had begun, condensing four weeks of passagemaking into a single sentence: "We continued our course toward England, without seeing any land by the way, all the rest of this month of October. And on the seventh day of November, being Saturday, by the Grace of God we safely arrived in the Range of Dartmouth in Devonshire, in the year 1609."

Once again, Juet left out an important piece of information: even on the return passage to England, Henry Hudson was unwilling to end his search for the Northwest Passage. His Dutch mate suggested they overwinter in Newfoundland and resume the search again the following spring, but Hudson knew that a winter spent in that harsh climate, with dwindling supplies, would likely result in another mutiny. As a compromise, he elected to make landfall in the British Isles before proceeding to Holland.

Juet's record leaves other questions unanswered. Why, after he had sailed as far south as Chesapeake Bay, did Hudson abandon his plans to reach the new colony at Jamestown and visit his friend Captain John Smith?

He may have been deterred by his Dutch colors and partially Dutch crew. Even with no flag flying, the *Half Moon*'s hull configuration would reveal her nationality, and she might be attacked before there was a chance to show she was under English command. And the Dutch crewmembers surely had no desire to end up in an English settlement.

Then, too, Hudson had discussed the Northwest Passage with the eminent Dutch geographer Peter Plancius, who did not agree with Captain John Smith's hypothesis that a route existed in these latitudes. Plancius's doubts stemmed from the knowledge that Smith's exploration of Chesapeake Bay and its tributary rivers had revealed one unbroken coastline.

Hudson ran aground in Delaware Bay and wrote, "He that will thoroughly discover this great bay may have a small Pinnace, that must draw but four or five foot water, to sound before him." He recognized that this bay was far too shallow to lead him to the Pacific Ocean, and he wasted no more time on it.

Long before the *Half Moon* arrived at the upper reaches of the Hudson River, it must have been apparent that this was not the passage to Cathay; yet Hudson persisted. Perhaps he was nourished by the thought that, although the Strait of Magellan is narrower in places than the Hudson River, it had made the South Pacific accessible to the Spanish.

When Hudson returned to England, he sent word to his Dutch employers that upon payment for services and supplies he was willing to set out immediately to search again for the Northwest Passage. He proposed to leave on March 1 so that he could spend April and part of May catching whales and fish off Newfoundland. Then, no matter what else happened, his promoters could at least be assured of the ship returning with a profitable cargo. He was also eager to leave early enough to avoid ice blockage and severe weather in the Arctic.

But Hudson and his English crew were forbidden from leaving England—or from being employed by another nation. The *Half Moon* and her Dutch crew were returned to Holland in July of the following year, along with Hudson's journals, logbooks, and charts.

Why did Hudson sail to England? Most likely no one on the *Half Moon* was eager to return to Holland. The crew would have feared punishment for their mutiny, and Hudson must have been uncertain about the repercussions of so totally disregarding the terms of his contract. Also, there are indications of still another mutiny, with the English crew, who outnumbered the Dutch, forcing a landfall with no more delay.

Some historians suggest Hudson was motivated by a shortage of provisions. But the passage east took only four weeks; at the outset of the expedition their first landfall was a full nine weeks after their departure. No food shortage is mentioned in the journal, and even if they were in need, they surely could have held off a few days longer to reach Amsterdam.

Perhaps there were deeper forces at play. A 1612 account by the Dutch historian Hessel Gerritz states that many in Holland believed that Hudson "purposely missed the correct route to the western passage" because he was "unwilling to benefit Holland and the directors of the Dutch East India Company by such a discovery."

Could Henry Hudson have been in the employ of the English all along? They appeared outraged that he was working for their Dutch rivals; but the morality of hiring a foreign national never bothered the English when John Cabot, an Italian, sailed for them. And Henry Hudson was in Amsterdam for months before he signed his contract and departed. Surely this news must have gotten back to England; Henry Hudson was one of their most famous navigators. Yet they did nothing to prevent his journey.

Could it be that English merchants, unwilling to invest any more money in the search for a northern route, let the Dutch do it for them? If the expedition failed, the English lost nothing. But if Hudson was successful, England could proclaim the rights and profits of the passage, since it was accomplished under the command of an Englishman. Perhaps Hudson stopped in England to let his true employers know of his findings.

Origin of Hudson's Geographic Notions

At the time of Hudson's voyage, the Virginia coast had not yet been mapped with any accuracy. Captain John Smith wrote of this "coast unknown and undiscovered":

I have had six or seven charts of those Northern parts, so unlike each other, and most so differing from any true proportion, or resemblance of the country, that they did me no more good than so much waste paper, though they cost me more.

Of these 2,000 miles, more than half is yet unknown to any purpose: not even so much as the borders of the Sea are yet discovered. As for the goodnes and true substances of the Land we are for the most part truly ignorant of them unless it be those parts about the Bay of Chisapeack and Sagadahock [Popham Colony on the Kennebec River, Maine]: but only here or there have we touched or seen a little of the edges of those large dominions, which stretch themselves into the Main, God knows, how many thousand miles.

When the new colony was formed at the mouth of the Sagadahoc River in 1607, its commander, George Popham, wrote to England telling of their good fortune. So little was known about the region that in his letter to Prince Charles he said cinnamon and nutmeg grew here, and that a large sea existed only seven days journey to the west, by which China could be reached.

For the purpose of navigation, charts by even the most authoritative mapmakers were nearly useless.

When Hudson encountered the "River of the Steep Hills" (Hudson River), as he called it, he truly believed he was the first to discover it. Hudson was not aware that since the voyage of Esteban Gomez three-quarters of a century earlier, Spanish maps had been showing this river as Rio de Gamas, or Rio Grande, or that in 1524 Giovanni da Verrazano had anchored in its mouth.

Though the Dutch claimed ownership of Hudson River territory by virtue of Hudson's statements that he and his men were the first white people the Indians ever saw, Verrazano's exploits, described in his letter to Francis I, invalidate this. From 1615 to 1665 Dutch maps gave this river a variety of names: Noort Rivier, Groote Rivier, Manhattan's Rivier, and Maurits (or Mauritius) Rivier.[27]

John Smith

His acquaintanceship with Captain John Smith may explain why Henry Hudson sailed as far south as 37°N latitude to search for the Northwest Passage. It is likely that the two men, with their similar sailing experience and mutual interest in the New World, had met in London to discuss the latest theories and information on the Northwest Passage.

According to Van Meteren, Smith wrote to Hudson from Virginia, expressing his belief that a strait, sound, or river north of the Virginia Colony, somewhere under 40°N latitude, might lead to a Western Sea. From there, perhaps by traveling through the Great Lakes, one would pass into the Pacific Ocean.

This notion arose from two separate sources. Smith had heard rumors about the vast waters of the Great Lakes (Erie, Ontario, Huron, Michigan, and Superior), whose true geography was hardly understood. (It was thought they entered into the large strait north of Canada.) And he had seen maps drawn from information brought back by Verrazano in 1524.

One of the best-known maps was created by Michael Lok, "citizen of London." Intended to show the geography of northern regions, it depicts as fanciful a

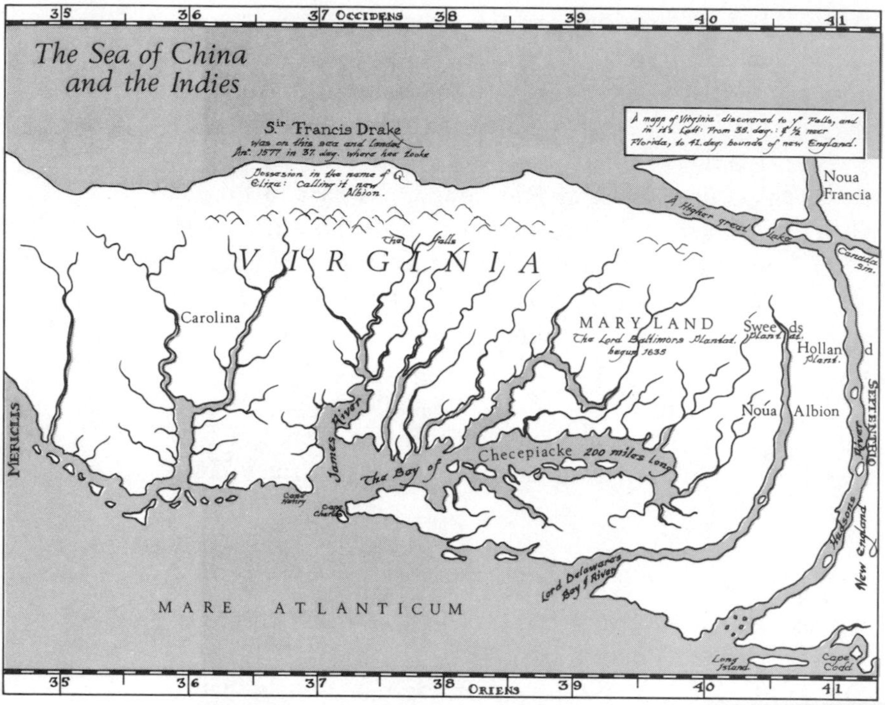
The Sea of China
and the Indies
S.ir Francis Drake
was on this sea and landed
An°. 1577 in 37. deg. where hee tooke
Possesion in the name of Q.
Eliza: Calling it new
Albion.
A mapp of Virginia discovered to ye Falls, and
in it's Latt: From 35. deg.: & ½ neer
Florida, to 41. deg: bounds of new England.
Noua
Francia
A Higher great Lake
Canada
Sin.
VIRGINIA
The falls
Carolina
MARY LAND
The Lord Baltimors Plantat.
begun 1635
Sweeds
Plantat.
Holland
Plant.
Noua Albion
SEPTENTRIO
Hudsons River
New England
James River
The Bay of Checepiacke 200 miles long
Cape Henry
Cape Charles
Lord Delawares Bay & River
MERICLIS
MARE ATLANTICUM
Long Island
Cape Codd
OCCIDENS
ORIENS

Figure 4-5. *The Sea of China. Belief continued in a waterway north of Virginia leading to an open-water passage to China and the Indies, despite lack of any confirming evidence. According to John Farrer, deputy treasurer of the Virginia Company who published this 1651 map of Virginia, both the St. Lawrence River, by way of the Great Lakes, and the Hudson River directly connected with the strait, while only a ten-day march separated it from the head of the James River.*

collection of places as could be imagined: the legendary islands of Frisland, Hy Brasil, Saint Brendan, Maide, Verde, and Island of the Demons. Frobisher's Strait is recognized, but the island of Queen Elizabeth Foreland, below the strait, is reassigned to part of the Canadian mainland. Captions acknowledge the 1497 voyage of John Cabot and the 1535 voyage of Jacques Cartier. The mythical kingdoms of Saguanay (peopled with winged men and rich with jewels and spices) and Norumbega are prominently depicted. But the most unusual aspect of this map is the sudden and complete constriction of the continent in its middle to a thin isthmus of land north of

Florida, beyond which a great sea—the Sea of Verrazano—opens out. This was due to Verrazano's mistaken belief that the open water he saw to the west of the outer barrier islands of the North Carolina coast was the Pacific Ocean.

It seems unbelievable that any credence could be given to such a tortured geography, but one must realize that the vast interior of the American continent had not yet been explored.

Peter Plancius

While Hudson was waiting in Amsterdam to sign his contract during the winter of 1608–1609, he spoke at length with Peter Plancius, a clergyman and scholar with

---

Figure 4-6. *Michael Lok map. Michael Lok, "citizen of London," shows the legendary sea reportedly discovered by Giovanni da Verrazano in 1524. As Verrazano sailed along the outer banks of Carolina, he saw open water extending all the way to the horizon on the far side of this narrow strip of land. In his letter to Francis I, Verrazano says "here is an isthmus a mile in width and about 200 long, in which from the ship we could see el mare orientale . . . this sea "is the same which flows around the shores of India, China and Cataya . . ." Printed in Richard Hakluyt's 1582 Divers Voyages, its projection plan is identical to that used by Mercator in his 1569 Atlas.*

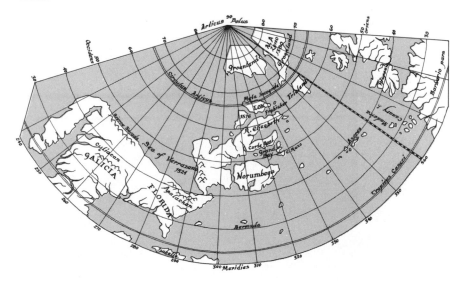

much scientific enthusiasm. Born and raised in west Flanders, Plancius was forced to seek refuge in Holland to avoid religious persecution. There, as one of the leaders of the Calvinist party and minister of the Reformed Church of Amsterdam, he pursued his interest in cosmography.

Plancius also started a school of navigation. The training it provided to Dutch mariners allowed Holland to became a serious commercial rival to Spain. One of Plancius's best-known pupils was Willem Barents, who brought glory to Holland in his exploration of the Arctic.

Figure 4-7. *Peter Plancius and the declination compass. Plancius, Dutch geographer and a leading force in Holland's school of navigation, worked on the problem of determining longitude by magnetic variation. Drawn by Jan van der Straat around 1600, the print is one of a series of 20 under the general title of "New Discoveries." Reproduced from* Dutch Sailing Ships, *the original engraving is in the Rijksmuseum of Amsterdam.*

Plancius's studies made him a recognized authority on geography, especially on routes to the Far East, and earned him the role of official cartographer for the Dutch East India Company. In this capacity he produced almost eighty maps. As one of the founders of both the Dutch East India Company and the Dutch West India Company, he had a personal financial stake in the creation of accurate charts.

Although Hudson told members of the Dutch East India Company exactly what they wanted to hear—that there was every likelihood of finding a Northeast Passage to the Indies—to Plancius Hudson admitted his most fervid belief that the real route lay to the northwest, probably through Lumley's Inlet or the Furious Overfalls—both north of 60°N latitude. He even sketched a map for Plancius on which he showed the intended route. Several years later Plancius related to Hessel Gerritz, a mapmaker and publisher of a brief history of northern discovery, that Hudson, in his final voyage of 1610 "*again* embarked *with no less determination* to explore the Western route than he had on the previous voyage."[28]

During the same winter that Hudson discussed his plans with Peter Plancius, he also met with another important man, Jodocus Hondius.

Jodocus Hondius

Josse de Hondt, better known by the Latinized version of his name, was born in Ghent in 1563. Like Plancius and many other Flemish citizens, he fled his country for religious reasons. He settled briefly in London, where he established a name for himself as an engraver of portraits and as a cartographer. Among his friends were English geographers and others interested in maritime explorations: William Sanderson, John Davis, Richard Hakluyt, and Gerardus Mercator.

Hondius returned to Amsterdam in 1593 or 1594 and became Holland's leading map publisher. His maps were admired not only for their geographical information and accuracy, but also for their great beauty. When Mercator died in 1594, Hondius purchased the plates of his maps and, with the addition of maps of his own, produced a new and enlarged version of Mercator's atlas.

While in Amsterdam, Hudson gave Hondius details about his 1607 attempt to sail over the North Pole, and his 1608 effort to reach Cathay by a Northeast Passage. Hondius later included this information in his chart of the Arctic regions. As further evidence of their friendship and trust, Hondius acted as Hudson's advisor and interpreter in the negotiations for the forthcoming voyage—signing as witness at the bottom of the contract.

Open Polar Sea

Hudson still believed that a completely open polar sea might be reached by keeping to open water as much as possible. In the open sea, he reasoned, the greater depth of the water and its agitation by waves and currents would prevent the formation of ice. With no ice blockage, he could sail as far north as 83°, or even farther, where the sea would not be frozen. He would then be free to sail eastward, where he could pass through the Strait of Anian, "thereby reaching the Kingdom of Cathay, to China, to the Islands of Japan, and also to the Spice Islands and the Philippines. For east and west join on account of the spherical shape of the earth."

Pierre Jeannin

Another source, a rather unusual one, documents some of Hudson's geographic notions. While Hudson was negotiating with the Dutch East India Company, an intrigue was brewing to have France hire him to discover the Northeast Passage.

France, like other northern European countries, was prevented from the lucrative Far East trade by Spanish and Portuguese control of the southern oceans. Furthermore, French ventures in the New World—expeditions to Canada—were a great disappointment, yielding neither profit nor glory. By the time of Hudson's third voyage, the Dutch were not only serious rivals with England for the Russian trade, but the scope of their maritime activities was growing. Dutch vessels were already making their way to the Indies around the Cape of

Good Hope, usurping Portuguese power there. Eager to gain a share in the fortunes of the East, King Henry IV of France sought to hire those in Holland who had experience in the India trade.

He confided this plan to his ambassador in the Hague, Pierre Jeannin, asking him to make discreet enquiries. Jeannin, who was in Holland to aid in peace negotiations between the States General and Spain, contacted Isaac Le Maire, an influential Amsterdam merchant and a director of the East India Company. Le Maire's involvement with the company was minimal, and he ceased activity in it after a year or two. His interests lay in forming his own enterprise to discover new routes to the East Indies in order to compete directly with the monopoly of the East India Company.

Le Maire was well acquainted with Hudson and conferred with him about a northern passage, thinking he might wish to hire Hudson for his own ventures. Jeannin met directly with Plancius to confirm the facts, not admitting the true reason for the discussion, but only, "in the way of scientific discussion on the northern passage, and as if I were desirous to instruct myself, and to learn what he knows about it, or what he concludes on scientific grounds." All this information was conveyed in full from the Hague in a letter from Jeannin to Henry IV, dated January 25, 1609. Jeannin wrote:

Plancius maintains, according to the reasons of his science, and from the information given him, both by the Englishman [Hudson] and other pilots, who have been engaged in the same navigation, that there must be in the northern parts a passage corresponding to the one found near the South Pole by Magellan.[29]

Apart from the geographic advantage of a northern route, there were political considerations in its favor.

This whole voyage, both out and home, can be finished in six months, without approaching any of the harbours and fortresses of the King of Spain; whilst by the road, round the Cape of Good Hope, which is now in common use, one gen-

erally requires three years, and one is besides exposed to meet and to fight the Portuguese . . . with regard to the northern passage, your majesty might undertake the search openly, and in your majesty's name, as a glorious enterprise. It belongs to your majesty to command me what I am to do in this affair. The truth is, that one cannot guarantee the success of this enterprise with certainty; but yet it is also true, that Le Maire has for a long time inquired into the charges of the undertaking, and that he is generally considered to be an able and industrious man. Besides, the risk would not be very great. When Ferdinand of Spain received the offer of Columbus, and caused three ships to be fitted out for him, to sail to the West Indies, the proposal seemed still more hazardous, and all the other potentates, to who he had applied, had laughed at him, considering his success as impossible, and yet he has obtained such great results. It is also the opinion of Plancius, and of other geographers, that in the northern parts there are many countries which have not yet been discovered, and which God may be keeping for the glory and the profit of other princes, unwilling to give everything to Spain alone.

Nothing came of France's overtures to Hudson, but they did spur the Dutch East India Company into signing his contract.

George Weymouth

Captain George Weymouth's two voyages to the New World also figured prominently in Hudson's geographic notions. The first voyage, made in 1602, had as its goal the discovery of the Northwest Passage. In this attempt, Weymouth sailed 100 leagues into Hudson Strait before ice forced him to return to England.

Weymouth's second voyage had far different objectives. The primary purpose of this 1605 venture, planned and equipped by Sir Thomas Arundell and some Plymouth merchants, was to find a suitable place for Catholic settlers. (In the early seventeenth century, England and other northern European countries considered America a good place to rid themselves of their unwanted Irish and English Catholics.) Weymouth also was charged with seeking out good fishing grounds.

In the 1500s, the North American coast was visited

regularly by boats from every nation, fishing for the plentiful cod off Newfoundland and Nova Scotia. Toward the end of that century, with the discovery of the cod's winter spawning grounds along the coast of Maine, the fishing industry moved close inshore. Ships from England, France, Spain, and Holland now headed for Maine's harbors—Boothbay, Damariscove, Monhegan.

Weymouth set out on his second voyage to create a permanent habitation in the northern region—beyond Spanish power to the south and out of reach of French power to the north—and to take part in this new inshore fishery.

He left England on March 5, 1605 with the vessel *Archangell*, and sailed as far south as 41°30', making his landfall at Cape Cod. From there he sailed across the Gulf of Maine to Monhegan Island, a whale-shaped landmark rising high above the sea. He anchored there, went ashore with his crew to explore, and noted that there were fine trees that could be used to make masts and planks for boats, fresh water, and abundant fish. Nearby, to the north, were two other islands that provided good anchorage and had strong potential for the new settlement. These were Burnt and Allen islands, near the western approach to Penobscot Bay.

Weymouth and his crew continued to explore the region in a small shallop, going well into the nearby inlet and the large river that he called Pentecost Harbor, known today as St. George River, after the patron saint of England. An attempt to reach the mountains (Camden Hills) they saw from Monhegan Island was unsuccessful; the weather was too hot and the distance farther then they had surmised. They returned to the boat, and Weymouth continued to explore and chart the coast.

James Rosier kept a record of the voyage, which was published later that year as *A True Relation of the most Prosperous Voyage made this Present Yeare 1605, by Captain George Weymouth in the Discovery of the Land of Virginia*. Rosier thought the St. George River, with its attractive woods, gently rolling grassy lands, and numerous coves, "a fairer river than the Severn or the Thames."

There is no doubt that when Henry Hudson made

his own exploration of this area, he was well prepared with the necessary charts, for he knew exactly what soundings would show his position on the Newfoundland Banks. He took the *Half Moon* almost due west to Cape Sable at the southwest extremity of Nova Scotia, where they sighted land. From Cape Sable the *Half Moon* sailed west northwest across the Gulf of Maine until the water quickly shoaled to twenty fathoms. "Then we made account we were neere the Ilands that lie off the shoare. So we came to an Anchor. . . ." They didn't just happen upon islands; they sought them out. Dense fog hid the islands until the next morning, when they could be seen lying north and northwest, about six miles off. Judging from the distances sailed and the soundings made, these were Burnt and Allen Islands, north of Monhegan Island. Further confirmation is derived from the journal entry on July 18, which reads: "fair weather, we went into a very good harbour, and rode hard by the shoare in four fathoms of water. The River runneth up a great way, but there is but two fathoms hard by us . . . we found the height [latitude] of the place to be 44° 1′." This observation was taken in calm seas, while at anchor in a protected harbor, and is probably quite reliable. It places them at the mouth of the St. George River, where Captain Weymouth had anchored only four years earlier. Obviously, Henry Hudson made good use of Rosier's journal and of Weymouth's logbooks and detailed charts of this coast.

Bartholomew Gosnold

Captain Bartholomew Gosnold sailed from Dartmouth, England, on March 26, 1602, in the *Concord*, a small bark. His was a purely exploratory expedition, since a crew of 32 men was hardly sufficient to start a new colony. The voyage was short—Gosnold returned to England on June 18 of the same year—but significant: Cape Cod, which Gosnold named, was the first English appelation in the region. He also discovered and named Martha's Vineyard and the Elizabeth Islands.

A full account of Gosnold's voyage was published in

London in 1602, so it was available to Henry Hudson; and Juet referred to it in his August 6 journal entry: "Upon this Risse [shoal] we had an observation, and found that it lyeth in 40°10′. And this is that Headland which Captaine Bartholomew Gosnold discovered in the yeere 1602 and called Cape Cod; because of the store of Cod-fish that he found thereabout."[30]

After his stay in Maine, Hudson sailed south until he again sighted land. He steered in, thinking to go north of it, but first he sent a shallop ashore to take soundings. This was on August 3, and although no observations were taken that day, the description of depth and currents places them near the northern end of Cape Cod. Their observation for the previous day, when still out of sight of land, was 41°56′. So far there are no inconsistencies, for the northernmost tip of Cape Cod stands at 42°05′N latitude. And in the footnotes of the journal, Samuel Purchas explains, "They goe on Land neere Cape Cod." On August 4, they "came to an Anchor at the Northern end of the Headland."

A disparity in the facts begins here, for according to Robert Juet, "the bodie of this Headland lyeth in 41° 45′." Though still abeam of Cape Cod, they were closer to Chatham at its southern end than near its northern headland. On August 5 and 6 their general course was south-southeast, but during this time tidal currents and fog made it difficult for them to determine their position. It also makes it hard for us to reconstruct their course.

When Juet wrote that this was the headland called Cape Cod by Captain Bartholomew Gosnold, and that it "lyeth in 40° 10′," he got the latitude wrong: this latitude would place them at the inlet to Barnegat Bay on the coast of New Jersey.

Samuel Purchas says "This dangerous Risse is in 41°10′, and lyeth off East from Cape Cod into the Sea." When corrected by the obvious error of 60 nautical miles (one full degree of latitude), they were just south of Nantucket on the Nantucket shoals, not off Cape Cod. What Purchas was referring to as the dangerous rise was

Georges Bank, much farther offshore; but we know the *Half Moon* was close enough to Nantucket for land to be sighted from the top of the mast, and this would not be possible from Georges Bank. From the description of the currents and depths, they were definitely caught on the reefs of Nantucket, with their shallow, irregular bottom, and swift, erratic currents.

Figure 4-8. *Cape Cod and the Great Rise. Hugo Allard's map, of which only a portion is reproduced here, is a reworked version of Jan Jansson's 1650 map "New and Exact Map of All New Netherland." It showed, as the result of Hudson's voyage, the new colony stretching from the Chesapeake Bay all the way up to Penobscot Bay, Maine.*

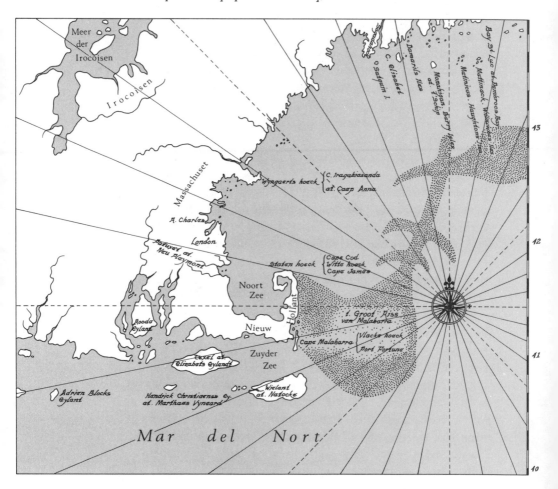

Charting the Sea of Darkness

Samuel Mace

In the same month and year that Captain Gosnold sailed (March 1602), a second ship set out for the coast of Virginia. Sir Walter Raleigh had purchased a bark and hired a crew, paying their wages by the month. In command of the ship was Samuel Mace, "a very sufficient mariner, an honest sober man, who had been at Virginia twice before." He was to see if anything could be found of the people left at Raleigh's Roanoke Colony in 1587. In addition, Captain Mace had two other objectives. One was to start a new colony "to plant Christian people and religion upon the northwest countries of America, in places temperate and well agreeing with our consitution." The other was to find a convenient passage into the "South Sea" — the Pacific.

At first, these two goals seem to be incompatible. But Captain Mace's approach to finding a way into the South Sea was radically different from that of other explorers. Instead of searching in the frozen, outermost bounds of America for a Northwest Passage, he intended to incorporate overland travel, rivers, and lakes into his route. By first planting a colony, he would "learn as much by inquisition of the natural inhabitants, as by his own navigations." Based in a temperate, habitable region, they would avoid being frozen in the seas, or "forced to winter in extreme colde and darkenesse like unto hell," where even in summer the ships were in peril of being "overwhelmed or crusht in pieces by hideous and fearefull mountaines of yce floting upon those seas."

Trade with Cathay was to be accomplished by having two sets of ships, one in the Pacific, the other in the Atlantic. In between, goods would be transported by carriages and flat-bottomed river boats. An entire passage was expected to take no more than four or five months.

Nothing came of this expedition — neither the finding of the Roanoke colonists, nor the realization of a combined sea and overland route to Cathay. It was important, however, in that it reflected yet another line of thinking by English merchants in their attempts to reach the Orient. And it may have been a factor in Hudson's decision to start a search at the coast of Virginia instead of heading directly for Davis Strait.

Busse Island

Explorations in the Canadian Artic by Martin Frobisher in 1576, 1577, and 1578 provided new information about the geography of Baffin Island. Unfortunately, they also were directly responsible for geographic misconceptions shown on maps and charts well into the nineteenth century.

On his return passage in 1578, one of Frobisher's vessels, the *Emmanuel*, came upon an unknown island. The *Emmanuel* was a busse (a type of herring boat, often referred to as the Busse of Bridgewater), and the crew named their discovery the Island of Busse in its honor. George Best, one of the passengers, first described the island in his *A True Discourse*:

The Busse of Bridgewater, as she came homeward . . . discovered a great Ilande in the latitude of . . . Degree, which was never yet founde before, and sayled three days alongst the coast, the land seeming to be fruitful, full of woods, and a champion countrie.

The omission of latitude figures is common throughout Best's *Discourse*, and was perhaps intended to conceal the whereabouts of gold mines Frobisher thought he had discovered. Later "sightings" of Busse Island gave it a definite location—about 420 miles southwest of Iceland in the latitude of $57^1/2°$N—and a coastline with named harbors and mountains.

Thomas Wiars, another passenger, also gave an account of the discovery. It contained a more detailed description of the island, and gave it a latitude of "57 degrees and 1 second part [$57^1/2°$], or thereabout." The longitude was not given, but surmising from their last known position it was approximately $38^1/2°$W, or 350 miles southeast of Cape Farewell, Greenland.

The earliest map to show Busse Island was the renowned Molyneux Globe of 1592. Though undoubtedly taken from Wiars' account, the position of Busse Island was shifted somewhat toward the southeast. Two years later, Peter Plancius produced a map that moved the island still farther south and east. He showed it at 57°30′ to 58°30′ N latitude and 23°W longitude. Hudson must have studied these maps and discussed them with Plancius when the two were together in Amsterdam. The position of Busse Island was variously displayed on other charts at the beginning of the seventeenth century, but generally it was located at 58°N latitude, and 27° to 31°W longitude.

When Henry Hudson failed to complete the Northeast Passage and headed west in search of the Northwest Passage, he made a brief stop at the Faeroe Islands. He set sail again on May 31. Two days later, Juet wrote:

The second [June], mystie weather, the wind at northeast.
At noone we steered away south-west to find Busse Iland,
discovered in the yeere 1578 by one of the ships of Sir
Martin Frobisher, to see if it lay in her true latitude in
the chart or no.

The third. At noone we observed and found our height
to bee 58° 48′. . . We accounted our selves neere Busse Iland:
by mid-night we looked out for it, but could not see it.

Though Hudson's latitude was a trifle high to be looking for the island, it was within a creditable range. But in longitude, he was considerably off course. Only two days out of the Faeroe Islands, the farthest Hudson could have reached was 10° W longitude — far away from 27 or 30 degrees.

Busse Island serves as a marvelous example of how unknown were the vast reaches of the Atlantic, how total was the lack of comprehension about longitudinal (east/west) distances, and how inadequate was the geographical information depicted on charts. There is a 900-mile distance between the island's presumed location southeast of Greenland and the place where Henry Hudson looked for it.

Although he didn't hesitate to show it on the map he drew in 1610, Hudson never saw Busse Island. Nonetheless, he must be given credit for attempting to verify the island's existence and reconcile the discrepancy in its location.

Whether it actually existed or was a mirage playing tricks on the eyes of mariners will never be determined. But even though it was never seen again after 1670, cartographers continued to depict the Sunken Island of Busse until well into the nineteenth century, attributing its disappearance to a cataclysmic event, such as a volcano or subsidence of the ocean floor.

CHAPTER FIVE

The Great Bay of Ice: 1610

Prologue

*H*enry Hudson finally did receive official sanction to do what he had attempted three times before against the wishes of his employers and the will of his crew: search for the Northwest Passage. This time his financial backers were an independent group of merchant adventurers—not the Muscovy Company. Among the investors were Sir Thomas Smythe, an influential London merchant and one of the original members of the English East India Company; Sir Dudley Diggs, an educated and wealthy gentleman; and Master John Wolstenholme, collector of customs revenues and ardent promoter of voyages of discovery.

In 1610 Hudson took command of the bark *Discovery*, Captain George Weymouth's old ship. It was larger than either the *Half Moon* or the *Hope-Well*, and carried a crew of twenty-two, at least five of whom (including Robert Juet) had been with Hudson on his other voyages.

Hudson had learned on his last journey that the Northwest Passage did not lie along the eastern seaboard of America. Therefore, it had to be somewhere north of 60° latitude in one of the straits through Arctic Canada. Accordingly, Hudson headed directly for Greenland and Davis Strait to enter the Furious Overfall, which had been visited earlier by Captain John Davis. He entered Hudson Bay, and for three months the *Discovery* struggled through a labyrinth of ice. Daily they fought to keep the ship from being trapped by floating islands of dense pack ice, or destroyed by immense icebergs thrust at them by storms or furiously rushing currents.

When they reached the southernmost part of James Bay, Hudson decided to overwinter, hauling the boat aground and building a temporary shelter. The severity of the winter and lack of food began to affect the emotional and physical health of the men. As supplies ran out, they "went into the woods, hills and valleys in

Figure 5-1. *Reconstruction of Hudson's route to Hudson Bay on his fourth and last voyage in 1610.*

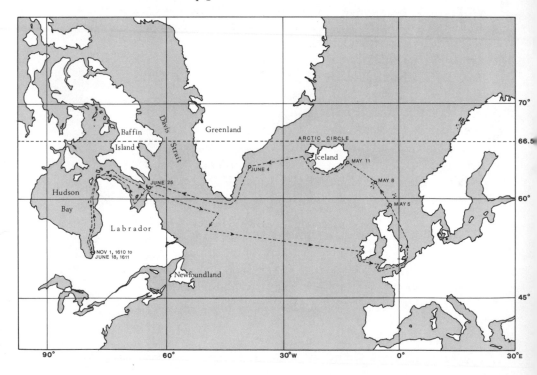

Charting the Sea of Darkness

Figure 5-2. *Detail of Hudson Bay portion of Hudson's 1610 passage. Labels in italics are names Hudson used. Approximate position of the first mutiny is indicated by an open circle at "1" in Ungava Bay. "2" is where Hudson and his men overwintered, and "3" is the general location where Hudson and a portion of his crew were forced into the shallop and cut adrift.*

search of anything that had any substance to it, no matter how vile: nothing was spared." The sailors contracted scurvy, and their blackened gums rotted around their teeth. Their limbs swelled; legs lame with the disease, made worse by frostbite and foot rot, no longer supported their undernourished bodies. The desolate surroundings intensified their misery. Ice and snow united land and sea into nothingness. The few hours of light given by a low, pallid sun brought no warmth.

In the spring, what had been a quiet undercurrent of dissatisfaction surfaced as a full-fledged mutiny. Henry Hudson, along with eight others of the crew, was bound, put into the shallop, and set adrift. Those who remained with the *Discovery* headed back to England. There the mutineers were tried in the High Court of Admiralty. Four were briefly imprisoned, but eventually all were acquitted.

Only a small portion of Henry Hudson's journal has survived. It ends abruptly on the first of August, when the *Discovery* sailed between Cape Wolstenholme and Cape Diggs in Hudson Bay. Before their return to England, the mutineers destroyed any part of the journal that contained incriminating evidence. However, another journal, written by one of the passengers, survived.

Abacuk Prickett's journal tells us little about the geography of this region, but it does detail the events of the voyage and the personalities of the men who shaped them. Journals of the previous voyages hardly mention the actions and thoughts of individual crewmembers, but Prickett's record provides an intimate view of strange characters and stranger deeds.

Crew of the bark Discovery, *1610*

Henry Hudson, master; put in shallop
Robert Juet (Ivett), mate; died on return voyage
John King (Henry King), quartermaster, and mate after Bylot; put in shallop

Robert Bylot (Billet), mate after Juet, and master on return voyage

Edward Wilson, surgeon; returned to England

Francis Clements (Clemence), boatswain, displaced by William Wilson; returned to England

Silvanus Bond, cooper; returned to England

Philip Staffe (Stacie), carpenter; put in shallop

Arnold Lodlo (Ludlowe, Ladley); put in shallop

Michael Butt (Bucke, Bute); put in shallop

Adame Moore; put in shallop

Syracke Fanner (Funer); put in shallop

John Williams, gunner; died in November, 1610

William Wilson, boatswain on return voyage; killed by Indians

John Thomas; killed by Indians

Michael Perse (Pierce); killed by Indians

Adrian Motter (Mowter), able-bodied seaman, boatswain's mate on return voyage; killed by Indians

Abacuk Prickett, passenger, author of journal; returned to England

Bennett Matthew, cook; returned to England

Thomas Wydowse (Woodhouse), passenger, mathematician; put in shallop

John Hudson, Henry Hudson's young son; put in shallop

Nicholas Simmes (Syms); returned to England

Henry Greene, passenger; killed

Master Coleburne (Colbert), advisor; put ashore at beginning of voyage.

The Journal

The following transcription is taken from Book III of *Purchas His Pilgrimes*, by Samuel Purchas. This journal of the 1610 voyage is all that remains of what was written by Hudson.

For the Discoverie of the North-west Passage, begunne the seventeenth of April, 1610, Ended with his End, Being Treacherously Exposed by Some of the Companie.

April 17, 1610 We broke ground, and from Saint Katharines Pool the tide took us down to Blackwall, where we worked our way with the ships to Lee; arriving there on April 22nd.

April 22 I put Master Coleburne (Colbert) aboard a pinke bound for London, along with a letter to the Merchant Adventurer Company telling them the reason for putting him off the ship; so doing, we proceeded with the voyage.[1]

May 2 The wind was southerly, and by evening we were opposite Flamborough Head.

May 5 We were at the Orkney Islands, and here I

set the north end of the needle and the north of the fly to be the same.[2]

May 6 We were in the latitude of 59°22', and noticed that the northern end of Scotland, Orkney and Shetland are not as far north as shown on the charts.

May 8 Faeroe Islands sighted today, in latitude of 62°24'.

May 11 We came upon the eastern side of Iceland, and worked our way along its southern shore until reaching the Westman Islands [islands south of and close to Iceland] on the.15th.

May 15 With contrary winds, we continued to work our way along the main island until the last of July. We were able to get some fowls of various sorts.

June 1 We put out to sea from a harbor on the westernmost part of Iceland and worked our way westward in the latitude of 66°34'.

June 2 Sailed with a light, easterly wind, and found ourselves in 65°57'.

June 3 We found ourselves in 65°30', with the wind out of the northeast; a little before this we sailed near some ice.

June 4 We saw Groneland [Greenland] over the ice perfectly, and tonight the sun went down due north, and rose in the north northeast.

June 5 Still encumbered with much ice which hung upon the coast of Groneland, but by tacking back and forth we arrived at the latitude of 65°.

June 9 We were off Frobisher's Strait, and with a northerly wind we worked our way southwestward until the 15th.[3]

Frobisher's Strait.

June 15 Today, in the latitude of 59°27', we were in sight of the land which was called Desolation by Captain John Davis, and found he was in error in charting its position. Then for the next five days we sailed northwestward, reaching the latitude of 60°42' on the 20th. We saw much ice, many ripplings or overfalls on the water, and a strong current setting from the east southeast to west north-west.

Desolation.

West Greenland Current.

June 21-23 We worked our way northwestward in variable winds and in sight of much ice, reaching the latitude of 62°29' [near Cape Elizabeth, Labrador].

June 24, 25 We sailed west, and about midnight saw land to the north, but suddenly we lost sight of it again and so continued our westward course in 62°17'.

Entrance to Hudson Bay.

July 5 We worked our way along the southern side [of Resolution Island], seeking the shore, but we were prevented by the quantity of ice. We finally reached the shore, and observed our latitude to be 59°16'. Then we worked our way off the shore again until July 8, when we found our latitude to be 60° and no minutes. Here we saw land; it was a fine land, covered with snow, and we called it Desire Provoketh. We continued to sail west, as much as the land and ice would allow us, until the 11th; then, fearing a storm, we anchored in uncertain depth (between two and nine fathoms) by three rocky islands. But we found it a poor harbor due to the sunken rocks, one of which by next morning was 12 feet above water. We called them the Isles of God's Mercies.

Eastern shore of Ungava Bay.

Desire Provoketh.

The tide here flows greater than four fathoms, and at the change of day the flood tide is from the north, flowing eight [fathoms]. The latitude here is 62°09'. Then, working to the southwest, we were in the latitude of 58°50', but found ourselves embayed with land and much ice: sailing northwest, until the 19th, we reached 61°24' and saw land, which I named Hold with Hope. From there, I continued the course north-

Isles of God's Mercies.

Hold with Hope.

west, with variable winds, until the 21st. Here I found seas greater in height than any we had seen since leaving England.

July 23 By observation our latitude was 61°33'.

Magna Brittania.

July 25 Today we saw land and named it Magna Brittania.

July 26 We took observations and found our latitude to be 62°44'.

July 28 Today we were in latitude 63°20, and worked our way south of west.

July 31 Working westward, we found ourselves at noon to be in 62°24'.

August 1 We had sight of the northern shore. Its northern part about 36 miles, and its western part about 60 miles from us. Taking soundings, we found no ground here at 180 fathoms. I think I also saw land bearing east northeast on the sun [south] side, but could not make it out perfectly. Here I found the latitude to be 62° 50'.

Salisbury Island.

A great and whirling sea.

August 2 We sighted a fair headland on the northern shore about 18 miles off, which I called Salisburies Foreland. We ran about 42 miles west southwest, but midway we were suddenly caught in a great and whirling sea; whether it was caused by the meeting of two tidal streams or not, I don't know. Then, sailing west by south 21 miles farther we arrived at the mouth of a strait, and sounded, finding no ground at 100. The western part of this strait is about six miles broad, and approximately 750 miles distant from the eastern part of Davis Strait.

Cape Wolstenholme and Cape Diggs.

August 3 After our men had been ashore and had well observed that the tide did come from the north, and that it flows by the shore five fathoms, we went through the narrow passage. I named the head of this entrance on its south side Cape Wolstenholme, and the head on the northwestern shore as Cape Diggs. After we had sailed west for 30 miles (with an easterly wind) the land fell away to the south, and the other islands and land left us to the west. Then at noon I took ob-

servations and found the ship in 61°20' latitude, with a
sea to the west of us.

*[The following journal is of the same voyage, the author
this time being one of the passengers, Abacuk Prickett.]*

A LARGER DISCOURSE OF THE SAME VOYAGE, AND
THE SUCCESS THEREOF, WRITTEN BY
ABACUK PRICKETT

We began our voyage for the Northwest Passage
the 17th of April, 1610. When we were opposite Shep-
pey Island [at the mouth of the Thames] our master
sent Master Colbert, along with a letter, back to the
owners. The next day we weighed anchor, heading for
Harwich, where we arrived on the 28th of April. From
Harwich we set sail on the first of May, following the
coast north until we came to the Orkney Islands, and
from there to the Faeroe Islands and finally Iceland. We
anchored at Iceland, but although we were close
enough to hear the roar of the sea breaking on shore,
we could not see land on account of the fog. Here we
were in a bay in the southeast part of the island. We
weighed anchor and sailed north along the west side of
the coast; but one day, being without wind, we used
the time and caught a great many cod, ling, butte, and
various other kinds we couldn't identify.

*Orkney and
Faeroe Islands.*

*Southeastern part
of Iceland.*

The next day we had a good gale of wind out of
the southwest and raised the Isles of Westmonie where
the King of Denmark has a fortress; passing that, we
sighted what is called Snow Hill, a mountain on the
northwest part of the land. Along the way we saw
that famous hill, Mount Hekla, which cast out much
fire—a sign of foul weather in short time. We left Iceland behind us, but when meeting the pack-ice which
hangs on the north coast of Iceland, stretching down
to the west, our master turned back for Iceland to find
a harbor.

Westman Islands.

*Mount Hekla
eruption.*

Figure 5-3. *Westman Isles. A tormented looking, dangerous group of rocks off the southern coast of Iceland. From G. Hartwig,* The Tropical and Polar Worlds.

We found one on the northwest coast, called De-refer [Dyrefiord], where we anchored, and here we killed a good many fowl. From here we put to sea again, but with both the wind and weather against us, our master decided to return to the harbor, but was unable to reach it. However, we found another to the south of it, called by the English Louise Bay. On shore we found a hot bath where we all bathed ourselves, the water being so hot it could scald a fowl.[4]

A *hot bath in the sea.*

From here, we put to sea for Groneland on the first of June; for the better part of a day we thought we saw land to the west of us, but it turned out to be only a fog bank. So we disregarded it and continued toward Groneland, which we raised on the fourth of June. There was so much ice along the coast that in no way could our master reach shore. The land in this part is very mountainous, and filled with little hills covered with snow, looking much like sugar-loaves.

Greenland.

Upon reaching the south side of the land, we turned and followed it as closely as the ice would allow us. For the most part our course was between west and northwest, until we raised Desolation, which is a great island in the western part of Groneland. Along this coast we saw a great many whales. Three of them came so close we could hardly avoid them; then two passed very near, with a third going under our ship; but we received no harm by them, praised be God.

Desolation Island.

Encounter with many whales.

From Desolation our master made his way northwest. He would have gone more to the north, but the wind was against him. Along this course we saw our first great island or mountain of ice; afterward, we saw a great many. About the latter end of June we raised land to the north of us which our master took to be that island which Master Davis laid down on his chart. Our master would have gone to the north side of the island in this strait to reach the west, but the wind would not allow it, so instead we fell to the south of it where we entered a great rippling or overfall of current which sets to the west. We went into the current, making our way to the north of west, until we met with ice which clung about this island. By tacking, our master cleared this ice and stood to the south, then west, through a great amount of floating ice upon which were many seals.

First iceberg.

Resolution Island.

We gained entrance to a clear sea and continued our course until we should again meet ice; first there were great islands of it, then much ice of the smaller sort. We made our way between them on a northwest course until we met with ice again. While sailing between the ice we saw one of the great islands of ice overturn, which was a good warning to us not to come close to them or be within their reach. We sailed into the ice ahead as though it was between two lands. The next day we had a storm that brought the ice upon us so fast that finally we were forced to attach ourselves to the largest piece of ice, and let the ship lie there. Today some of our men fell sick, I will not say it is on account of fear, but I did see some signs of other trouble.

Sign of trouble.

With the storm ceasing, we stood out again from the ice into the sea, going wherever there was a clear space. Our course took us wherever the ice would allow, but we were always enclosed with ice. When our master saw this, he changed his course to the south, thinking in this way to clear himself of the ice: but the more he struggled, the more he became enclosed, and the worse off he was, until finally we could go no farther.

Despair.

Here, our master was in despair, for (as he told me after) he thought he would never have got out of the ice, but would perish there. Therefore he brought forth his chart and showed all his crew that he had entered the strait more than 300 miles farther than any Englishman had, and left it to their choice as to whether or not they would proceed any farther.[5]

Entered 100 leagues farther than Capt. Weymouth.

Discord.

About this, some were of one mind and some of another, some wishing themselves at home and some not caring where they were, so long as they were out of the ice; but there were some who said things which were remembered a great while after.

There was one man who told the master that if he had 100 pounds, he would give 90 of it to be at home; whereas the carpenter answered that if he had 100 pounds, he would not give 10 upon such condition, but would think it as good money as any he ever had and would bring it home, by the leave of God. Much was said to no purpose, then all hands had to get to work to clear the ship and get ourselves out of the ice. After much work and time spent we were able to gain enough room to turn our ship in, and little by little gained a few miles to a clear sea, where our course was north and northwest. Finally we raised land to the southwest, a high land covered with snow. Our master named this land Desire Provoketh.

Akpatok I., Ungava Bay.

Lying here, we heard the noise of a great tidal overfall coming from the direction of land, but now, having been embayed before, we had some experience and were well enough acquainted with the ice to know that if foggy or foul weather overcame us for the night, to seek out the broadest island of ice and anchor to it. Then we could exercise and amuse ourselves, and fill our casks with the good, sweet water that stood in ponds on the ice.

Profit and pleasure on the ice.

But after we brought this land to bear south of us, the tides and currents opened the ice, carrying it first one way then another, which showed we were not in a bay, for there the ice lies without moving, as if in a pond. In the bay where we were previously troubled with ice, we saw many mountains of ice so large that they touched bottom in water 120 to 140 fathoms deep.[6]

Difference between a strait and a bay.

In our present course we saw a bear on a solitary piece of ice; the men tried to give chase to it in their boat, but before they could get near her the tide had carried the ice with its bear, joining it with other ice; so with their efforts useless, they came aboard again.

A Polar bear chase.

We continued our course northwest and raised land to the north of us, toward which we headed. Coming close, we found a great many islands of floating ice clinging to its easternmost point, one of which had a bear on it. She came toward us, moving from one island of ice to another, until she was ready to come aboard, but when she saw us looking at her she put her head between her hind legs and dived under the ice, moving from one piece to another until she was out of our reach. We sailed along the south side of the land until we saw clinging to a southerly point of land more ice than we had previously seen on land.

When our master saw this he headed toward shore. At the western end of the island we found a harbor and came in over a rock which at high tide was covered by 15 feet of water, but at low tide was bare. By the great mercy of God we cleared it and anchored nearby: our master named these islands the Isles of God's Mercy. This harbor was all right for their needs, but they had to be careful how they entered. Here, my master sent me, along with others, to explore to the north and northwest; and in going from one place to another we sprung a covey of young partridge. Thomas Woodhouse shot at them, but killed only the old one.

Dangerous rock.

Isles of God's Mercies.

This island is a most barren place, having nothing on it but violently split rocks and splashes of water, as though it were subject to earthquakes. To the north there is a great bay or sea (for I don't know what it will prove to be) where I saw a great island of ice that had been brought in to this bay or sea to the northwest by the spring tide, and set aground between two lands, there to stay. Here we took in some driftwood that we found ashore.

Jackman's Sound.

From here we sailed southwest, through much floating ice, to pass the land to the west of us; finally we found a clear sea, and continued our course until we raised land to the northwest. Then our master changed his course more to the south, but it was not long before we met with the ice that lay ahead of us. Our master would have sailed to the north of this ice, but he could not; and in the end had to enter it to the southwest, and then to the south, where once again we were embayed. Our master attempted to reach the shore, but could not on account of the great amount of ice on the coast.

We sailed north, leaving this bay, and were soon out of the ice; then we sailed southwest, and west, where we were enclosed (as far as we could see) by land and ice. For on one side we had land from the south to the northwest, and on the other from the east to the west; but the land that lay east and west of us was but an island. We continued until we could go no further on account of the ice: so we anchored our ship to the ice that the tide had brought upon us. But with the ebb tide, the ice opened up and gave way, so that except for some of the great islands that carried along with us, we were clear of the ice.

Three capes raised.

Having a clear sea, our master sailed west along the southern shore, and raised three capes or headlands lying one above another. The middle cape is an island and it makes a bay or harbor, which will prove a good one. Our master named them Prince Henry's Cape or Foreland. Passing these, we raised another, which was

the extreme point of land looking toward the north. *North Bluff.*
Upon it are two hills, but one (above the rest) which
looked like a haycock, our master named King James *Cape Weggs.*
his Cape.

To the north of this lie other islands which our
master named Queene Anne's Cape or Foreland. We *Northeast of
Charles Island.*
continued to follow the north shore. Beyond the
King's Cape there is a sound or bay that has some islands in it; and this should not be forgotten in case the
need for a harbor arises. Beyond this lies some broken
land close to the mainland, but what it is I do not
know, because we passed by it in the night.

We sailed north and then west to round this land,
until we met land that stretched from the mainland
like a skewer. Before reaching this land a storm, with
wind from the west, came upon us; we sailed north
until reaching land, which when our master saw it
turned south again, for he was loath that at any time
we should see the north shore.

With the storm continuing, we came to the south
shore again, but much farther to the west, which made
him wonder, considering the direction of our leeway.
On the mainland, to the southwest of this land, there
is a high hill which our master named Mount Charles. *Charles Island.*
Beyond this, to the north, lies an island with a fair
headland on its eastern side; beyond it to the west is
other broken land which forms a bay and a good road-
stead for ships. Our master named the first Cape Sals- *Salisbury Island.*
burie.

When we had left this to the northeast, we fell
into a rippling or overfall of a current which at first
we took to be a shoal, but when we cast the lead we
found no ground. We continued our way within sight
of the southern shore until we sighted land lying about
six miles from the mainland. Our master took this to
be a part of the northern shore, but it is an island with
the north side stretching out to the west more than the
south. This island was quite high and had a fair headland on its eastern side, which our master named *Cape Diggs.*

Deepes Cape. The land on the southern side, now falling to the south, makes another cape or headland, and
this he named Wolstenholme Cape.[7]

When we were close to the North or Island Cape,
our master sent the boat ashore, with myself (in
charge), the carpenter, and others to explore to the
west and northwest, and to the southwest; but there
was more to it than we thought, for the land was very
high, and we were overtaken by a storm of rain, thunder and lightning. But we made it to the highest part
of the northeast side by going from one rock to another. Here we found level ground, and saw some
deer; at first, four or five, and then a dozen or 16 in a
herd, but could not reach them with a musket shot.

Thus, going from one place to another, we saw to
the west of us a hill higher than all the rest and quite
close: but it proved to be farther than we had figured,
for when we got there, the land was so steep on the
east and northeast part that we could not land there.
But we saw a place to the southwest where we could
alight, and headed there. Under the east side of this hill
was a large pond of water with a stream running out
of it. Falling down the south side of a high cliff into
the sea, this stream of water was sufficient to drive an
over-shot mill. In this place a great many fowl breed,
and there is the best grass that I have seen since leaving
England. Here we found sorrel, and that which we call
scurvy-grass in great abundance.

Breeding place of
many fowl.

Moving along, we saw some round hills of stone
looking like small grass mounds, which at first I took
to be the work of some Christian. We passed by them
until we came to the south side of the hill, then, finding still more, we went over to them, and being close
I removed the topmost stone and found that they were
hollow and full of fowl hung by their necks. Then
Greene and I went to fetch the boat to the southside,
while Robert Billet [Bylot] and the others got down a
valley to the shore, where we took them in.

Unusual storage of
fowl.

In the meantime our master brought the ship in
between the two lands and fired a few shots to call us

back, for it was foggy. We came aboard and told him what we had seen, trying to persuade him to stay a day or two here, telling him what refreshments were available; but he was not pleased with the idea and by no means would he stay. So we left the fowl and headed southwest, losing the mainland (which now bears to the east of us) that we had been following all along. It falls off to the east, out of sight, after some 75 or 90 miles. Now we came into shallow water that we had not encountered since we left Iceland, with broken ground and rocks through which we passed heading south. In this passage we had a storm, and the water shoaled considerably, so we anchored in 15 fathoms.

We weighed anchor, and because of the lay of the land, headed southeast. When we came to the point on the western land, for now we had land on both sides of us, we again anchored. Our master sent the boat ashore to look the land over and see if there was any way through. They soon returned, and described a large sea beyond the point of land to the south. This land on the west side was a very narrow point. We weighed anchor from here and sailed between the two lands, which from here to a great way south is but six miles broad. We lost sight of the eastern shore and did not see it until we came into water six or seven fathoms deep at the bottom of the bay. At this point we headed over toward the western shore until we came to an island in 53° latitude, where we took in water and ballast.

From here we headed north, but some two or three days later there were arguments concerning our coming into and going out of this bay, and our master took occasion to revive old matters, and to displace Robert Juet from being his mate, and the boatswain from his place, for the words spoken previously in the great bay of ice. Then he made Robert Billet his mate, and William Wilson our boatswain. Up to the north we sailed until we sighted land, then down to the south, and up to the north, then down again to the south; then, on Michaelmass day, because we came into

Strife revived and duties changed.

and went out of certain lands on that same day, our master named it Michaelmass Bay.

From here we sailed north and coming into shoal water, with the weather thick and foul, we anchored in seven or eight fathoms of water, lying there for eight days. In all that time there was not one hour in which we could raise anchor. But on the eighth day the wind began to lessen and our master decided he would have the anchor up, this, against the mind of those who believed otherwise.

Well, we went to it, and when we had nearly brought the anchor up, a sea took the ship and threw us all off the capstan, hurting some of us. We lost our anchor, and if it hadn't been for the quick thinking of the carpenter we would have lost our cable too, but in already fearing such a matter he was ready with his axe and so cut it.

Anchor lost.

From here we headed south and to the southwest, through a sea clear of ice and of various depths, and came to a sea of two colors, one black and one white. We went between them for 12 to 15 miles in water 16 or 17 fathoms deep. With night coming on we took in our topsails, and sailed downwind with our mainsail and foresail, until we came to water five or six fathoms deep; we saw no land, for it was dark. Then we headed east, gaining deep water again, then to the south and southwest, and thus came to our most westernmost bay of all; here we anchored closest to the northern shore.

Sea of two colors.

Our boat went out to the land nearest us, but as the men got close to the shore the water was so shallow the boat wouldn't float; yet they got ashore. Here our men saw the footprints of a man and a duck in the snowy rocks, and a good amount of wood which they took and brought back to the ship. While at anchor here we saw a ledge of rocks to the south of us, lying in a line north and south; some were as much as three miles in length, but a strong tide sets in here so they are covered at high water. At midnight we weighed anchor, planning on leaving the same way we came in,

Charting the Sea of Darkness

but after a short while the carpenter came and told our master that if he continued on this course we would be upon the rocks. The master believed he was past them, when presently we ran onto them and were stuck fast for 12 hours; but by the mercy of God we got off unhurt, though not unscarred.

We sailed east and sighted three hills lying north and south. We headed to the farthest, leaving it to the north of us, and entered a bay where we came to anchor. Here our master sent myself and the carpenter to search out a place in which to spend the winter; for it was that time, with the nights being long and cold and the ground covered with snow. Being the last of October now, and having spent three months in a labyrinth without end, we struck out toward the east, at the bottom of the bay, returning slowly in search of a place. The next day we went to the south and southwest, and here we found a place where we then brought our ship and hauled her aground: this was the *Winter haven.* first of November. By the 10th we were frozen in, and it was now time to assess what we had (which we knew) and what we did not have (which was uncertain).

We had sufficient food to amply last us for six months time, which was good; indeed, if our master had more, it was at home or in other places. Now it was best to plan for the future, and to get to the capes where the fowl breed [Cape Diggs and Cape Wolstenholme], for that was all the hope we had for food for the return journey. Therefore our master organized the disbursement of what we already had, and the increase of it by proposing a reward to anyone that killed either beast, fish or fowl.

About the middle of this month of November, John Williams, our gunner, died: God pardon the mas- *John Williams* ter's uncharitable dealing with this man. Therefore, not *dies.* to wrong the living nor slander the dead, I will try (by the leave of God) to deliver the truth as close as I can in speaking of that unhappy deed out of whose ashes (as it were) brought a scandal upon all who returned home, and upon the action itself, causing the crew to react to the event and not the cause of the event.

Henry Greene's history.

You should understand that our master kept in his house in London a young man named Henry Greene; though born in Kent of worshipful parents, this man had spent all he had, and lost the good will of all his friends through his lewd life and words. Our master gave him meat, drink and lodging, and by means of one Master Venson, with much trouble, got four pounds from his mother to buy him clothes. Master Venson would not trust him, making sure he saw it laid out himself.

This Henry Greene was not listed in the ship owners book [as crewmember], nor were any wages made for him. He first came aboard at Gravesend, and at Harwich should have gone in the field with Wilkinson. At Iceland, the surgeon and he had an argument in Dutch, but Greene sorely beat him in English, which set the crew into a rage, and it was difficult to get the surgeon to come back aboard. I told the master about it, but he told me to let it alone, for the surgeon had a tongue that would wrong the best friend he had. But Robert Juet (the master's mate) decided to get involved, and when he was drunk told the carpenter a long tale about how our master brought Greene along to discredit anyone whose actions and words would displease Hudson.

When this conversation got to the master's ears, and he understood what was being said, he was set to turn the ship around and head back to Iceland, though it was 120 miles away, to send Robert Juet home in a fishing boat. But he was persuaded otherwise, and all was well.

So Henry Greene stood upright, very close with our master, and in every way a good man: as for religion he said he was like a clean paper where he could write upon it what he would. Now, when the gunner died, his belongings were brought to the mainmast (as is the order in such cases) and if any of the crew should need anything of the deceased, the article could be bought by the highest bidder. This gunner had a gray cloth gown which Henry Greene asked our master to let him have, saying he would pay for it as much as any other would give. The master said he would, and to the others who wanted it he replied that Greene should have it, and none else, and so the matter rested.

Disposal of the gunner's gown.

Now, being late in the year, the master called upon the carpenter to go and build a house on the shore, which earlier, when it might have been done, the master would hear nothing of it. The carpenter told him that the snow and frost were such that he neither could nor would do it. And when the master heard this he sought him out of his cabin to strike him, calling him many foul names and threatening to hang him. The carpenter told our master that he knew his job better than he, and that he was no house carpenter. So this passed, and the house was finally made, with much labor, but of little use.

Rebellion of the carpenter.

The next day, after the argument between the master and the carpenter, the carpenter took his gun and Henry Greene with him, for it was an order that no one go out alone but should have a gun and be accompanied by another person with a spear. This angered the master so much against Henry Greene that he took away the gray gown from him and gave it to his new mate, Robert Billot.

When Greene saw this he challenged the master's promise; but the master turned abusively upon Greene, with many words of disgrace, and telling him that none of his friends would trust him with so much as 20 shillings, so why should he. As for wages he had none, nor would he have any if he did not act better to please him. Yet the master had promised Greene before that he would make good his wages equal to that of any other man on the ship, and that upon returning home he would make him one of the prince's guards.

This so worked the devil with Greene that he did whatever mischief he could to our master to discredit him; eventually as to thrusting him and many other honest men out of the ship. To speak of all our trouble

Greene's conspiracy.

---

in this time of winter, which was so cold that it lamed
most of the crew (myself still feels it) would be too
tedious.

But also, I must not forget to show how merci-
fully God dealt with us during this time; for in the
Succour by space of three months we had so many partridge (white
partridge and fish. as milk) that we killed more than a hundred dozen,
besides others of different kind, and we had all the fish
that we could net. Although the partridge left us in
the coming spring, they were with us through all the
extreme cold. In their place came various kinds of
other fowl, such as swans, geese, ducks and teal, but
they were hard to get. Our master hoped that they had
come here to breed, but they did not, and were only
on their way from the south to a place much farther
north than we ever reached on this voyage. Yet if the
wind is against them, coming from the north, northwest or northeast, they will land and stay until the
wind is more favorable for them to continue their
flight north.

By now, these fowl are gone, with few or none to
be seen. Then we went into the woods, hills and valleys in search of anything that had any substance to it,
Miserable diet. no matter how vile: nothing was spared, including
moss of the ground, compared to which rotten wood is
better, and the frog, which in breeding time is as loath-
some as the toad. But among the various kinds of
plants, Thomas Wodhouse brought back the bud of a
tree full of a turpentine substance. The surgeon made a
A scurvy medicine. concoction of this to drink, and applied the buds hot to
those who were troubled with ache in any part of their
body. For my part I confess I received immediate and
great ease from my pain.

At about this time, when the ice began to break
out of the bay, a savage came to our ship to see and be
seen; he was the first we had encountered and our master treated him well, giving him much attention, and
promising there was much he could do for him. Our
master requested all the knives and hatchets that any
man had for his private use, but received none other

than that which John King (the carpenter) and myself gave. Our master gave this savage a knife, a mirror and some buttons, which were thankfully received, and he made signs that after he had slept he would come again, which he did.

Trade with a savage.

When he came back he brought with him a sled on which were two deer skins and two beaver skins. He had a pouch under his arm out of which he drew those things the master had given him. He took the knife and laid it upon one of the beaver skins and the mirrors and buttons upon the other, then he removed them, putting them back in his pouch and gave the skins to our master. Then the master showed him a hatchet, for which he would have given our master one of his deer skins, but our master wanted both, which he got but not willingly. After many signs indicating that there were people to the north and to the south, and that after so many days he would come again, he went on his way; but he never came back.

Now that the ice was out of the sounds we were free to move again, and a group of men was appointed to go fishing with our net; their names were as follows: William Wilson, Henry Greene, Michael Perce, John Thomas, Andrew Moter, Bennet Mathewes and Arnold Lodlo. On the first day they went out these men caught 500 fish, as big as good herrings, and some trout; which gave us all some hope of supplying our needs and improving our common good. But this was the most they ever got in one day, and many days they got only a quarter as many. While they were fishing, Henry Greene and William Wilson, with some others, plotted to take the net and the shallop (which the carpenter had now set up) and shift for themselves.

Fishing.

But the shallop being ready, the master decided to make use of it himself to sail to the south and southwest to see if he could meet with the savages, and to see the woods which were set on fire by them; this was the reason the shallop was set up. So the master took the shallop and the seine, along with as much food as would be needed for eight or nine days, and went off to the south. Those that remained behind were to take in water, wood, and ballast, and to have everything in readiness when he came back. He set no time for his return, for he was sure that if he met up with the people he would be able to get a good amount of meat from them; but he returned worse off than when he left. Though they were close by, and would set the woods on fire in his sight, by no means was he able to meet with them.

Having returned, he fitted out the ship for the return journey, but first he brought all the bread out of the bread room (which came to a pound each for every man's share) giving them also a receipt, insisting they have it to show, if it pleased God that they came home: and he wept when he gave it to them. In order to help us in this poor condition, and provide some relief, the boat and seine went to work on Friday morning, staying until Sunday noon, at which time they came back, bringing 80 small fish; a poor relief for so many hungry bellies.

Then we weighed anchor and sailed out of the place we had wintered in, dropping anchor at the mouth of the bay, and again in the sea outside the bay. Now that the bread was gone, the cheese, of which there were five, was given out, which caused some complaint, for by the crew's account there were nine. The remaining cheese was equally divided by the master, although he was cautioned otherwise, for there were some men who were unable to ration themselves, quickly eating all that was given them.

Henry Greene gave half his bread, which was sufficient for 14 days, to another crew member to keep, telling him not to give him any until next Monday; but before Wednesday night he wouldn't leave its keeper alone until he had it all back again, having already eaten up his first week's bread. And Wilson, the boatswain, had eaten his two week's ration of bread in one day, which made him sick for two or three days. The reason the master decided to give out all the cheese was because they were not all of the same quality.

Every man would have the same, the best and the worst together, which amounted to three and a half pounds of cheese for seven days; therefore they would have no cause for complaint.

The wind being favorable, we weighed anchor and sailed northwest, but by Monday night (the 18th day of June) we were into ice, and with the wind being out of the west the next day, we remained here in sight of land until Sunday. While there, the master told Nicholas Simmes that there would be a breaking up of sea-chests and a search for bread, telling him that if he found any to bring it to him; which he did, delivering to the master 30 loaves in a bag. This deed of the master (if it was true) made me wonder why he did not stop the offense right at the beginning, but let it grow to the extent that it would overthrow himself and many other honest men: but *"there are many devices in the heart of man, but the counsell of the Lord shall stand."*

During the night on Saturday (the 21st of June), while still trapped in the ice, Wilson the boatswain and Henry Greene came to me while I was lying lame in my cabin, and told me that they and the rest of their associates would change the crew, and turn the master and all the sick men into the shallop, letting them shift for themselves. There was only 14 days worth of food left for all the men, and a meager ration at that, while the master stayed here not caring to go one way or another. For three days they had not eaten anything and were therefore resolute to either mend or end, but once begun they would go through with it or die. When I heard this, I told them I couldn't believe what I was hearing, considering that they were married men with wives and children, and that for their sakes they should not do such an evil thing in the sight of God and man, as they intended to do. Furthermore, why should they want to banish themselves from their native country?

Henry Greene told me to hold my peace, saying he knew the worst, which was to be hanged when he came home; of the two choices, he would rather be

hanged at home then starved abroad. For the good will
they felt toward me they wanted me to remain with
them on the ship. I thanked them, and told them I
would stay with the ship, but did not want to hurt
myself and others by being involved in such a deed.
Henry Greene told me then that I must take my fortune in the shallop. If there is no other remedy I said,
then the will of God be done.

*Wilson and
Greene's
wickedness.*
Henry Greene went away in a rage, swearing that
if anyone should try to stop them they would have
their throat cut. Wilson was left with me and I had a
long talk with him, but it didn't do any good, for he
was persuaded that there was no other solution now,
and that it was best to do it immediately while everyone was so worked up; otherwise they might lose
heart, and the mischief they intended to do to the
others would instead be done to them.

Henry Greene came back and demanded to know
what I had said to Wilson. Wilson answered: he is
keeping with the same old song — still patient. Then I
spoke to Henry Greene, asking him to refrain from any
action for three days, during which time I would con-
fer with the master so that all would be well. Then I
begged him to give me two days, or even 12 hours;
there was no other way they said, but to do it immediately. Then I told them that if they would hold off
until Monday, I would join them on the ship, sharing
the food, and would justify it when I got back home;
but this would not serve their purpose.

I told them that what they were planning to do
was much worse than what they were telling; that it
was blood and revenge they were after, or else they
wouldn't be undertaking such a deed in the middle of
the night. With that, Henry Greene took the bible
that was lying before me and swore that he would not
harm any man, and that what he was doing was for
the good of the voyage, and for nothing else; and that
all the rest of the crew should take the same oath —
which they did.

Henry Greene went away, then Juet came in, and because he was an older man I thought I could reason with him; but he was worse than Henry Greene, swearing that he would justify this deed when we came home. After him came John Thomas and Michael Perce, as birds of one feather; but because they are not living I will let them go, as I did then.[8] Then came Moter and Bennet and I asked them if they were well advised of what they were doing. They answered that they were, and had come to take the oath.

Now, since I am much condemned for this oath, in that causing it to be taken, it bound the men together to perform what they had begun, as well as making me one of the members of their plot, I thought it would be best to write down everyone's views, and show how well their oath and deeds agreed. Thus it was: "You shall swear truth to God, your prince and country: you shall do nothing, but to the glory of God and the good of the action in hand, and not harm any man."

This was the oath, without adding or diminishing. I looked for more accomplices, although these were already too many, but no more came. It was dark, and they were in readiness to put this evil deed into action. I called to Henry Greene and Wilson, imploring them not to begin their action in the dark, but at least to wait until morning. I had hoped that every man would rest, but wickedness does not sleep: Henry Greene kept the master company all night (and gave me bread which was given him by his cabin-mate), and others were equally watchfull. I asked Henry Greene who he would put out with the master?

The carpenter [Phillip Staffe], John King, and the sick men, he replied. I said it would not be in their best interest to part company with the carpenter, for they might need him later. The reason the carpenter was held in disregard by the crew was that he and John King were thought guilty in the matter of food. But the main reason was the affection that he was held in by the master, and being made his mate when they had left the wintering place, thus displacing Robert Billet [Bylot] as mate.

This made them bitter, because the carpenter could neither read nor write, and therefore (they said) the master and his ignorant mate would take the ship wherever the master pleased. The master had forbid any man to keep an account of their position, removing from them whatever means they had to do so. I was able to get Henry Greene and Wilson to agree to let the carpenter remain, hoping that eventually (after they had been allowed to have their own way) the master and the other poor men would be taken back on the ship again. Or at least, I hoped, one of the more forward men of the crew (as it might have happened) would warn either the carpenter, John King, or the master.

Now it would be in order to show how we were lodged, beginning with the cook's room; there lay Bennet and the cooper, lame; outside the cook's room, on the starboard side, lay Thomas Wydhouse [a student of mathematics], sick; next to him lay Sydrack Funer, lame; then the surgeon and John Hudson with him; next to them lay Wilson the boatswain, and then Arnold Lodlo next to him; in the gun room lay Robert Juet and John Thomas; on the port side lay Michael Bute and Adria Moore, who had never been well since we lost our anchor; next to them lay Michael Perce and Andrew Moter. Next to them, outside the gun room, lay John King and Robert Billet; next to them myself, and next to me Francis Clements. In the midship, between the capstan and the pumps, lay Henry Greene and Nicholas Simmes. John King was up late tonight, they thought he was with the master, but instead he was with the carpenter who lay on the poop deck; coming down from him he was met by his cabin-mate, quite by chance as it were, and together they went to their cabin. It was not long before it was day; then Bennet came for water for the kettle, and when he went into the hold they shut the hatch on him. I don't know who kept it down, but Bennet got back up on deck.

In the meantime Henry Greene and another engaged the carpenter in conversation until the master came out of his cabin (which he soon did); then John Thomas and Bennet stood in front of him, while Wilson bound his arms behind him. He asked them what they meant by this? They told him he would know when he was in the shallop. While this was going on, Juet went into the hold where he came upon John King who had gotten a sword of his own. He kept Juet at bay, and might of killed him; but others came to his aid, and so he came up to the master. The master called to the carpenter and told him that he was bound, but I heard no reply.

Hudson is bound.

Now Arnold Lodlo and Michael Bute turned on them and told them their dishonesty would show itself. Then the shallop was brought up to the ship's side, and the poor, sick and lame men were made to get out of their cabins and into the shallop. I came out of my cabin as best I could to speak to the master at the hatchway when he called me; on my knees I begged them, for the love of God, to remember themselves, and to do onto others as they would have others do onto them. They told me to take care, and get back into my cabin, not allowing the master to speak with me. But when I returned to my cabin he called to me by the horn and told me that Juet would overthrow us all; no, I said, and not softly either, it is the villainy of Henry Greene.

Evilness perpetuated.

Now the carpenter asked them if they knew they would be hanged when they got home; as for himself he said, he would not stay with the ship unless he was forced to. They told him to go then, for they would not keep him. I'll go, he said, if I may have my chest with me and all that's in it; they said he could, and shortly put it into the shallop. Then he came down to me to say goodbye. I tried to persuade him to remain

The carpenter let go.

with the ship, that he might be able to accomplish some good; but he said he did not think they would be glad to take him in again.

He was quite convinced by the master that there was not a single man aboard the ship who had the ability to bring her home: but, he said, if we must part (which we will not willingly do, but intend to follow the ship), if you arrive at the capes [Cape Diggs and Cape Wolstenholme] before us, to leave some token near where the fowls breed that we will know you had been there, and that they would do the same for us: and so, with tears we parted. Now the sick men were driven out of their cabins; but John Thomas was Francis Clements's friend, and Bennet was Cooper's, so there were words between them and Henry Greene; one saying that they should go, and the other swearing that they shouldn't go, but that those in the shallop should be brought back. When Henry Greene heard that, he had to relent, and with much protest put out Arnold Lodlo and Michael Bute.

In the meantime, there were some men who acted as though the ship had been taken by force, giving them free leave to break up chests and search and rob everywhere. One of them passing by asked me what they should do. I told him he should stop what he was doing, for he was nothing but a swindler. Now, all the poor men were in the shallop, their names as follows: Henry Hudson, John Hudson [Henry's young son], Arnold Lodlo, Sidrack Faner, Phillip Staffe, Thomas Woodhouse (or Wydhouse), Adam Moore, Henry King, and Michael Bute. The carpenter got for them a gun with powder and shot, some spears, an iron pot with some grain, and a few other things. They sailed out of the ice with the shallop tied fast to its stern, and when they were well out (for I cannot say they were *Shallop cut adrift.* clean out), they cut her adrift; then they set the ship's topsails and sailed eastward in a clear sea. Finally, they took in her topsails, brought the ship up into the wind, and lay there until they had searched and ransacked every place in the ship.

Charting the Sea of Darkness

In the hold they found one vessel of grain completely unused, and one other half used (for we had but two): we also found two small barrels of butter, some 27 pieces of pork, and half a bushel of peas; but in the master's cabin we found altogether 200 biscuits, a quarter bushel grain, and a large cask of beer. They noticed now that the shallop had come into sight, so they set the mainsail and topsails, and flew away as though from an enemy.

The wicked flee where none pursuith.

Then I prayed them to take account of what they were doing; but William Wilson (more than the rest) would hear of no such matter. As they approached the eastern shore they tacked and headed west until they came to an island; there they anchored in 16 or 17 fathoms of water. They then sent the boat and net ashore to see if they could get anything, but could not on account of the rocks and great stones. On shore, Michael Perse killed two birds, and they found a large amount of that weed which we called cockle-grass where we were wintering; getting as much as they could, they came aboard again. We stayed here that night and the best part of the next day, never seeing the shallop then, or ever after.

Last sight of the shallop.

Now Henry Greene came up to me and told me that it was the crew's decision that I should come up into the master's cabin and take charge. I told them that Robert Juet was more fit for the job, but he said he would not enter the cabin, nor meddle with the master's chart or journals. So I came up, and Henry Greene gave me the key to the master's chest, and I was told I would also be in charge of the bread. Henry Greene had laid out the master's best things together which he planned on using for himself when the proper time came.

With the wind being favorable, we set a course to the northeast; this was Robert Billet's course, and was contrary to that of Robert Juet who would have gone to the northwest. We still had the eastern shore in sight, and during the night we had a strong gale of wind; we ran with it until we met ice; finally it was so

thick we could go no farther. At the same time the
wind was pushing the ice upon us from astern, so that
we could not move. We lay here for 14 days in worse
ice than we have ever had to deal with before.

Although we had been where the ice was thicker,
never did it cover such a wide area as this; here, in a
deep sea and a tide of ebb and flood (which set northwest and southeast) this floating ice encompassed many
miles. Robert Juet wanted to go to the northwest, but
Robert Billet was confident that we should head northeast, which we did. Being clear of the ice at last, he
continued his course in sight of the eastern shore until
he raised four islands which lay north and south; but
we passed within 18 to 21 miles of them, the wind not
allowing us to get any closer.

Then we tacked to regain them, and anchored
between the two northernmost islands. We sent the
boat ashore to see if there was anything to be had
there, but found nothing except cockle-grass, which
was gathered and brought back. Before we got to this
place I became aware that my presence on the ship was
against Henry Greene's wishes, because I was not more
in favor than I was of their actions.

He began (very subtly) to have me search for those
things that he himself had stolen, and accused me of no
less than treason against them, and that I had deceived
the crew of no less than 30 cakes of bread. They began
to talk among themselves about how England was not
a safe place to return to, but Henry Greene swore that
the ship would not go into any port, remaining instead
in the open sea, until he had the Kings Majesties hand
and seal for their safety. They had many plans in their
heads, but since Henry Greene was captain, in the end
he made the decisions.

From these islands we sailed northeast, still keeping the eastern land in sight, until we came to those
islands that our master called Rumnies Islands. Our
master entered the first great bay that lay between
these islands and the shallow ground to the east of
them. We continued keeping the eastern shore in sight,

but coming opposite the low land we ran upon a rock Almost stranded.
that lay underwater. We struck only once, but God
soon sent us off without any harm to the ship that we
could see; otherwise we might have been made permanent inhabitants of the place. We continued our course
and raised land ahead of us which stretched out to the
north.

When they saw this they were sure that Robert
Billet's northeast course had taken them north of the
capes they were searching for, and that they had to
head back down south to find them, and quickly too,
for there was not much food left. But Robert Billet
continued following the land to the north, saying that
he hoped God would provide relief in this direction
just as much as to the south. I told them that this land
was part of the mainland of Wolstenholme Cape, and
that the shallow, rocky ground was the same that our
master entered when he went into the great bay.

Robert Juet said it was not possible unless the
master had brought the ship over land, and insisted
that they look at the master's chart and compare it
with their own course. We sailed east, leaving the main
land to the north, and past many small islands into a
narrow gut where we anchored. The boat went ashore
on the northern side, where we found a large antler,
but nothing else.

The next day we went to the southern side, but
found nothing there except cockle-grass which we
gathered. This grass was a great relief, for without it Saved by
cockle-grass.
we couldn't have made it to the capes for want of
food. We left with a favorable wind, but before we
could get clear, the wind came around to the west and
we were forced to anchor again, on the northern side.
The next day we weighed anchor and rounded the
point of North Land (which is high land) and so continued to the capes lying north and south, which were
some 75 or 90 miles away.

We headed for the northern cape to obtain the
great many fowl that breed, to kill them with our shot
and bring them back to the boat. We raised the capes

with joy, and headed for them, coming to the islands that lay in the mouth of the strait. But coming in between the rocky isles we hit an underwater rock, and were stuck fast there for eight or nine hours. It was an ebb tide when we hit, and with the help of God guiding wind and sea so as to have fair weather and calm water, the flood tide set us afloat: the ebb came from the east and the flood from the west. When we were afloat we headed closer to the eastern shore and anchored there.

The next day, being the 27th of July, we sent the boat ashore to fetch some fowl; the ship was to get as close as it could, but the wind was against us and it had to tack back and forth. They had such a great way to row that they were unable to reach the breeding grounds, but they did find a good many gulls on the rocks and cliffs. Though still hard to come by, they killed about 30 of them, and toward night returned to the ship. By now we had brought the ship closer to the mouth of the strait, and found a place on a rise or shelf in which we could anchor in some 18 or 20 fathoms of water. We left here and sailed closer to the birds' breeding ground, but the water was so deep there was no place to drop anchor; neither could we find the place again where we had anchored before, so we were forced to sail back and forth within the strait, always in danger of the rocks.

On the 28th day the boat went to Cape Diggs for birds, heading directly toward the place where they breed; as they drew close they saw seven boats come around the eastern point toward them. When the savages saw our boat they drew themselves together and put their smaller boats into a larger one. When they had done that they came rowing over to our boat, making signs to the west, but being ready for any other attempts.

The savages came to our men, and by signs grew familiar with one another, so that our men took one of theirs into our boat, and they took one of ours into their boat. Then they carried our man to their tents

which stood to the west of the cove where the fowl
breed, taking him into a tent where he remained until
our men returned with theirs.

Our boat went to the breeding place, wishing to
find out how the savages killed their birds, and were
shown how it was done in the following manner: they
take a long pole with a noose at the end which they
put around the bird's neck, and simply pluck them up.
When our men knew they had a better way, they
showed them how with the use of a gun a single shot
would kill seven or eight. To keep the story short, our
boat returned to their cove for our man and to deliver
theirs.

When they arrived, the savages put on a great
display of joy; dancing and leaping and stroking their
breast. They offered various things to our men, but
they only took some walrus teeth, for which in return
they gave a knife and two glass buttons. Our men
returned aboard ship, rejoicing that by chance they had   *Rejoicing.*
met the most simple and kind people in the world.

Henry Greene (more than the others) was so con-   *Greene's confidence.*
fident of their good nature that he felt there was no
need whatsoever to stand guard. God had blinded him
so, that when he expected a great deal from these
people he received more than he looked for; by ignor-
ing the possibility of evil he was suddenly made a good
example of for all men, and we learned to take heed of
the savage people no matter how simple they may seem
to be.

The next day, the 29th of July, they quickly got
ready to go ashore. Because the ship was anchored so
far out, they hoisted the anchor and sailed in as close as
they could get; and because I was lame I was to go in
the boat, carrying with me an assortment of things I
had in the cabin. With more haste than good speed,
and not without some swearing, off we went; Henry
Greene, William Wilson, John Thomas, Michael Perse,
Andrew Moter and myself. When we approached the
shore, the people on the hills were dancing and leaping. We came into the cove where they had beached

their boats, bringing our boat to the east side of the cove close to the rocks. After making the boat fast to a large stone on the beach, everyone went ashore with something in his hand to barter with the people who came. Henry Greene swore that he would not give them anything until he got the venison they had promised him by signs before.

When we came, they made signs to their dogs, of which there were many and as big as hounds, and pointed to their mountain, and to the sun, clapping their hands. Henry Greene, John Thomas and William Wilson were standing close to the bow of the boat, while Michael Perse and Andrew Moter were up on a rock gathering sorrel; not one man had so much as a stick or any kind of weapon with him except Henry Greene who had a piece of spear; nor was there anything the savages had that could hurt us. Henry Greene and Wilson had mirrors, Jew's harps and bells that they were showing the people.

Savage's assault. One of the savages that was standing around them came over and got in the bow of our boat to show me a bottle. I made signs to him to get out, but he pretended he had not understood me, whereupon I stood up and pointed him ashore. In the meantime, while I was getting the man at the bow of the boat ashore, another had crept around behind, and when I sat down again I suddenly saw the leg and foot of a man near me. I looked up and saw the savage with a knife in his hand, striking over my head at my breast; whereupon in raising my right arm to protect myself he wounded my arm and struck me in the body below my right nipple. He struck a second blow which I met with my left hand, and then struck me in the right thigh, almost cutting off the little finger of my left hand. I got hold of the string of the knife and wound it about my left hand, while he with both hands was striving to make an end of what he begun. I found he had a weak grip, and with God's help got hold of the sleeve of his left arm and was able to pull him away from me. His left side was exposed to me, and when I saw that I got hold of the sleeve of his arm in my left hand, holding the string of the knife there also, while with my free right hand groped for something to strike him with. I had forgotten about my dagger at my side, but when looking down I saw it, and therewith struck him in the body and throat.

While I was being assaulted in the boat, our men on shore were being set upon. John Thomas and William Wilson had their bowels cut, and Michael Perse and Henry Greene, being mortally wounded, came tumbling into the boat together. When Andrew Moter saw this jumble he came running down the rocks, and leapt into the sea to swim to the boat. He hung onto the stern of the boat until Michael Perse, who was protecting the bow of the boat against the savages attacking there, was able to pull him in. Then the savages set upon us with their bows and arrows, whereupon Henry Greene was slain outright, and Michael Perse and the rest received many wounds. Michael Perse cleared the boat, starting to move it away from the shore, and pulled Andrew Moter in. But in turning the boat around, I received a cruel wound in my back with an arrow. Michael Perse and Andrew Moter rowed the boat away; the savages seeing this ran to their boats and I was afraid they would launch them and follow us, but they did not. Our ship was in the middle of the channel so they could not see us.

When we had rowed a good distance from shore, Michael Perse fainted, and couldn't row anymore. Then Andrew Moter stood in the bow of the boat and waved to the ship; at first they didn't see us, but when they did they didn't know what to make of us, but finally they sailed over and picked us up. Henry Greene was thrown out of the boat into the sea, while the others, including the savage who was still alive but unconscious, were brought aboard. But they all died there that day, William Wilson swearing and cursing in a most fearful manner. Michael Perse lived for two days longer, then he died. Thus you have heard the tragic end of Henry Greene who they called captain,

Just treachery to unjust traitors.

Greene slain.

Wicked and wretched end to wretched and wicked men.

and his mates; these four being the only strong men on the ship.

The poor few who were left had to work the ship back and forth in the strait, for there was no place nearby to anchor. Besides, they still had to go in the boat to kill enough birds to supply us on our return home: which they did, although with danger to everyone, for if the wind came up there would be a high sea, and the eddies of the tides would carry us so close to the rocks that our master [Robert Billet] (as I called him now) was afraid. After much labor they killed about 200 on the south cape [Cape Diggs] and then sailed eastward. But when we were 18 to 21 miles from the capes the wind came around to the east and we had to sail back to the capes again. There, we killed another 100 birds. After this, the wind came out of the west, which allowed us to get away from the capes. For the most part, our master followed along the northern shore until he came to broken ground near Queen's Foreland, and there he anchored.[9]

From there we sailed to the Isles of God's Mercies, and on to Rose Islands which lie in the mouth of our strait, not seeing land on account of the fog until we practically put our bowsprit on the rocks. But then it cleared a little and we could see that we were enclosed by rocky islands, and we couldn't find any ground to anchor in; there our master lay-a-trie all night. The next day we still had the fog with us and sought for some ground to anchor in, which we found in a hundred and some fathoms of water. The next day we weighed anchor and sailed eastward, but before we came here we had already placed ourselves on short rations, allowing half a bird a day with the pottage.

Pursued by misery. As yet we still had some grain left, but nothing else. Then began the testing of our qualities. We began to skin the birds, for the feathers would not pull out, and Robert Juet was the first to make these skins edible by burning off the feathers, so that they became a great dish of meat. As for the garbage, it was not thrown away.

After we were clear of these islands, which lie out with two points, one to the southeast and the other to the north (making a bay with the appearance of no way through), we continued our course east southeast and south by east until we raised the Desolations. From there we shaped our course for Ireland. Thus we continued for many days, until the wind coming against us made us change our course. With this change, Robert Juet persuaded the crew to stop in Newfoundland, saying that if our countrymen were still there [fishing] we would find great relief, and even if they had already left, there would be a large amount of bread and fish left by them; but how true, I give God thanks we didn't try.

Still, we had sailed southwest until reaching almost 57° latitude, when (by the will of God) the wind came up out of the southwest. Then the master asked me if we shouldn't take advantage of this wind and reshape our course toward Ireland. I said it was best to go where we knew grain grew, and not to seek it where it is cast away and not to be found.

We sailed towards Ireland with prosperous winds for many days in a row. By now all our grain was gone, and our remaining fowl dried out; since there was no other choice, we were content with the salt broth for dinner, and half a fowl for supper. Next, our candles were brought out, and Bennet, our cook, made a meal of marrow from the bones of the birds, frying them with candle wax until they were crisp, and with vinegar put on them they made a very good meal. We shared our vinegar, and every man was given a pound of candles each week as a delicacy.

Diet of candle wax and bird bones.

By Robert Juet's reckoning, after having sailed 600 miles, we were now 180 or 220 miles away from Ireland. There is no doubt that our course was made much longer than need be, through bad steering, for our men became so weak they could not stand at the helm, but had to sit.

Then Robert Juet died miserably for mere want, and all the men were in despair, saying we had already

Juet's demise.

passed Ireland—and with our last bird in the deep tub. Since our master had to look out for himself, as much as the rest of the crew, they didn't care which end of the ship went forward. Some would just sit, watching the foresail or mainsail break free, the sheets either flying or broken, and not bother to do anything about it or even call for help, which much grieved the master.

In this adversity it pleased God to give us sight of land, not far from the place where our master said we would be—the Bay of Galway. We came to the west of Dursey Island [on the southwest coast of Ireland] and sailed along the coast to the southwest.

Finally there was a joyful cry, "a sail, a sail," and we headed toward it. Then we saw more sails, but continued toward the nearest, calling out to him; it was a bark from Fowey, Cornwall, and was at anchor, fishing. He came over and guided us into Beer Haven. We stayed there a few days and dealt with the Irish to supply our needs, but found no relief, for they had neither bread, drink nor money amongst them. They advised us to deal with our own countrymen who were fishing there, which we did, but found them so cold in kindness that they wouldn't do anything without first being paid, and we had no money on the ship.

In the end we got John Waymouth, the master of the bark that brought us into the harbor, to furnish us with money; in return which he received our best cable and anchor in pawn. With this money, our master, with the help of John Waymouth, bought bread, beer and beef.

Just as we were under obligation to Waymouth for his money, so were we to Captain Taylor for making our contracts with Waymouth, by whose means he took a bill for our cable and anchor and for the mens' wages. Although he had guaranteed their wages, they indicated that they were unwilling to go with us for any amount of money. Whereupon Captain Taylor swore he would force them, and then if they wouldn't go, he would hang them.

Refuge in Ireland.

In conclusion, we agreed on three pound 10 shillings per man to bring our ship to Plymouth or Dartmouth, and to give the pilot five pound. But if the wind was unfavorable, and instead they had to put into Bristol, they were to have four pound 10 shillings per man, and the pilot six pound. Omitting further circumstance, we arrived at Plymouth from Beer Haven and anchored in front of the castle. From Plymouth we had fair winds and weather, and without any delay or stopping, we came to Downes, and then to Gravesend where most of our men went ashore. From Gravesend we came to Erith, and there we stopped. Our master, Robert Billet, came aboard, and the two of us went up to London together to Sir Thomas Smith.

Arrival at Plymouth.

In as much as my report may be suspected by some as not being so friendly to Hudson, since I stayed with the crew that so cruelly exposed him, and therefore imply that there was more to my actions than stated, I have also added the report of Thomas Wydhouse, one of those put in the shallop, who ascribes those occasions of discord to Juet. It is not up to me to examine or to pronounce sentence; I have presented the evidence just as it occurred. Let the court censure, hearing with both ears, that which both eyes may see in these notes and the following report of Thomas Wydhouse.

A Note Found in the Desk of
Thomas Wydhowse

Student in the Mathematickes, hee being one of them who was put into the Shallop

The 10th day of September 1610, after dinner our master called the crew together to hear and bear witness of the abuse of some of the crew (having been the request of Robert Juet), that the master should redress some of the abuses and slanders, as he called them, against this Juet. After the master had examined and heard with fairness what Juet could say for himself, there proved to be so many great abuses, mutinous matters, and action against the master, that there was danger in letting them go on any longer; that it was time to punish and cut off any later occasions of such mutinies.

Juet accused.

It was proved to his face, first by Bennet Mathew, our trumpet,[10] upon the first sight of Iceland, who confessed that if it came to action he supposed there would be manslaughter, and prove bloody to some.

Secondly, after leaving Iceland, within hearing of the rest of the crew, Juet threatened to turn the boat around and head it back home after the mutiny (which at that time our master had wisely pacified in hope of some change).

Thirdly, it was deposed by Phillip Staffe, our carpenter, and Ladlie Arnold [Arnold Ludlow] that he persuaded them to keep muskets charged and swords ready in their cabins, for they would be used before the voyage is over.

Fourthly, when we were much pestered with the ice, he used words tending to mutiny, discouragement, and slander of the action, which easily took effect on those who were timid; and if the master had not prevented it in time, it might easily have overthrown the voyage. And now lately being embayed in a deep bay, which the master desired to see (for some reasons known to himself), his words tended to put the crew into an extreme fright about wintering in the cold. He jested at our master's hope of seeing Bantam by Candlemass.

Juet disposed.

For these and various other base slanders made against our master, Robert Juet was disposed, and in his place Robert Bylot, who showed himself honestly respecting the master's purposes, was made the master's mate.

Also, Francis Clement, the boatswain, was discharged from his office, and William Wilson, a man thought more fit, was put in his place. This man [Clement] had basely carried himself to our master and to the action.

Also, Adrian Mooter [Moter] was appointed boat-swain's mate, and was promised by the master that from now on, Juet's wages would be given to Bylot, and the boatswain's excess of wages would be equally divided (to the owners' satisfaction) between Wilson, John King, and one of the quartermasters, who had all carried themselves well in the furtherance of the voy-age.

Also, the master promised that if the offenders behaved themselves honestly for the remainder of the voyage, that he would do well for them, and forget the injuries, with other admonitions. These things just stated relating to Hudson's exposing, and God's just judgement on the exposers, as Prickett has related, was taken to mean that Sir Dudley Digges [Prickett's mas-ter] would procur their pardon when they returned to

---

Figure 5-4. *Map of Hudson Bay. The map drawn by Hudson on his voy-age in 1610–1611, survived the mutiny and, on the return of the Discovery to England, was sent to Peter Plancius in Holland, where it was engraved and published by Hessel Gerritz. It was so successful that within one year there were five editions. Hudson recognized and corrected many errors in Greenland's geography, and in spite of its several shortcomings in topo-graphic details, it was far more accurate than those of any other contempo-rary cartographers. The implication that Hudson Bay was the passage to China and Japan sparked the public's interest.*

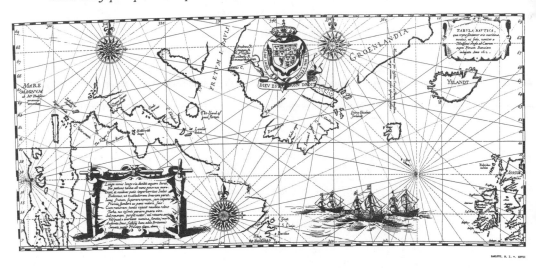

England. I think I should also add information which I have received from a knowledgeable source, that when the ship ran aground at Digges Island in 62°44' latitude, a considerable flood tide, coming from the west, set it afloat.

Support for the Northwest Passage.

Further support.

This supports the premise of an open passage from the South Sea [Pacific] to that region, and therefore to these seas [Atlantic]. Also, the observed weapons and arts used by these savages were different than those used by other savages, which provides further support. The one who assaulted Prickett in the boat had a weapon that was broad and sharply indented, made of bright steel (such as they use in Java), riveted into a handle made of walrus tooth.

Epilogue: 1610

Before the *Discovery* left the Thames River, Henry Hudson made two changes in the ship's company. He summarily dismissed Master Coleburne, sending him back to London aboard a pinke with a letter of explanation; and he took Henry Greene aboard.

The very presence of Coleburne, who was signed on as an "advisor" by the Merchant Adventurers, must have galled Hudson, who seized upon the first opportunity to be rid of him. In *North West Fox*, a description of his own 1631 explorations for the Northwest Passage, Luke Foxe wrote "Coleburne was a better man than Hudson." He also credited Coleburne with the decision to search for the passage north of 61° latitude—a conclusion that flies in the face of overwhelming evidence to the contrary. Perhaps Foxe sought to discredit Hudson in order to advance himself.

In character and background, Henry Greene was totally different than Hudson's other associates. Greene was a man of the underworld who "preferred above everything the company of bawds, panders, pimps, and trollops." Why did Henry Hudson want Greene on the *Discovery*? Clearly Hudson knew of his reputation, for

Greene was taken aboard furtively at Gravesend after the directors of the company had made their formal visit, and his name did not appear on the ship's crew list. Yet he was not only given a berth on the passage, but was promised a post as one of Prince Henry's guards upon return to England.

In Iceland, when Greene picked an argument with the ship's surgeon, Edward Wilson, Hudson came to Greene's defense. Later, he gave Greene the deceased gunner's gray cloth gown, bypassing the normal custom of allowing it to be sold to the highest bidder.

Robert Juet divulged to the carpenter that Greene was given a berth on the ship to act as an informer, "to crack the credit" against anyone who displeased Hudson. The informer's role called for someone in whom the crew would be likely to confide, and with his crude, rough background, Henry Greene certainly fit the bill. Hudson's strong reaction to these accusations—he considered turning around to put Juet ashore in Iceland—lends credence to Juet's charges against Greene. But in the end Hudson lost faith in Greene, "telling him that none of his friends would trust him with so much as 20 shillings, so why should he." After this, Greene allied himself with those whose discontent he could channel into mutiny.

If Hudson's selection of Greene as a crewmember was questionable, so was his choice of Robert Juet. Juet's background is obscure, and we know nothing about his previous activities. Llewelyn Powys describes him as "an elderly man, cynical, skeptical, and dangerous."

Although he was Hudson's mate on the previous journey, in 1609 Juet held some other rank. It is odd that he now accepted a lower status; but perhaps the Dutch East India Company, in order to impose control on its foreign captain, had insisted that his mate be Dutch. Juet may have been offered higher wages—sure balm to an injured pride—to compensate for his lesser role.

In Hudson's journal for the 1608 voyage he neither indicates his feelings about Juet nor comments on his competence. Juet's own journal of this voyage, which no longer exists but was available to Samuel Purchas, is more revealing. Purchas noted that on June 22, Juet noticed a sudden change in variation of the compass. Whereas on the previous day it had been 22° to the east, it shifted suddenly to the north by 11°. On that same date, Hudson's calculation of the ship's latitude was 74°34', but he remarked that the ship's way and the observations were not in agreement, "though careful heed were taken of both." Juet's observation about the change in magnetic variation of the compass would account for the discrepancy between the dead reckoning and the celestial sighting—a change Hudson had overlooked.

The celestial observations in Juet's journal of the 1609 voyage were clearly his own, not a transcription of Hudson's records. They were complete and concise, and judging from his accompanying descriptions of the localities visited, his calculations appear to be as true and correct as contemporary navigational science would allow. Although Juet almost certainly had been involved in the mutiny of the previous year, his proficiency in navigation most likely outweighed Hudson's fear of insubordination, and in 1610 Juet was reinstated as first mate.

This may also help to explain Hudson's vehement reaction to Juet's disclosure of Henry Greene's purpose on the ship. He was angry at Juet for subverting the stratagem of keeping an ear open to the crew's thoughts, and felt betrayed. Hudson showed more forbearance than was perhaps prudent, and allowed the matter to rest, but when arguments arose later in the voyage, he demoted Juet to punish him and prevent any further occasion for mutiny. Later, though, Juet would voice his mutinous thoughts through the mouth of Henry Greene. He met his deserved end on the return voyage, when nearly within sight of England, he "died miserably for mere want."

Was the crew warranted in taking the extreme action of mutiny? Even before they reached Greenland the men had begun to doubt Hudson's integrity. The favoritism he showed toward Greene later in the voyage only intensified their distrust. And as the journey pro-

Charting the Sea of Darkness

gressed, they grew alarmed by Hudson's apparent incompetence as a navigator and by his vacillating behavior.

At the first dangerous encounter with ice, when they were 120 miles into the strait, Hudson displayed a singular lack of determination by bringing out his chart, showing the crew how far they'd sailed, and leaving it up to them whether or not to continue. With this show of weakness, Hudson all but relinquished his command.

His apparent indecision showed itself in other ways. When he entered James Bay, Hudson spent several weeks sailing north and south looking for the westward passage. The sailors and Prickett became concerned about this apparently purposeless wandering, and Thomas Wydowse wrote that Hudson acted "for some reasons [only] to himselfe knowne." Their safety—indeed their very lives—were in the hands of a man who seemed to have lost his way.

Inconsistency and shows of anger were not in keeping with Hudson's past behavior, but the extremity of their situation had made him volatile. One moment he threatened discipline by hanging; the next he promised to forgive the miscreants if they behaved themselves in the future. Where firmness and reason might have averted disaster, displays of false force alternating with appeasement only served to feed the crew's mounting apprehension.

They survived the winter, but the following spring their situation worsened. Trapped in the ice once again, the ship lay immobile; only 14 days of food remained, and a poor allowance at that. And just when the crew most needed a master to give them courage in their adversity, Henry Hudson, utterly disheartened, completely withdrew, "not caring to goe one way or other." The crew were forced to take matters in their own hands in order to survive.

Whatever its causes, mutiny was the most serious offense a sailor could commit, punishable by hanging. Contrary to all expectations, when the *Discovery* returned to England and Bylot with Prickett went to the directors of the Merchant Adventurers in London to make their report, an immediate inquiry was not made. A month later, in a preliminary report, the masters of Trinity House expressed the opinion that "they deserved to be hanged." But with the exception of Wilson, the surgeon, they weren't even brought before the High Admiralty Court until six years later.

On January 25, 1611,

Edward Wilson of Portsmouth, surgeon, aged 22 years [was] sworn and examined before the right Worshipfull Master Doctor Trevor, Judge of his Majesties High Court of the Admiralty concerning his recently being at sea in the Dis-covery, of London, whereof Henry Hudson was master for the Northwest discovery; sayeth as follows:

Their victuals were so scant that they had only two quarts of meal allowed to serve 22 men for a day, and that the master had bread and cheese and aquavite in his cabin and called some of the company whom he favored to eat and drink with him in his cabin, whereupon those who had noth-ing did grudge and mutiny against the master and those who he gave bread and drink to; these visits thus being the begin-ning. William Wilson, then boatswain of the Discovery, *but later slain by the savages, went to Philip Staffe, the master's mate, and asked him the reason why the master should so favor to give meat to some of the company, and not the rest. Staffe answered it was necessary some of them be kept up; whereupon Wilson went down again and told Henry Greene what Philip Staffe had said; whereupon they with others consented together, and agreed to pinion the master, and John King the quartermaster, and put them into a shallop. Philip Staffe could have stayed on the ship, but he voluntarily, for the love he bore Hudson, went into the shallop upon the condition they would give him his clothes (which he had).*

There were also six more, beside these three put in the shallop. They thought they were put there only to keep Hud-son and John King in the shallop until the victuals were properly shared. They went willingly, but later, when they found they were not allowed to come back on the ship again they desired that they might have their clothes, of which a part of them was delivered. The rest of their apparel was sold at the main mast to whoever would bid the most for them, and an inventory of every man's particular goods was made, and their money was paid by Mr. Allin Cary to their friends here in England, and deducted from the wages of those that bought them when they returned to England.

(He knew nothing of the mutiny) until the master was brought down pinioned and set before his cabin, whereupon he [Wilson] looked out and asked what was wrong, and the master replied that his arms were bound. I would have come out of my cabin to have given some food to them, but those who had bound the master told me that if I were well enough off, I should keep myself so. . . . neither did Silvanus Bond, Nicholas Simmes or Francis Clements consent to this practice . . . .

(The Company in the Shallop) . . . put out sail and followed after the ship for half an hour, but when they saw the ship put up more sail and realized they could not follow them, they headed toward shore . . .

No other depositions were taken until 1616. Then an indictment for murder was finally brought by the High Admiralty Court, and the following charges set before the men:

Be it enquired for our Lord the King if Robert Bylot, Abacuk Prickett, Edward Wilson, Benett Matthew, Francis Clemence, Adrian Motter, Sylvanus Bond, and Nicholas Simms on June 22 in a certain ship called the Discovery of the Port of London, *at that time being on the High Seas near the Straits of Hudson, etc., not having God before their eyes, by force and arms place cruel hands upon Henry Hudson, master and governor of the* Discovery, *and did pinion his arms. And that John Hudson, his son, along with Arnold Ludlo, John King, Michael Butt, Thomas Woodhouse, Philip Staffe, Adam Moore, and Sidrack Fanner were placed in a certain shallop in the ice, without victuals, drink, fire and clothing, by reason thereof they came to their death and miserably did perish. And that Robert Bylot and etc., did kill and murder Henry Hudson.*

Like many of the court documents, records of the questions put to the expedition's survivors are gone; their answers, however, have survived. On February 7, 1616, Abacuk Prickett of London, haberdasher, made his statement to the Worshipfull Master Doctor Amy, deputy to the judge of the Admiralty:

To the first article . . . Henry Hudson, John Hudson, Thomas Widowes (Woodhouse), Philip Staffe, John King, Michael Butt, Sidrack Fanner, Adam Moore and John Ladlo, mariners on the Discovery *in the voyage about six years ago for finding the Northwest Passage were put out of the ship by force by Henry Greene, John Thomas, John Wilson, Michael Pearce and others, and into the shallop in the strait called Hudson's Strait, in America. They would not allow those on the shallop to return to the ship, the reason being that they [the mutineers] were sick and in need of food; if all returned, there would not be enough food and they would all starve. The only exception [to those put out by force] was Philip Staffe, who left the ship of his own accord for the affection he bore for Hudson.*

Greene, with eleven or twelve of the company, sailed away in the Discovery *and left Hudson and the rest in the shallop in the ice, in the month of June. What became of them afterwards he does not know. At the time of putting the men out of the ship he [Prickett] was lame in the legs, unable to stand or move; neither did he have a hand in the mutiny, but greatly lamented it, for Henry Hudson and Philip Staffe were the best friends he had on the ship.*

Five weeks after Hudson and the rest were put into the shallop, Henry Greene, John Wilson, John Thomas and the rest in the ship came to Sir Dudley Digges Island. There, Greene, Wilson, Thomas, Pearse and Mowter went ashore to trade with the savages, but were betrayed by them and all were sorely wounded in sundry places. They were brought back to the ship before they died, but almost immediately Greene died, and a few hours later so did Wilson, Thomas and Pearse. Two of them had their bowels cut out, and the blood which was upon the clothes and other things brought home was the blood of the persons so wounded and slain by the savages, and no other.

Greene and the others turned out Hudson and the rest only for want of victuals, and for no other cause to my knowledge. For my part I made no means to hinder the proceedings that might have been taken against them, nor know of any other who did."

Depositions of the other crewmembers were, for the most part, in accord with those quoted above. Each of the deponents protected himself in his own way, being careful to deny having had knowledge of the mutiny until it was already in motion, or claiming to have been somewhere else on the ship when it occured. Even Abacuk Prickett blamed the mutiny and Henry Hudson's death entirely on the men who had been slain by the savages. This conveniently eliminated the threat of counteraccusations.

The mutineer's main defense was imminent starvation—a defense that could not be argued against. To have justified their action on the grounds of their master's incompetence would almost certainly have led to their hanging.

Prickett maintained "that no one was shot at or hurt in any way." Bylot implied that those in the shallop had departed by mutual agreement; he said that Greene and the rest would not allow them to come aboard the ship again, "and so Hudson and the others in the shallop went away to the southward, and the ship came to the eastward." Bennet Matthew swore to the court that "the nine persons went into the shallop without any violence offered, save for that Hudson was pinioned." He even claimed that after being put in the shallop Hudson and many of the others came back on the ship again to warm themselves and gather some of their personal belongings, "and then went again into the shallop."

But the reported equanimity with which Hudson and the others allowed themselves to be placed in the shallop and cast adrift without food, water, or clothes is suspect. Even sick men will put up a struggle against certain death. In fact, the *Discovery* returned to England so drenched in blood that months of rain and wave had not washed it away.

On Friday, July 24, 1618, four prisoners were brought forth from the gaol and arraigned in Southwark. Abacuk Prickett, Edward Wilson, Francis Clements, and Bennet Matthew were charged "for feloniously pinioning and putting Henry Hudson, master of the *Discovery*, out of the same ship with eight more of his company into a shallop in the Isle in (the parts of) America without meat, drink, clothes or other provision, whereby they died." All four pleaded not guilty. Charges against Matthew and Clements were thrown out by the jury. Wilson and Prickett were found not guilty of the charges and not guilty of fleeing from justice. Robert Bylot already had been pardoned for his feat of seamanship in bringing the *Discovery* and the remaining men safely back to England.

Why did it take five years for the crew of the *Discovery* to be brought to trial—and why were they then exonerated? The guilt or innocence of the men seemed less important than the claim that they discovered the Northwest Passage.

The strength of flow of tides in Hudson's Strait, which could only have come from a connection between the two great oceans, was offered as evidence. Thomas Woodhouse had supported this premise in his letter, in which he described the considerable flood tide that set the ship afloat after it had been grounded on Diggs Island. Although they destroyed most of his journal, the mutineers left untouched the map Hudson had made of his explorations. To those eager to believe, the lack of delineation of a western shore to Hudson Bay served to confirm that this was the way to the Pacific Ocean. As final proof, the *Discovery* survivors had noticed that the weapons used by the savages who had attacked them appeared to be the same as those used in Java.

Before the trial began, Bylot, Wilson, and Prickett had been made members of a new company called "The Discoverers of the North-west Passage." On July 26,

1612, King James I provided a charter to some merchants of London, investing them with the power to establish trade by way of this route.

They sent out two ships in May, 1613 — the *Resolution* and the *Discovery*, that "good and lucky ship."[11] Prickett and Bylot were passengers aboard the *Discovery*, with Thomas Button as its captain. They were as sure of the existence of this passage, and as confident that it would take them to the East Indies, as they were about a passage between Calais and Dover. That they might also find and rescue the abandoned Hudson and his men was at best an afterthought.

They did neither. Five men were lost on Diggs Island, and after overwintering on the western shore of Hudson Bay, the ships returned to England the following year. Their expedition showed that there was a definable western limit to Hudson Bay — that it was not a strait or passage continuing all the way across the North American continent — but this in no way reduced the fervor of their belief that the Northwest Passage lay in this direction. Not until after his second exploration in the Great Bay of Ice was Robert Bylot convinced that no navigable passage would be found here.

In 1616 the *Discovery*, with Bylot as captain and William Baffin as pilot, searched Baffin Bay for the Northwest Passage. They managed to sail 300 miles farther north than Davis had, exploring and mapping the entire bay. Bylot returned to England with the conclusion "there was no passage, no hope of a passage." Altogether, the *Discovery* made a total of six voyages into the Arctic, and Robert Bylot made four.

In the meantime, ships' captains and fur trappers for the Hudson Bay Company reported finding stakes in the ground and the ruins of a house assumed to be built by Staffe, Hudson's carpenter. The rumors were never validated, but it may provide a small measure of relief to think, as Llewlyn Powys did, that "the forsaken men did manage at least to regain land . . . and were not left to wash backwards and forwards under the ice, below the dim white abdomens of cod and halibut, on the floor of 'green ooze and gross gravel' of that forlorn remote coast."

Origin of Hudson's Geographic Notions

Henry Hudson's information about the northwest Arctic contained contradictions about the location of islands and straits. Some of this was due to inaccurate navigation, and some responsibility fell upon the cartographers, who erred when piecing together information from many sources.

Yet the information was sufficient to establish where the Northwest Passage lay, and how to find it. Hudson was convinced that there must be a strait in the western continent leading from the Atlantic to the Pacific, its position almost certainly north of 60°N latitude. To reach it, he must first double the cape at the southern extremity of Greenland, then sail north and west across Davis Strait to explore the two possible entrances to the strait leading across the top of North America—the Furious Overfall (at the mouth of Hudson Bay) and Lumley's Inlet (Frobisher Bay at Baffin Island).

There is no solid evidence that Hudson had access to geographic information gained by French and Portuguese mariners. However, the journals, logbooks, and charts of English explorers into the Canadian Arctic definitely were available to him.

Martin Frobisher

Sir Humfry Gilbert's *A Discourse of a Discoverie for a New Passage to Cataia*, published in 1576, prompted a group of eminent Englishmen to back Martin Frobisher's first voyage in search of the Northwest Passage. They included Stephen Burrough, explorer of Nova Zembla and the Kara Sea; Dr. John Dee, scientist and official advisor of the Muscovy Company; and Richard Hakluyt, cosmographer and navigator.[12] Queen Elizabeth, while providing no official support, took a strong interest in the expedition. One of the passengers exclaimed, "her Majesty had good likings for our doings, and thanked us for it."

Martin Frobisher's first voyage, in 1576, took him to the southern and southwestern shores of Greenland. From there, with the barks *Gabriel* and *Michael*, he sailed west toward the coast of Labrador, searching for the strait that would lead him to Cathay. He reached land somewhat north of Labrador, at Resolution Island—which he named Queen Elizabeth's Foreland—off the southeastern cape of Baffin Island. Sailing north past a "great gutte, bay, or pasage," he came to another headland, which he was convinced formed part of the continent of Asia.

Frobisher, like other geographers of the time, believed that the Arctic regions of North America were connected to Asia, and that a passage into the Pacific lay between these two. He concluded that this new strait or bay between the headlands, at a latitude of 62°N, was the passage to Cathay. To prove his assertion, Frobisher entered the bay and sailed as far west as he could. After 150 miles, he was forced by ice-choked water at the head of the bay to retreat to its mouth.

Figure 5-5. *In his* True Discourse (1578), *George Best showed Martin Frobisher's 1576 discovery of the strait, which Best believed led to Cathay.*

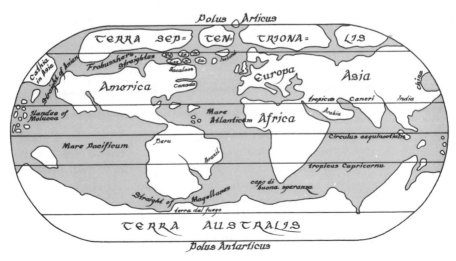

Certain that he had found the Northwest Passage, he named this body of water Frobisher's Streytes, "lyke as Magellanus at the Southwest end of the Worlde, havying discovered the passage to the South Sea . . . called the same straites Magellanes Streights." Before returning to England, being "so tyred and sik with laboure of their hard voyage," Frobisher sent part of his crew ashore to collect rocks and other souvenirs as proof of their having taken possession of this new land.

When a piece of black stone they brought back was assayed and said to contain gold ore, there was no problem raising money for a second voyage. This time Queen Elizabeth provided money for the expedition and made available an additional ship, the *Aid*. A royal charter was granted to the merchant's group, now officially called the "Company of Cathay."

Their goals for the forthcoming voyage were:

1. To set the miners to work collecting 'gold ore' on Hall's Island [near the north side of Frobisher's Strait] or elsewhere.
2. In one of the barks, to sail no more than 100 leagues up his 'Strait,' but not so long as to jeopardize returning home the same year.
3. To leave some of his company to winter on the Strait, with a pinnace and supplies.
4. If no more promising ore were forthcoming, to send his flagship [*Aid*] home and go on to China with the two barks."

Obviously, geographical exploration was secondary to the gathering of gold ore. The Northwest Passage and the route to Cathay were all but forgotten. As for the ore, it turned out to be worthless—fool's gold—a mistake resulting in much recrimination (from which Frobisher was not exempt) among members of the now bankrupt Company of Cathay.

Although Frobisher never completed his passage through the strait he named after himself, he remained convinced that it was the way to the Orient. George Best, a passenger on the expedition, published his detailed description of the three voyages in *A True Discourse* in 1578. It contained a world map that "confirmed" that Frobisher's Strait continued all the way across the top of

Canada to enter the Pacific by way of the Strait of Anian. Crude as the map may appear today, it shows evidence of considerable rethinking of the geography of the Arctic regions. The strait above Canada no longer separates Asia from America, while Cathaia and Greenland are now separate lands, unattached to Asia.

Basically, this map is a reworking of the 1569 Polar projection map by Gerardus Mercator. The major difference is that the strait above Canada, Americae Pars, is now called Frobisher's Strait. The four large islands across the top of the map are the same mythical islands seen on the Mercator map (in turn derived from the Ruysch map of 1507), but on George Best's map they are strung out in a line due to the difference in projection. Furthermore, the two large islands on the left are transformed from mythical status to actual land masses, based on direct observation. The island with the partial label Terra Sep presumably represents Baffin Island, since it is the land to the north of Frobisher Strait, and that with the partial label Ten is Greenland. All of Terra Septentrionalis balances in a perfect manner the land mass of Terra Australis, and each is completely surrounded by a circulating ocean—as ancient cosmography would dictate. The Straits of Frobisher are the northern counterpart to the Straits of Magellan, connecting the Atlantic and Pacific Oceans.

How much Martin Frobisher's discoveries increased the knowledge of the northwest Arctic is less important than the impetus his voyages provided for others to continue searching for the passage.

John Davis

In 1585, Captain John Davis departed on the first of three expeditions into the Canadian Arctic. After a six-week crossing, Davis reached the southeast coast of Greenland, but dense fog blocked sight of land. He was first aware of it when he heard "a great whirling and brustling of a tyde . . . a mighty great roaring of the Sea." This, he found, was caused by ice rattling together. When the fog cleared next morning, he beheld the coast of Greenland, "which was the most deformed, rocky and mountainous land that ever we saw." The mountain tops were snow covered, and dense pack ice extended for three miles off the shore. Believing that Greenland lay farther north, and that he had therefore discovered a new land, Davis aptly named it Land of Desolation.

After doubling Cape Farwell at the southern tip of Greenland, Davis sailed north along its western coast until he reached the latitude of 64°11'. From there he sailed south in search of any deep inlet that would take him west. A most promising entrance, with 60 miles of open water across it, appeared south of 65 degrees. He entered, sailing 180 miles into the sound, and found the signs most auspicious for its being the sought-after passage. The farther he sailed the deeper the water became, and strong tidal currents strengthened his conviction. But with winter approaching he had to make his return to England and save further exploration of this sound, which he named Cumberland Sound, for the following year. Davis claimed that "the Northwest Passage is a matter nothing doubtful, but at any tyme almost to be passed, the sea navigable, voyd of yse, the ayre tolerable and the waters very depe."

On his second voyage, in 1586, Davis explored these regions again, finding two potential inlets besides Cumberland Strait, Frobisher's Strait, and Hudson Strait. These new straits, both on the Labrador coast, were Davis Inlet, at 56°, and Hamilton Inlet, at 54°30'.

In spite of the seeming failures of the first two voyages, Davis's backers were sufficiently encouraged to provide support for a third voyage, with John Davis as "Chiefe Captaine & Pilot Generall, for the discoverie of a passage to the Isles of Molucca, or the coast of China, in the yeere 1587." Convinced that the Northwest Passage had to be in one of these major inlets, Davis set out to "see an end of these businesses."

This time, his main goal was to explore the more northerly portion of Davis Strait, presently called Baffin Bay. He was able to sail as far north as 72°46°, 356 miles north of the Arctic circle, before the ever-present pack ice in Baffin Bay forced him to turn the bow of his boat south. At one point he saw a gap in the ice with clear water beyond, in which there was "no ice, but a great sea, free, large, very salt and very blue," and "it seemed most manifest that the passage was free and without impediment toward the north." But in entering it, he found himself surrounded by icebergs and could not pursue this promising lead. As he continued sailing south he attempted to explore Cumberland Strait again, but was stopped by a solid barrier of ice.

When passing Frobisher's Strait, he apparently did not recognize it from his charts, or else had not been able to take accurate latitude sightings, for he gave it a new name—Lumley's Inlet. Shortly thereafter he was caught in the great current discharged from Hudson Bay, where "to our great admiration, we saw the sea falling down into the gulfe with a mighty overfall and roaring, and with divers circular motions like whirlpools."

In his journal he referred to this inlet as the Furious Overfall. Undaunted, fully expecting that the next voyage would be the one in which he could complete the passage, he wrote to his chief backer, William Sanderson, "the passage is most probable, the execution easie."

Thanks to the efforts of Richard Hakluyt, Davis's detailed accounts of these voyages, as well as the journals of the masters of Davis's other vessels, were available to Henry Hudson. Although they weren't printed until 1599 and 1601, they preceeded Hudson's departure in sufficient time for him to study them. Davis not only kept journals of his voyages, but made charts that were incorporated into two maps: one, the celebrated Molyneux globe; the other, a planisphere map printed in 1599. The Molyneux Globe was commissioned by William Sanderson and engraved and printed by Dutch cartographer Jodocus Hondius. It was the first globe ever made in England, and when completed in 1592 was much publicized. Either the globe or its variation in a map form, the Wright-Molyneux map of the world, must have been well known to Henry Hudson.

This map, containing "a true hydrographical description of so much of the world as hath beene hereto discovered, and come to our knowledge," was published in Richard Hakluyt's *Principal Navigations*. Though pri-

Figure 5-6. *Detail of a world map derived from the Molyneux Globe and published in Richard Hakluyt's* The Principal Navigations *in 1598-1600.*

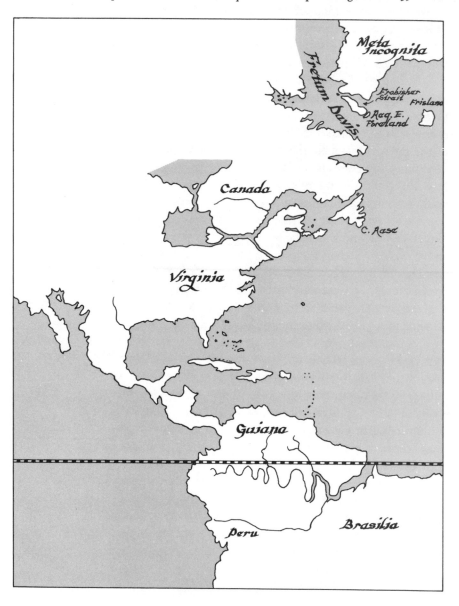

Charting the Sea of Darkness

marily intended to show the recent discoveries Sir Francis Drake had made in his 1577–1579 circumnavigation, and the voyages of Pedro Sarmiento de Gamboa and Thomas Cavandish, it also included information brought back by John Davis. One is immediately struck by the apparent accuracy of this map, especially when compared to George Best's map of Frobisher's expeditions. But though the general proportions and outlines have a fair degree of verisimilitude, even here there is much evidence of geographic uncertainty and misrepresentation.

On North America's northeastern coast, we see that the fictional island of Frisland is still retained from the original Zeno chart of 1558, while some remarkable changes were made to Greenland's geography. When Davis first approached the southern part of Greenland, he mistakenly thought there was a large island south of the mainland, the tip of which he called Cape Desolation. This is the configuration we see on the Wright-Molyneux map. But instead of its being captioned as Cape Desolation, it is called Queen Elizabeth Foreland, the name Frobisher gave to that large island on the northern side of Hudson Strait. The strait between the southern part of Greenland and the island to the south of it is labeled Frobisher's Strait, while the southern tip of Greenland is called Meta Incognita—the name Frobisher reserved for that part of Baffin Island south of his strait. Thus, the cartographer, in attempting to reconcile information from these two sets of voyages, has transposed some of the geography described by Frobisher on the western shore of Davis Strait over to its eastern shore, appending it to Greenland.

Delineations of Newfoundland and its environs—the Gulf of St. Lawrence, Belle Isle Strait, and the River of St. Lawrence—demonstrate a definite familiarity with the region. Newfoundland is depicted as a single large island with deep indentations; earlier maps showed it as a group of islands. Its two labels, Cabo Raz (Cape Race) and Cabo Baccalaos (Cape Codfish), indicate the Portuguese origin of this portion of the map. The coast of Labrador is labeled: "This land discovered by Sebastian

Cabot for King Henry VII, in the year 1497." There are several deep indentations at its northern end—then nothing. The deepest indraught is Cumberland Strait. Lumley's Inlet is not present, but the Furious Overfall is. The map ends here, for that is where the known world ended. North America's northern boundary is missing; only the east and west coastlines, the only portion of the continent that had been explored, are delineated. The possibility of a strait leading from the Atlantic to the Pacific is neither affirmed nor denied. The Great Lakes, amalgamated into a single, large body of water, empty into blank space, suggesting the possibility that they enter into a northern strait.

Evidently, Hudson's knowledge of this region depended on the Davis voyages, and approximated what is represented on the Wright-Molyneux map. On his 1608 voyage, after his attempt at the Northeast Passage failed, Hudson turned westward, "to make triall of that place called Lumley's Inlet, and the 'furious over-fall' by Captain Davis, hoping to runne into it an hundred leagues, and to returne as God should enable mee."

George Weymouth

In 1602, within a year of the publication of the journals of John Davis's voyages, George Weymouth secured the support of the English East India Company to finish what Davis had started. "So confident was he of success, that in case of failure he waived all claim to pay or renumeration."

Weymouth arrived at Davis Strait, then sailed diagonally north and west toward the American shore, hoping to find the continuation of open water that Davis had seen. If necessary, he was prepared to overwinter so as to have a second chance the following year. But by the time he reached 68°53', his crew refused to go any farther, and Weymouth was forced to retreat south. He entered Hudson Strait at its northern side, and in his own words, "sailed an hundred leagues west and by south" into the strait.

Hudson had James Rosier's journal of George Weymouth's 1605 voyage, but he did not have Weymouth's logbook for the 1602 voyage in which he had entered Hudson Bay.[13] Hudson doubtless had heard of Captain Weymouth's exploits, and entreated Peter Plancius to obtain the logbook for him. Plancius was not convinced that the route to Cathay lay to the northwest, believing that it was more likely to be found to the northeast, past Nova Zembla; still, he obliged his friend "in fairness to investigating of new matters."

Greenland

Greenland continued to stymie mariners and cartographers alike. Whether it was completely surrounded by water, or attached at its northern end to Asia, was still undetermined. Even the latitude of its southern extremity, which had been coasted and charted by Davis and other voyagers, was shown differently on various charts. The almost continuous presence of cloud banks and fog made the taking of latitude observations very sporadic. Furthermore, strong and contrary currents along its shores produced errors in dead-reckoning position. For the most part, the delineation of Greenland was still based on the Engroneland of the Zeno brothers—unchanged from their voyage in 1380.

In 1625 the Reverend Samuel Purchas published a treatise, written by Greenlander Iver Boty, whose title reveals the source of Henry Hudson's information, and how he came to receive it:

A Treatise of Iver Boty a Gronlander, translated out of Norsh language into High Dutch, in the yeere 1560. And after out of High Dutch into Low Dutch, by William Barentson of Amsterdam, who was chiefe Pilot aforesaid. The same copie in High Dutch is in the hands of Jodocus Hondius, which I have seene. And this was translated out of Low Dutch by Master William Stere, Marchant, in the yeere 1608, for the use of me Henry Hudson. William Barentsons Booke is in the hands of Master Peter Plantius, who lent the same unto me.

A small portion of the treatise is sufficient to give an idea of the fragmentary nature of the information Hudson had at his disposal.

IMPRIMIS, it is reported by men of wisedome and understanding borne in Gronland, that from Stad, in Norway, to the east part of Island [Iceland], called Horn-nesse, is seven dayes sayling right west.

   Item, if you goe from Bergen in Norway, the course is right west, till you bee south of Roke-ness in Island, and distant from it thirteene miles, or leagues. And with this course you shall come under that high land, that layeth in the east part of Groneland, and is called Swafster. A day before you come there, you shall have sight of a high mount, called Huit-sarke; and betweene Whitsarke and Groneland lyeth a head-land, called Hernoldus Hooke; and thereby lyeth an haven, where the Norway merchant ships were wont to come; and is called Sound Haven.

   Item, somewhat more east, toward the ice mountayne, lyeth a high land called Corse Hought, upon which they hunt white beares, but not without the bishop's leave, for it belongeth to the cathedrall church. And from thence more easterly, men see nothing but ice and snow, both by land and water.

   Item, in Groneland runneth great streames, and there is much snow and ice: but it is not so cold as it is in Island or Norway. All this before written was done by one Iver Boty, borne in Groneland, a principall man in the Bishop's Court, who dwelt there many yeeres, and saw and knew all these places. [14]

Conclusion

As a result of Henry Hudson's 1609 voyage, Holland lay claim to a large portion of North America. Although slow to start, Dutch colonization eventually extended all the way from Delaware, up to and including Penobscot Bay, Maine. Dutch dominance over this vast territory lasted well into the second half of the seventeenth century. Gradually, through treaties with England, this domain contracted to the area we now think of as New Netherland — Delaware, New Jersey, Pennsylvania, New York, and Connecticut.

At first, it might seem that Hudson failed. He discovered no new continents, revealed no passages between oceans, and never realized his goal of finding a northern route to the Indies. But taken collectively, Hudson's voyages were a great achievement. Uncompromising in his conviction that a passage could be found, he explored the Arctic region of the western hemisphere in all directions, to the farthest limit of a solid ice barrier. True, others had led the way, but only Henry Hudson explored the Arctic in its entirety. It was Hudson who proved, if only by negation, what was navigable. Unlike Columbus, who voyaged in southern waters, powered by balmy trade winds, Hudson sailed through vicious cold, blinding snow, treacherous ice, enveloping fog, and unknown currents. Yet he persevered almost to the death in his quest to achieve what he had undertaken, or, as he put it, "to give reason wherefore it will not be."

Appendix One
The *Half Moon*

From her construction in a Dutch East India Company (V.O.C.) shipyard until her likely demise in the Far East less than a decade later, little is certain about the ship that carried Henry Hudson to America in 1609. No contemporary paintings or engravings were made of the *Half Moon*, nor did shipwrights use blueprints when they built her in 1608.

But by studying Dutch construction methods, contemporary literature, and V.O.C. records—which include the *Half Moon*'s construction order—one can deduce her lines and her rigging and sail plans, as did the builders of a replica *Half Moon* in 1988.

Two main sources provide information on ship design in Hudson's time. One is a superbly illustrated 144-page manuscript written in 1586 by Matthew Baker, an English master shipbuilder who relates the critical dimensions of several ships. The second is Josephum Furttenbach's 1629 *Architectura Navalis*, which discusses in great detail a Dutch ship he saw in Genoa. The ship, which had completed a remarkably quick voyage from Amsterdam, had been built in 1628, and is close to the type of ship Hudson would have sailed. Furttenbach's description is complemented by illustrations showing forward and aft views of ships both in and out of the water.

Both books show a ship with a broad, flat floor. Called Vlie boats, they are described in van Meteren's *Historie der Nederlanden* as being flat-bottomed yachts, built to ease the difficult navigation of the sandy, shallow entrance to the Zuyder Zee (called the Vlie), which lies between the island of Vlieland and Texel on the mainland.

The Dutch stayed with these flat bottoms even for oceangoing ships sailing in foreign waters. Without the slack bilges of typical vessels, a Dutch ship could carry some 30 percent more cargo than would be hinted at by its overall size, a decided advantage when it came to paying duty.

At the time the *Half Moon* was taking shape in a V.O.C. shipyard, England and the Dutch were fierce commercial rivals—with the Dutch holding the upper hand. Holland's fleet of 1,680 merchant ships not only outnumbered England's 350, but those ships were superior in sailing ability, an advantage noted by the Earl of Northumberland, who complained: "Holland has so many and are so fast, that if we ever went to war, England would certainly lose."

Dutch ships were faster than English ships primarily because they were lighter and narrower. At 47 pounds per cubic foot, the tightly spaced oak frames of English ships provided strength—but also added substantial weight. Dutch ships, on the other hand, not only used much wider spacing between frames, but also used lighter wood such as pine for topside planking. All structural members on Dutch ships were graduated in thickness; the higher they were, the smaller and lighter they became. On larger ships it wasn't unusual to have clinker-built (lapstrake) topmost strakes to reduce weight while maintaining strength.

Early seventeenth-century Dutch construction methods were governed by rules of proportion that included a stipulation that the ratio of keel length to the width of the ship was always 3:1. Keel length was established as ending forward of the "touch," where the stem is scarfed to the keel. If one knows the width of the vessel, the keel length is automatically known, and vice versa. The Dutch measured a ship's length between stern and stem, its width to the inside of the planking, and its depth to the top of the keelson. Another rule called for one-half-inch thickness of keel for every foot of beam. Proportions of the spars were also based on the ship's beam.

For convenience, ships were built with

the keel set horizontally, with the frames set plumb. (English ships were built with the keel laid parallel to the waterline.) When the ship was afloat, the frames thus raked aft. It was not an exaggerated rake, for there was little drag to the keel, and the ship tended to set down by the bow due to the forces acting upon it while under sail. The mainmast was set at right angles to the keel, close to the midsection, which was the exact middle of the waterline. Computer analysis shows that this midsection was the center of buoyancy and center of gravity through all ranges of load—without changing the sailing characteristics of the vessel. This eased loading, since the vessel's trim was always maintained.

Some Dutch practices arose from necessity rather than preference. The archaic Dutch word for spars is *rondhout*, which literally translates into "round wood." Because of the expense of importing the larger timber necessary to build square or octagonal mast sections, Dutch ships featured round, tapered spars, with no hounds, squaring, or octagonals at the deck level.

In profile, though Dutch ships had a tremendous amount of sheer, decks were kept straight—unlike today's common practice of following the sheer's sweep. Our modern eye has a difficult time getting used to this, but these straight decks were eminently functional. In battle, with gunports in line and guns on the same level, they could be easily handled and interchanged if needed. The level decks could also be easily flooded if necessary, reducing the risk of explosion and fire.

In all ships of this period, hulls were strengthened by the "corrugated" surface produced by the tumblehome and reverse tumblehome. Narrow decks at the height of the tumblehome added additional strength by creating an egg-like structure in the transverse section. The combination of straight decks and steep sheer on Dutch ships allowed the wales and planking to be set in one direction relative to the frame, while clamps, decking, and ceiling planking were parallel to the waterline in another direction. This triangulation further

reinforced the hull—one reason Dutch ships lasted so much longer and could be built with much less wood than their English counterparts.

With their flat bottoms and shallow keels, Dutch ships made a great deal of leeway, and with no centerboard or leeboards to counteract this, the amount of lateral slippage could be as much as 15 or 20 degrees. Close hauled, under a fair gale, ships of this period were capable of speeds no greater than three knots. Performance improved as the wind moved aft, with the best speeds of seven knots achieved in a following wind. On the average though, in a transatlantic crossing, a ship like the *Half Moon* had a speed of three and a half knots.

Unique among contemporary shipbuilders, Dutch boatwrights of Hudson's time used the tangent arc system. Crucial to this system is a midsection in the vertical plane through the ship in which a number of arcs are tangent. These lines are either parallel to the waterline or parallel to the keel. The midsection line is very important, for the shape of the ship is determined either by reducing the ship's width or raising its sections. Not surprisingly, these are called narrowing and raising lines and are shown in profile and overhead views.

Curvature of the stem was tangent to the keel, with its center located along a line vertical to the keel, usually corresponding with the beginning of the forecastle. All were drawn with tangent arcs. When an arc needed extending, a line perpendicular to the tangent at another location was extended and a new arc struck. Any arc can be found from perpendicular tangents by knowing only two points. If there is no tangent, then any three points can define any specific arc.

Everything is related to that midsection in the vertical plane and to arcs from that plane at different heights at critical points such as rabbet location, maximum beam location, deck wale (point of inflection, where tumblehome starts), and zenith line. The length of radii of these arcs is determined by general proportional rules.

In designing the frames, rising and narrowing lines automatically define the shape by themselves, with no mathematics or any subdivision proportions. Ordinates from these lines are simply plotted directly onto the lofting floor, and arc centers for the frames are determined by tangential rules. All that's needed is a straightedge and a compass. Even deck beams are a segment of a circle determined by an arc. In contrast, the English system used constantly changing proportions, to which one had to continually apply mathematical rules to determine where the arcs change; in the Dutch system, everything is automatic.

Dutch builders abandoned the system after 1638 because of mathematical discoveries that allowed builders to calculate areas within a complex curve, or volumes of a curved surface. Other mathematical and physical concepts provided by Isaac Newton improved the ability to project the physical characteristics of a shape.

The tangent arc system:
1. Establish defined points by transferring half breadths at the centerline, rabbet, floor, deck wale, and maximum beam, and heights of the zenith, castles' wale, waist-tree, gunwale, upper deck, deck wale, gun sill wale, orlop deck, maximum beam, floor, rabbet, and keel. 2. Extend beam at maximum beam. 3. Extend plane at zenith. 4. Construct perpendicular bisector to chord between deck wale and maximum beam. 5. Extend bisector to find the center of great arc. 6. Strike great arc from deck wale down. 7. Extend radian from great arc center through deck wale to intersect zenith plane. 8. Strike top timber arc from deck wale up to height of hull at that station (in this case the waist-tree). 9. Construct perpendicular bisector to chord between rabbet and floor point. 10. Extend bisector to centerline to find rising arc center. 11. Strike rising arc from rabbet to floor plan. 12. Draw radian from rising arc center to floor. 13. Floor arc is found along line 10–12 when side of radian tangent at floor point is equidistant from great arc. This means radian from great arc center and radian from rising arc center intersect at 13, giving center of floor arc, which is tangent to the great arc and the rising arc, even when rising arc becomes a straight line or a curve.

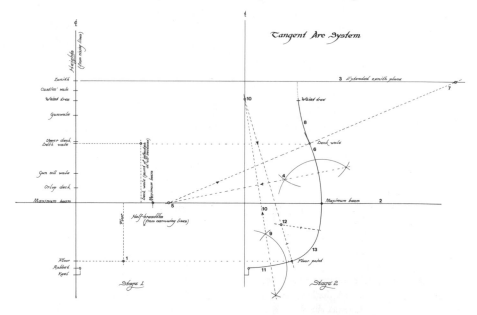

Charting the Sea of Darkness

The Dutch were pioneers in the development of the tangent arc system, yet they abandoned it after these discoveries, preferring to use blueprints by this new method. It is interesting to note the cyclical nature of events—for now, computers use the tangent arc system in large ship design. Our technology has finally caught up with what was already in practice centuries ago.

ORIGINAL HALF MOON

Specifications for the original *Half Moon* are sparse and subject to interpretation. V.O.C. documents show that she was built in Amsterdam in 1608. The V.O.C. built its ships with German and Danish lumber, hiring shipwrights to work under company supervision, a practice the company continued until it went out of business in the 1790s.

Since the original *Half Moon* was designed using the tangent arc system there were no blueprints (and since espionage from competitors was common, this absence carried an added benefit). The V.O.C. contract gave Hudson a vessel of about thirty lasts burden, the last being a measure of volume. However, port records indicate that Hudson's ship was closer to 40 lasts, a difference amounting to about 60 to 80 English tons.

But this still does not give us the *Half Moon's* dimensions: Different combinations of numbers can produce the same result. Furthermore, rules for determining lasts and tonnage—both in Holland and England—changed constantly, as did the methods by which a ship's dimensions was determined. Even within Holland there was no uniformity, with each of the seven provinces using its own system for measuring lasts. It wasn't until 1693, when the V.O.C. hired Peter van Dam to review its documents and bring order to chaos, that a consistent code for constructing and managing ships was established. His results were published as *The Writings of the East India Company.*

In sorting through the company's material, van Dam found the *Half Moon's* construction order. The *Half Moon* was 70 feet long, measured from sternpost to stem at the deck, with a beam of 16 feet, measured inside the ceiling planking; the depth of the hold was 8 feet. It is not certain whether the depth measurement was taken from the top of the keelson to the underside of the deck beams, but this is a reasonable assumption since the object of the measurement was to determine cargo-carrying capacity. The construction order further added that the vessel have a cabin aft the mizzenmast, like that on a large ship.

Its rig and sail plan—which likely allowed the square-rigged *Half Moon* to sail within five points on either side of the wind—can be deduced from various comments made in Robert Juet's journal of the *Half Moon's* 1609 voyage. Her rig was typical of the period, consisting of a square foresail and topsail on the foremast and foretopmast, square mainsail and topsail on the mainmast and main topmast, lateen sail on the mizzenmast, and a spritsail hung from the bowsprit—a sail area of some 2,800 square feet.

Her builders added waist-boards and waist-trees, removable railings between the sterncastle and forecastle in the waist of the ship. The waist-boards were set up temporarily in the space between the gunwale and the waist-tree to keep heavy seas from breaking onto the ship, and for protection in case of Indian attacks.

FATE OF THE VESSEL

The 1609 voyage to "the Great River of the Mountains" ended with the *Half Moon's* return to Dartmouth, England, on November 7, 1609. Hudson was forbidden to leave the country and from any further exploration for the Dutch. With renewed energy toward finding the Northwest Passage, the Muscovy Company quickly hired Hudson for another voyage. It was not until after his departure from England that the *Half Moon* was permitted to return to her owners in Holland.

News of Hudson's exploits in the New World reached Amsterdam ahead of the ship. Dutch merchants, quick to realize the potential for profits in Indian fur trade, immediately sent a vessel guided by some 1609 crewmembers back to the Hudson River. Within a few years the Dutch had established forts and were involved in a burgeoning fur trade. The *Half Moon* was not part of that trade, and was instead re-outfitted for service in the East Indies.

Early in May of 1611, the *Half Moon* sailed for India under the command of Captain Laureus Reale, a Dutchman. Her fate after that date is a matter of speculation. Varying accounts have her listed as part of a fleet of four ships wrecked off Mauritius in 1611, sighted in Mauritius and elsewhere after 1611, disappearing off the coast of Sumatra in 1616, and set afire in 1618 along with other Dutch ships by English merchants in Jakarta harbor.

It is likely the *Half Moon* was destroyed by the British, if not in Jakarta in 1618, then within a few years and in that region. The once friendly rivalry between Holland and England gave way to open hostility in their competition for world trade. In the North Sea and

off the coast of Greenland, the Dutch grew wealthy taking large quantities of herring— herring the English felt came from her waters. Farther from home, the English, Dutch, Spanish, and Portuguese competed for the lucrative trade in the Spice Islands, and the Malay Archipelago became a frequent battleground.

In 1617, a dispute over ownership of the island of Pularoon resulted in the Dutch capture of an English vessel. Most of the sailors were put in chains, and their captain, Nathaniel Courthope, was thrown into the sea. The hatred and indignation sparked in England by this incident intensified after a Dutch massacre at Amboyna in 1623. The Dutch shared the island, which they had taken from the Portuguese in 1605, with English merchants. Fearing an English conspiracy to have them expelled from their settlements on the island, the Dutch took a number of Englishmen prisoner and tortured them into confessing such a plot existed. This gave the Dutch merchants an excuse to behead twelve Englishmen.

In these waters, beyond any measure of influence by treaties, and far from the control of any government, open warfare existed. And it was here that the *Half Moon* likely fell victim to combat.

1909 *HALF MOON* REPLICA FOR THE HUDSON-FULTON CELEBRATION

In 1909 the Dutch gave a replica of the *Half Moon* to the United States for the Hudson-Fulton Celebration in New York. The citizens of Amsterdam wished "to assist in keeping before the coming generations of Americans the memorable fact their glorious river (Hudson) was discovered, and New Amsterdam founded by men bent on discovery, who hailed from Amsterdam and sailed under the Netherlands tricolor and badge of the 'Oost-Indische Compagnie.' "

The event also honored Robert Fulton, who 100 years before had successfully used steam power to propel a boat. Within four years his invention became a practical mode of

transportation, and by 1807 the steamboat *Clermont* made a 150-mile trip up the Hudson River in thirty-two hours. The world's first seagoing steamship, the *Phoenix*, made a passage from New York to Philadelphia in 1809.

By linking Henry Hudson's passage up the Hudson River with the accomplishments of Robert Fulton, the New York Commission promoted the river's role in the momentous change from the age of sail to that of mechanical power.

When the Dutch undertook the job of building a *Half Moon* replica for this celebration, they encountered the problems previously discussed in trying to determine the vessel's shape and dimensions—the lack of blueprints chief among them. Manuscripts we now have access to, such as Matthew Baker's 1586 illustrated work on ship design, were unavailable in 1909. And although the Dutch did have Furttenbach's 1629 *Architectura Navalis*, they didn't know how to use it.

This lack of knowledge led to a fundamental misunderstanding during construction over references to a "vlock line" (flat line) in early drawings. The flat line is one of the major lines used as a reference for the tangent arc system. It refers to a basic breadth applied to the relatively flat and straight floor sections, and has nothing to do with flatness or chine construction. As a result, the 1909 *Half Moon* contained a major flaw: a hard chine running half the length of the ship at the turn of the bilge.

Blueprints for the 1909 *Half Moon* were based on two things: the appropriate size of forty lasts and an inventory from William Barents's expedition in 1593 that was used as a guideline for the ship's contents. While this gave the Dutch figures on the required amount of provisions and gunpowder necessary for a voyage, it did not provide even the general dimensions of the ship. It wasn't until the 1920s that Peter van Dam's manuscript containing this information was found.

With these extremely limited sources, builders created a set of plans by first making a half-model, then taking the frame shapes from it. This use of a half-model, strictly an American practice, shows how little those builders knew of their own shipbuilding heritage. The model is presently in Amsterdam's Scheepvaart Museum and shows all the framework (drawn on the half-model), the position of the ports and gun ports, and the aberrant chine construction. Despite these difficulties they produced a vessel quite similar to the original, though slightly smaller than what we now know it to have been.

Though capable of making the passage on its own, the new *Half Moon* was placed aboard the S.S. *Soestdijk* of the Holland America Line and transported as deck cargo to New York. She was sailed around the harbor and the Hudson River, and took part in ceremonies and re-enactments of the events of 300 years earlier. On one occasion, part of the *Half Moon*'s bowsprit was torn out when she collided with the reproduction of Fulton's *Clermont*. But sailors turned this into an advantage by reducing the damaged bowsprit into myriad carved reproductions of the ship, which were eagerly purchased by souvenir collectors.

FATE OF THE SECOND *HALF MOON*

When the festival ended, the *Half Moon* was towed across the Hudson River to Palisades Interstate Park, where she lay at anchor as a tourist attraction. In the spring of 1924 she was once again moved—this time to the town of Cohoes, on the Hudson River about six miles north of Albany, where in 1609 Henry Hudson gave up on any further exploration of the river.

The *Half Moon* was hauled out of the water to her final resting place at East Side Park. Over the years, interest waned; there were fewer visitors, and money for maintenance dried up. Eventually she became a derelict—used by vagrants for shelter, and

youngsters for parties. Fires aboard were a constant problem, and one on July 22, 1934, destroyed her.

But the *Half Moon* did not completely end her existence in Cohoes. Chief historian for construction of the 1909 *Half Moon* was Professor G.C.E. Crona, a man obsessed with his work. After the ship was built, he continued his research by designing new half-models. Crona did not make the models himself, but used F. Baay, chief modelmaker at the Prinz Hendrik Maritime Museum in Rotterdam. Baay published a book in the 1940's on how he felt the *Half Moon* would have looked.

The pair knew, for example, to avoid

the chine construction in their more recent models. When the writings of Peter van Dam were found, they used this new information to lengthen the ship and broaden it. They also changed the relationship of the whipstaff and the mizzenmast, moving the mizzenmast aft the whipstaff and stepping it on deck.

1989 HALF MOON

On July 23, 1988, shipwrights laid the keel for a new *Half Moon*, the centerpiece of the 1989 New Netherland Festival. Organized by North Carolina physician Andrew A. Hendricks, the festival sought to recognize Dutch contributions to America. The Dutch colony of *Nieu Nederlandt* covered an area of what is now New York, New Jersey, Connecticut, Delaware, and Pennsylvania, with the first settlements founded by the Dutch between 1624 and 1648.

After meeting with Dutch and American shipbuilders, Dr. Hendricks hired Nicholas S. Benton, an expert in the rigging and design of traditional sailing vessels, to create blueprints for the new *Half Moon* and supervise her construction.

After reviewing blueprints used for the 1909 *Half Moon*, with the chine and other odd detailing, Benton sensed that something was wrong and that further research would be needed. He and Hendricks met in Lelystad, Holland, with Wilhelm Voss, then building a replica of the *Batavia*, a 1628 Dutch ship. Voss confirmed Benton's suspicion about the chine construction and some of the other lines in the 1909 *Half Moon*. It became clear that if the new *Half Moon* was to be historically accurate, it would have to be designed by the tangent arc system.

The extremely limited information on the *Half Moon*'s dimensions on which to apply the tangent arc system presented some problems. All that was known was her cargo-carrying capacity (40 lasts), and her length, width, and depth. There was also the Furttenbach book with illustrations and a blueprint for a similar ship. Benton used Furttenbach's information in conjunction with the tangent arc system to develop the lines for the ship in the latter's book, then extrapolated data to produce the *Half Moon*. It became apparent that the lack of details in the book was strictly a matter of economy. All the necessary information was there, and by applying the tangent arc system to the known critical dimensions, a *Half Moon* true to its original lines could be designed.

Of course, mathematics, proportions, and rules alone do not create a fine vessel; the designer must identify with the ship. In blueprinting the *Half Moon*, a certain amount of empathy was required to produce a truly Dutch ship. Furttenbach, for example, did not provide all the points for ordinates of the forecastle, and some had to be interpolated. Since an infinite number of different curves could be made to fit those few points, it is incumbent on the designer to arrive at the best one.

With the designing and blueprinting finished, Ernie Cowan Enterprises of Mayville, New York, took the plans for the new *Half Moon*, shaped the wood, and brought the ship to life. Ironwork for the vessel was custom forged by Mitchell FitzGibbon, whose blacksmith shop is in Westfield, New York; sails were made by Dave Bierig Sailmakers of Northeast, Pennsylvania. The new vessel was assembled in Albany near a spot where Hudson had anchored 378 years before. Albany, with its predominant Dutch history and architecture, is also the site of the first Dutch trading post of Fort Nassau, established in 1614, as well as Fort Orange, one of Holland's early settlements, established in 1624.

As with the original *Half Moon*, oak was used for the keel, frames, deadwood, lower planking, and wales, while upper planking, ceiling, and decks were of pine and fir. In Hudson's time the Dutch did not have access to

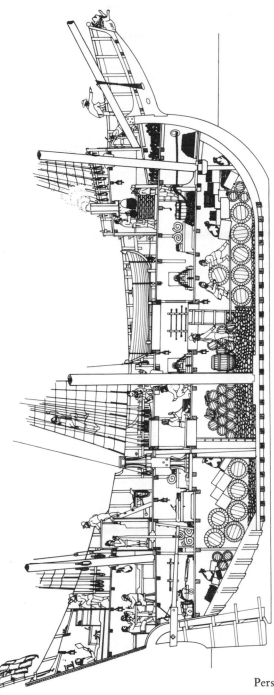

Perspective on the limited ac-
commodations aboard the *Half
Moon*, prepared by Nicholas
Benton.

tropical hardwoods and made blocks and dead-eyes of either ash or elm. Sails were flax, and the rope rigging made of hemp.

In the 1989 *Half Moon*, some concession to modern technology was made to cut costs and ease maintenance. Rather than using the traditional method of shaping them from single, large timbers, frames, keel, deadwood, and deckbeams were laminated from oak planks and bonded with epoxy resin to reduce the potential for dry rot. Sails for the new *Half Moon* were made from Duradon, a synthetic manufactured in Scotland that looks and feels exactly like canvas, yet is softer and easier to furl. All standing rigging was a composite of polyester treated with a net dip and with stainless steel wire insertions to eliminate stretch.

The *Half Moon* was launched on the Hudson River in Albany on June 10, 1989, and is now berthed near New York Harbor in Jersey City, New Jersey.

Appendix Two
North Atlantic Currents

Major surface currents of the North Atlantic. Cold-water currents are indicated by solid lines; warm-water currents by dashed lines.

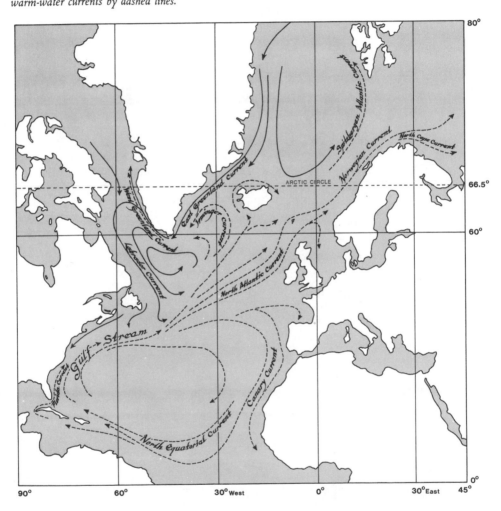

Appendix Three
Sixteenth-Century Distances and Boat Speeds

Sea League (Portuguese in origin)

Portuguese Measure

1 **league** = 4 Roman miles = 6,472 yards

1 **Roman mile** = 1,000 paces = 1,618 yards

17.5 leagues = 1 degree of latitude = 60 nautical miles

English Measure

1 **league** = 3 nautical miles = 6,080 yards

    20.0 leagues = 1 degree of latitude = 60 nautical miles

Statute mile (presently used in England and U.S.A.):

    1 mile = 1,760 yards = 5,280 feet

Nautical mile (presently used at sea):

    1 mile = 2,026.6 yards = 6,080 feet = 1 minute of arc of
    meridianal circle of earth (60' = 1°)

Knot = Unit of speed to cover 1 nautical mile in 1 hour

The average distance covered by sixteenth-century ships was approximately three to four miles per hour, or 84 nautical miles a day.

Endnotes

CHAPTER ONE

1. Nordenskiöld, 1973, p. 72. This quotation from Lactantius was used 12 centuries later at the Council of Salamanca to show the folly of Columbus' belief that the east could be reached by sailing west.

2. Cathay, popularized by Marco Polo, was the medieval name for China, although it usually applied only to that part of China north of the Yangtze River.

3. Magellan never lived to know the glory of his accomplishment, for part way through the voyage he was killed on the island of Mactan in the Philippines. Of the five ships that started out, only one, the *Victoria*, made it back to Spain in September 1522, completing the first circumnavigation of the world.

CHAPTER TWO

1. The streams Cabot encountered were those of the Labrador Current. Its velocity is scarcely more than 0.5 knot. The Gulf Stream the Spanish met at the Strait of Florida, has a velocity of 3.0 knots.

2. To measure the inclination, or dip, of the earth's magnetic field, a different kind of compass was used than the north-pointing magnetic compass. Whereas the needle of the magnetic compass swings horizontally, the needle of the dip compass was mounted to swing vertically. A scale provided graduated measurements in degrees below the horizon. In the journal of this voyage (1607) the measurement of the magnetic dip is mentioned only a few times, but in the 1608 voyage, Henry Hudson frequently recorded the amount of dip. In his last two voyages, Hudson took no measurements of the dip, evidently feeling them to be of little value.

3. Throughout the journal, there are shifts between the use of "I" and "we" as well as changes from a descriptive narrative of the voyage to a factual keeping of a ship's logbook. Samuel Purchas attributes this to its being written partly by John Playse (the section from May 1 through July 10) and partly by Henry Hudson (July 11th to September 15th). Purchas claims to have obtained firsthand information about this dual authorship. G.M. Asher, however, believes it was written entirely by John Playse, who made frequent use of notes from Hudson's journal. Asher attributes the occasional use of "I" instead of "we" to Playse forgetting to make the change when transcribing the notes. To me, the consistency of tone and style suggests single authorship.

4. In the sixteenth and early seventeenth centuries, any wind was termed a gale, with different descriptive terms for its strength. The word "breeze" was relegated to that wind found close along shore which results from differences in temperature between the sea and land. Today's mariner describes the force of wind in a continuing series of strengths from light breeze, through moderate, fresh and strong breeze until its

strength is gale-force at 28 to 33 knots. The designation of strength continues to storm-force and finally hurricane-force. It wasn't until 1806 that Admiral Sir Francis Beaufort devised a numerical scale for providing a standard reference for wind strengths.

5. It is the practice of mariners to account the beginning of a day at 12 noon, running until noon the next day, for this is the time when celestial observations of meridian passage of the sun are taken for determining position at sea.

6. It is difficult to determine the exact location of these places. The almost continuous presence of rain, snow, or fog frequently made it impossible to take celestial observations, and currents continually set them off course.

7. To "come about" is to change the heading of the ship so the wind moves from one side to the other—the same as "tacking," or "casting about," the term used in the journal. The position of sails have to be changed, with some "cast off" and others brought in.

8. Groneland was the name many cartographers used to designate Greenland.

9. Newland is the same as Spitzbergen—a group of islands astride the 80th parallel that have undergone many changes of name since Barents, the first to discover it in 1596, called it Greenland. It wasn't until 1613 that the name of Spitzbergen was ascribed to it by the publisher Hessel Gerard. Dutch geographers however, called it Nieuland, which later was changed by the English to King James his Newland.

10. The journal for this date is repeated, but in greater detail is given here.

11. It appears they were engaged in a little wishful thinking here, taking this improvement in climate to be a confirmation of the theory of Thorne and others that as the Pole was approached after passing through a cold zone, the weather would become warmer.

12. A "scant wind" is one coming from forward of the ship—scantly filling the sails. Under these conditions, the ship is sailing as close to the wind as she can. A ship is running "before the wind" or "with the wind" when the wind is coming from behind her. This is the most advantageous wind for a square-rigged vessel. A wind that is halfway between the two, slightly aft the beam, is called a "large wind." Here, the ship is neither by the wind nor running with it, but between the two—a quartering wind.

13. The grampus is a small, black, fierce variety of toothed whale, widely distributed in northern seas. It is closely related to, and much resembles a dolphin. The grampus is characterized by teeth in its lower jaw only, and has a length of nine to thirteen feet. Its great size, strength, and courage, combined with the formidable toothed jaw, makes it the dread of seals on which it preys.

14. Vogel Hooke (Voegl-hoeck) or Bird Cape, was discovered by Wm. Barents. It is the northwest point of Prince Charles Foreland Island, about halfway up the west coast of Spitzbergen.

15. The morse, a sea-horse, or walrus, takes its name from the Lapp word *Morsa.*

16. They were far enough north at this point (somewhere above 80°N latitude) to be able to see the sun throughout the night as well as during the day; its "north meridian" being that part of the sun's travel on the "back side" of the earth.

17. On this particular day there seems to be an error of one full degree in latitude observation. Whether it originated on Henry Hudson's part, or was

the result of transcription from the journal, is uncertain. However, in the context of Hudson's description of land sighted, and the track of the Hope-well for the next few days, there is little doubt about his true latitude. His stated latitude is left unchanged as printed in *Purchas His Pilgrimes*.

18. Mirages are common in the Arctic regions during the summertime, occuring whenever there is a mass of warm air over the cold water. Rays of light passing through layers of air of different temperatures in the atmosphere are bent backward toward the Earth, producing varying images or illusions. In some cases, the thin edge of an island on the distant horizon is expanded upward, appearing as a wall or rampart. Other times, one may see an inverted image on top of and separated from the primary image by a space between the two. These layers of air, when moved by the breeze in undulating waves, look like peaks of mountains and valleys. Temperature changes in the atmosphere can also make objects, such as islands or icebergs, which are beyond the real horizon, visible, and appear to be closer than they are. In this instance, the mirage showed Henry Hudson that land continued beyond the visible horizon.

19. A veering wind changes its direction in a clockwise fashion, that is, from north to east, or south to west. Its opposite, a backing wind, changes direction in a counterclockwise manner, that is, from north to west, or east to north.

20. The phenomenon of Arctic mirages (described in Note 19) enabled Hudson and his crew to determine from the sky when ice was present before it could actually be seen or encountered.

21. Cherie's Island (74°30'N, 19E) was discovered in 1596 by Willem Barents, who named it Bear Island. When the island was visited by Stephen Bennet in 1603, he believed he had discovered a new island and named it after Sir Francis Cherie, one of the Muscovy Company members who sponsored his voyage. G. Hartwig's *The Polar and Tropical Worlds* (1875, pp.144,145) gives the following description of the island: "The greater part of Bear Island is a desolate plateau raised about 100 or 200 feet above the sea toward the south it terminates in a solitary hill to which the first discoverers gave the appropriate name of Mount Misery. The general character of the island is a monotony of stone and morass, with here and there a patch of snow, while the coasts have been worn by the action of waves into a variety of fantastic shapes."

22. This group of islands, situated roughly 200 miles north of Scotland, was visited by Irish seamen in the sixth and seventh centuries. At the beginning of the ninth century they were explored and colonized by Norse men. Its name, "Faeroes," is derived from the Danish word Faar, meaning sheep. These animals have flourished here for many centuries, nourished by the island's rich grass. Several times, Henry Hudson replenished his water supply at the Faeroe Islands.

CHAPTER THREE

1. Since true, or geographic, north is not the same as magnetic north, some of the northern countries produced compasses in which the magnetic needle was mounted on the compass card (the Flye) in alignment with the amount of magnetic variation. Thus, the needle pointed to magnetic north,

while the fleur-de-lis on the compass card indicated true north. This was fine for voyages confined to limited regions where the amount of variation did not change appreciably. Some compasses even had an arrangement where the position of the needle (pointing to magnetic north) could be changed according to the amount of local variation. On long voyages across the Atlantic, magnetic variation significantly increased westward as one sailed west and north; while in northern waters east of Ireland it became an increasingly easterly variation. To avoid confusion, English mariners began using a "meridianal compass," one in which the needle and the fleur-de-lis were in direct alignment.

2. They had some help from the Norwegian Current, a branch of the Gulf Stream that sets toward the northeast, following the trend of the coast. Its velocity is about 0.3 knot.

3. The fathom is a unit of measure of depth. One fathom equals six feet.

4. Monsters, sea serpents, fairy maids, merfolk are all part of sailor's folklore dating back to earliest recorded times. Though the origin of these merfolk has been attributed to poorly identified sightings of seals, walrus, and manatees, the mythology surrounding them suggests a much more deeply rooted tradition. Underlying the mermaid legend is the belief that for every being that exists on land, there is a counterpart at sea. Thus, there are sea horses, sea lions and sea folk, mermaids and mermen. The interest exhibited in this mermaid by Hudson's crew also may have had to do with the belief, common in tales of merfolk, that she was a creator of weather. They would have been looking for any omen of good or foul weather.

5. During the daytime the passage of the sun is south of the observer, with its meridian marked by the point of highest elevation in the sky. But at night, if one is far enough north to see it, the sun's passage is in the northern sky, with its meridian marked by the lowest point in the sky.

6. We may safely assume the missing words are "in accord." This may have been due to currents setting them off course, errors in their dead reckoning, or a combination of both. A possible reason for their dead reckoning being off is provided in Juet's journal (available to Purchas). Juet mentions that the magnetic variation, which the day before was twenty-two and a half degrees easterly, suddenly shifted to a variation of eleven and a quarter degrees easterly.

7. Hudson meant to say "rise" here, rather than "fall." In other places of the journal he correctly says that he took observations of the sun's meridian at its lowest point.

8. A flightshot is the distance an arrow can be shot from a longbow.

9. Hudson believed, as did other geographers and cartographers of the time, that he could sail through the Tartaria Sea unobstructed, then round the Cape of Tabin and sail south through the Strait of Anian, reaching China and Japan—thus completing the Northeast Passage route.

10. A betacle [bittacle] is the box or enclosed stand that holds the compass and is placed on deck near the helm. Our contemporary word "binnacle," used for the same thing, is but a corruption of the word "bittacle." Having to "light a candle in the betacle" is an indication that now they were far enough south in latitude as to no longer have the midnight sun brightening the sky throughout the night.

11. Dr. G. Hartwig, in his book *The Polar and Tropical Worlds*, has little positive to say about the Samoïedes. He describes them as a group of "barbaric, poor wretches . . . whose physical appearance is as wild as the country they inhabit." He goes on to say, "A common trait in the character of all Samoïedes is the gloomy view which they take of life and its concerns; their material world is as cheerless as that which surrounds them."

CHAPTER FOUR

1. The seven provinces to join the Union of Utrecht were Holland, Zeeland, Utrecht, Gelderland with Zutphen, Over-Yssel, Friesland, and Groningen with Drenthe.

2. When the Dutch West India Company was formed in 1621, its charter gave it a monopoly of trade in the Atlantic Ocean with all countries west of the Cape of Good Hope, and east of the Strait of Magellan. The charter also gave it authority to protect trade by granting the right to wage war on Spanish colonies and to prey on Spanish ships in the New World.

3. The Compagnie van Verre's principal members were Hassalaer, Carel, Dirk Van Os and Jan Poppes. Van Os and Poppes are signatories on Henry Hudson's contract with the Dutch East India Company.

4. The V.O.C. predated its counterpart in the West Indies, the Dutch West India Company. See Note 2 above.

5. Various accounts place the number of crew at 16, 18, and 20, though most likely, 16 was correct.

6. As part of the archives of the Dutch East India Companies, Hudson's journals and all other books and documents relating to this voyage were sold at public auction in 1821. The state legislature in New York, in an attempt to locate the buyers and retrieve these papers so important to its own history, sent a representative to Holland in 1841. But no records were kept of the buyers, and in the intervening years the documents became widely dispersed and could not be found. They have been missing ever since.

7. Robert Juet begins dating his journal using the Julian calendar (*the old account*), but quickly changes to the new style (*stilo novo*) of the Gregorian calendar. Prior to the time of the Julian calendar, the Roman Republican year was based on lunar reckoning, creating a year containing 366.25 days. But by 50 BC, the vernal equinox, which should have occurred late in March, fell some eight weeks later and it was clear that this error would only continue to increase. To keep the calendar in phase with the seasons, Julius Caesar (mid-first century BC) abandoned the lunar calendar in favor of one based on the solar year. This created a year of 365.25 days, with one day every four years (leap year) added to correct the quarter-day increment. Though it was an improvement over the old system, it still created a year too long by 11 minutes and 14 seconds. Cumulatively, this amounted to 1.25 days in 200 years and 7 days in 1000 years. Pope Gregory XIII issued a new calendar reform in a bull in February 1582. A value of 365.2422 days was accepted for the year's length, with the centennial leap years eliminated. Though it differed from the Julian calendar by only 0.0078 days per year, it amounted to 3.12 days in 400 years and brought the calendar back into

better phase with the seasons. Due to religious conflicts between Protestants and Roman Catholics, the Gregorian calendar (which we now use) was not immediately accepted by many countries of the western world. The new style had been in use by France, Italy, Spain, Portugal, Luxemburg, and certain provinces of the Netherlands since 1582. By 1584 it was accepted by most of the German Roman Catholic states and Belgium. Britain did not accept the Gregorian calendar until September 2, 1752, starting that day as September 14, when there was exactly 11 days difference. Sweden adapted it in 1753 and Soviet Russia in 1918.

8. Exactly what Juet meant by "slake" is unclear. According to Llewelyn Powys, slake is a north country English word meaning an accumulation of mud or slime. From this he concludes Robert Juet observed a sunspot. If so, then he would be the first person to have seen and recorded this event, an honor history attributes to Thomas Hariot with his sunspot sighting one year later on December 8, 1610. There are some difficulties in accepting Powys interpretation. First, Juet would have had to make his observation with the naked eye. The telescope had been invented only the year before by a Dutch optician, Hans Lippershey, and a working model wasn't built until 1609 (by Galileo), the same year as the voyage. Nowhere in the journal (nor in that of the 1610 voyage) is any reference made to a telescope. Furthermore, the witnessing of the slake occurred at noontime when the sun was at its highest in the sky, and its apparent size was smallest. Had it been at sunrise or sunset, when refraction of the image of the sun through a much thicker layer of the earth's atmosphere makes it appear much larger, the possibility of his seeing a sunspot would be more plausible. Second, it would have been necessary to make some sort of filter, such as smoked glass, to look directly at the sun in order to avoid burning the retina. It is unlikely he did either of these, since there was no reason for doing so? Even if we are to suppose Juet saw a sunspot, we would also have to assume him to mention the discovery. He does not. It is much more likely that Juet was using slake to denote something other than an accumulation of mud or slime. Derived from the Old English word "slacian," slake also can mean "to diminish in activity, render less active, to reduce or lessen." The contemporary word "slack" in some senses replaces the earlier word "slake," though we still use the latter as in "slake one's thirst," or "slaked lime" (disintegration by the action of water). In this context the possibility of Juet's seeing a partial eclipse of the sun comes to mind. But as with the sunspot notion, an eclipse of the sun, even partial, would most assuredly have given rise to some further comment by Juet. The possibility of Juet's seeing a partial eclipse of the sun can be quickly dismissed. Through computer technology, motion of the planets can be checked back in time to find out whether there was an eclipse during the month of May, 1609. We find there was an annular eclipse on February 4, and a partial eclipse on July 30, but neither of these would have been visible anywhere in the region covered by their voyage. Therefore, we have to attribute some other meaning to slake. It has been suggested by meteorologist Charles Bosomworth, that in the context of "diminish in intensity," it is possible Juet was referring to some atmo-

spheric phenomenon. Perhaps in the course of taking sightings with the cross-staff the sun became obscured by cirrostratus clouds. This type of cloud creates a high, thin, transparent veil, and is usually accompanied by a solar halo. It signals the advent of an approaching warm front. Such clouds would have given Juet a large, diffuse image of the sun—not sufficiently vague to make it impossible to get an altitude reading—but certainly enough to make it difficult, and a great annoyance. This last interpretation—appearance of cirrostratus clouds—I believe best fits what Robert Juet meant by a slake of the sun.

9. See Chapter 3, Note 1.

10. A counterclockwise wind shift is said to be "backing," while a shift clockwise is "veering."

11. Busse Island is one of those mythical islands that filled the empty spaces on so many maps and charts of the seventeenth century. See Chapter 4, Epilogue, for a discussion of the origin of Busse Island.

12. Visibility of the stars was no longer masked by the brightness of the sky during the midnight sun.

13. Lay-a-trie is the procedure used to ease a ship in a storm by reducing sail (in this particular instance, the foresail) and bringing the tack (lower, windward corner of the sail) close aboard, the sheets close aft, and the helm tied close aboard. This makes the ship sail close to the wind. Should this fail, the mainsail would next be struck (taken in) and the same procedure used by mizzensail alone. If the storm should grow so strong that even this is too much for the ship, then all sail would be taken in and the ship left to lie-a-hull.

14. The bonnet is an additional piece of canvas laced to the foot (bottom edge) of the sail to increase the sail area, thus making it more effective in light winds.

15. In the sixteenth century, the North Star was not as close to the Pole as it is now. At that time, it described a circle around the North Pole of 3°30' radius. The star's location with regard to the North Pole was determined by its relationship to the two "guard" stars of the Little Dipper, Kochab (*Beta Ursae Minoris*) and Pherhad (*Gamma Ursae Minoris*). Since latitude is determined by the altitude of the North Star, these guard stars provided the proper values (taken from tables) to enable the navigator to make correct calculations.

16. It does not seem likely they would chase this vessel for twelve hours, just to speak with her. Rather, their intent was piracy. Here was a single, unprotected vessel that might yield some prize of commercial value. It has been suggested that Henry Hudson gained his competence as a mariner and navigator from his experience in preying on French vessels in the English Channel.

17. The difference between a heading and a course made good is the result of current and the amount of leeway (sideways movement) of the vessel, such as noted on the previous day. In this instance the amount of leeway was offset by the compass variation.

18. A ship in stays is headed directly into the wind. In this position the wind is on both sides of the sails bringing the vessel to a standstill.

19. The exact phrase used by Robert Juet is "and we steered away West Northwest, by our varyed compass." This means that the compass pointed toward magnetic north, and was not one of the corrected compasses which had the needle of the fly set at true

north. Later, on July 13, he gives the wind direction as being south "by our true [corrected] compass."

20. This would be the bright red star *Antares* in the constellation of Scorpio.

21. The sandglass measured a half hour. Each watch was eight glasses in length, or four hours.

22. A bowshot is the distance an arrow shot by a bow will travel.

23. A neap tide occurs just after the first and third quarters of the lunar month. At these times, the difference between high and low tides is smallest.

24. Cats were associated with witches and witchcraft. Evil deeds of witches were accomplished either by turning themselves into cats to achieve their ends in disguise, or by inflicting pain on cats, causing them to do the witch's bidding. Sailors believed witches were capable of stopping ships, diverting winds, or raising great storms. In Scotland, it was popularly believed that the defeat of the Spanish Armada was caused by witches from the Island of Mull in the Hebrides creating a great gale accompanied by black cats falling on the fleet. When the cat aboard the *Half Moon* began to exhibit strange behavior, it is little wonder it caused concern among the sailors.

25. John De Laet, in his *Nieuwe Werelt*, tells us that Hudson surmised that the strong current, numerous shoals, and sands here were caused by a large river discharging into the bay.

26. The grapnell is a small anchor with three or more prongs, used especially on small boats.

27. Maurits River was named after the Dutch Stadtholder Maurice, Prince of Orange. Maurice was a military leader of the United Provinces of the Netherlands in their war of independence from Spain. The Island of Mauritius in the Indian Ocean (now a British colony), was also named after Maurice when it was taken from the Portuguese (who called it Cerné) by the Dutch in 1598. In Hudson's time, the Mohican Indian name for the river was Muheakunnuk, or Mahakangéhtuc, meaning, "great waters constantly in motion." The Iroquois Indian name for it was Cahohátatéa. Henry Hudson called it the Great River, or Great River of the Steep Hills. Most Dutch maps called it the North River. The South River was what is now called the Delaware river.

28. *Description of the Country of the Samoeieds in Tartary lately brought under the dominion of the Mucovites. Translated from the Russian in the year 1609. Together with an account of the search and the discovery of the new passage or strait in the Northwest, to the kingdoms of China and Cathay. Also a memorial presented to the King of Spain, concerning the discovery and situation of the country called Australia Incognita.* Amsterdam: Hessel Gerritz, Bookseller. etc.

There were three editions of this treatise, more simply called *The Hudson Tract of 1612*: the first was printed in Dutch, the other two in Latin. Translations of all three can be found in Henry Murphy's *Henry Hudson in Holland* and in G.M. Asher's *Henry Hudson the Navigator*.

29. Isaac Le Maire eventually accomplished this, when in 1616 the expedition he promoted discovered two new passages around the southern tip of South America: the Straits of Le Maire, and Cape Horn.

30. Brereton in his *A Brief and True Relation of the Discoverie of the North Part of Virginia* wrote this on the naming of Cape Cod: "on account of the great number of cod found there," is well known. Following is the exact, and

complete description: ". . . in five or six houres absence, we had pestered our shipe so with Cod fish, that we threw numbers of them over-board againe: and surely, I am persuaded that in the moneths of March, April, and May, there is upon this coast, better fishing, and as in great plentie, as in Newfound-land: for the sculles of Mackerell, herrings, Cod, and other fish, that we dayl saw as we went and came from the shore, were wonderfull; and besides, the places where we tooke these Cods (and might in a few days have laden our shipe) were but in seven faddome [fathom] water, and within less than a league of the shore; where in Newfound-land they fish in fortie or fiftie faddome water, and far off."

CHAPTER FIVE

1. The Pinke was a fairly small (50-80 feet) vessel used in offshore fisheries of the Baltic and North Sea. Its distinguishing characteristic was the hull shape with its high, narrow transom and bulwarks carried out beyond the rudder, creating a long, false overhang. In the seventeenth century they were variously rigged as ships, brigantines, sloops, or ketches. Pinkies in this country, derived from these vessels, were schooner rigged; the two most well known types being the Essex, Connecticut, and the Eastport, Maine, pinkies.

2. This indicates that the compass they carried aboard was of the adjustable type that allowed compensation for the amount of magnetic variation in the region in which they were sailing. In this case it was set to read in degrees true.

3. Frobisher Strait was a geographic misconception carried on maps at this time. The strait supposedly separated the southern tip of Greenland from a large island south of it called Desolation. The origin of this notion is discussed in the epilogue of the 1610 voyage.

4. Asher identifies this as Breyde Fiord (mostly called Brede Bay on English maps). It is a large bay on the west coast of Iceland (65°20'N latitude, 23'00W longitude), where hot springs rise from the bottom of the sea.

5. The Englishman referred to was Captain John Weymouth, whose chart from his 1602 voyage Hudson had received from Peter Plancius.

6. Jacques Cartier encountered icebergs of similar size that reached to equally great depths in Grand Bay (Bay of St. Lawrence). A letter by the Cardinal of Seville to the Spanish Emperor reads, in part: "In Terra Nova the country is very cold, so much so that not until June is it possible to navigate or to enter Grand Bay because of the snow and cold and ice, and the mountains of ice which touch the bottom of the sea, through 100 fathoms deep." (Public Archives of Canada — 1930, Pub. #14, p. 462.)

7. These two capes on the opposite side of the strait were named after Sir Dudley Diggs and John Wolstenholme, two of the major contributors to the cost of fitting out the ship.

8. Both of these men died later, on the return voyage to England, when they were attacked by "savages."

9. This is Resolution Island, off the southeastern cape of Baffin Island.

10. In the various roles of a ship's crew, the trumpet [trumpeter] attended the

captain's command. He sounded the announcement of going ashore and returning aboard the vessel. He also announced the entertainment of strangers, as well as charging, boarding or entering another ship. His designated duty spot was the poop deck.

11. This seemingly unfitting designation for the Discovery was given by Samuel Purchas.

12. This Richard Hakluyt was a cousin to his namesake, the famous historian and collector of journals, logbooks and discoveries of England's mariners.

13. The publication of this did not occur until 1625, when it appeared in *Purchas His Pilgrimes* by Samuel Purchas.

14. That it was Captain John Smith referred to, we learn from E. Van Meteren (Dutch Counsel in London) in his *Historie der Nederlandern*, 1614.

Bibliography

Allen, John L. "The Indrawing Sea: Imagination and Search for the Northwest Passage," 1497–1632. Paper presented at Portland, Maine, International Conference on Norumbega, December 2 and 3, 1989.

Asher, G.M. *Henry Hudson the Navigator— The Original Documents in which his Career is Recorded, Partly Translated, and Annotated.* Originally published by the Hakluyt Society, 1855. Reprinted by Burt Franklin Publishing, New York, 1964.

Bagrow, Leo. *History of Cartography*, Revised and Enlarged by R.A. Skelton. Cambridge, Massachussets: Harvard University Press, 1964.

Barnouw, A.J. *The Making of Modern Holland—A Short History.* New York: W.W. Norton & Company, Inc., 1944.

Biggar, Henry Percival. *A Collection of Documents Relating to Jacques Cartier and the Sieur de Roberval.* Publication of Public Archives of Canada, Pub. #14., 1930.

Blacke, Jeanette D. "Mapping the English Colonies; from *The Compleat Plattmaker: Essays on Chart, Map, and Globe Making in England in the Seventeenth and Eighteenth Centuries*, Norman J.W. Thrower, editor. Berkeley: University of California Press, 1978.

Boyle, Robert H. *The Hudson River: A Natural and Unnatural History.* New York: W.W. Norton & Co., 1969.

Brereton, John. *A Briefe and True Relation of the Discoverie of the North Part of Virginia.* Originally published 1602. Reproduced in facsimile by Dodd, Mead & Company, 1903.

Bricker, Charles. *Landmarks of Mapmaking—an Illustrated Survey of Maps and Mapmakers.* Amsterdam: Elsevier, 1968.

Bruce, Wallace. *The Hudson—Three Centuries of History, Romance and Invention.* New York: Walking News, Inc., 1982.

Bryant, William Cullen, and Gray, Sydney Howard. *A Popular History of the United States—From the First Discovery of the Western Hemisphere by the Northmen, to the End of the First Century of the Union of the States*, Vol. I. New York: Scribner, Armstrong, & Co., 1876.

Cole, Rufus. *Human History—The Seventeenth Century and the Stuart Family*, Vol. II. Freeport, Maine: The Bond Wheelwright Company, 1959.

Ewen, C. L'Estrange. *The Northwest Passage: Light on the Murder of Henry Hudson from Unpublished Depositions.* London: Printed for the Author, 1938.

Gosch, C.C.A., editor. *Danish Arctic Expeditions, 1605–1620.* In Two Books: Book I, *The Danish Expeditions to Greenland*; Book II, *The Expedition of Captain Jens Munk.* Works issued by the Hakluyt Society, First Series No. 7., 1897.

Hartwig, G. *The Polar & Tropical Worlds: A Description of Man and Nature in the Polar and Equatorial Regions of the Globe.* Chicago: C.A. Nichols & Co., 1875.

Hudson-Fulton Celebration Commission. Report Submitted. New York: 1910.

Irving, Washington. *The Life and Voyages of Christopher Columbus — to which are added those of his Companions*, Vol. I. New York: G.P. Putnam; Hurd & Houghton, 1865.

Johnson, Donald S. "Henry Hudson and the *Halve Maen*," *Maine Coastal News*. Brewer, Maine: May 1989.

Manwayring, Henry. *The Seaman's Dictionary*, from *A Collection of Facsimile Reprints*. Originally published in 1644. Menston, England: The Scholar Press, Limited, 1972.

Miller, Samuel. "A Discourse Designed to Commemorate the Discovery of New York by Henry Hudson, Being the Completion of the Second Century since that Event," Vol. I. Delivered before the New York Historical Society, September 4, 1809. New York: Collections of the New York Historical Society, 1811.

Morison, Samuel Eliot, *The Great Explorers — The European Discovery of America*, Oxford: Oxford University Press, 1978.

Murphy, Henry C. "The Representation of New Netherland, Concerning its Location, Productiveness and Poor Condition." From Collections of the New York Historical Society, Second Series, Vol. II. New York: Printed for the Society, 1849.

Murphy, Henry C. *Henry Hudson in Holland — An Inquiry into the Origin and Objects of the Voyage which led to the Discovery of the Hudson River*. Reprinted from 1859 original edition in University of Illinois at Urbana, Library. New York: Lenox Hill Pub. & Distrib. Co., 1972.

Nordenskiöld, A.E. *Facsimile Atlas to the Early History of Cartography — with Reproductions of the most Important Maps Printed in the XV and XVII Centuries*. Originally published in Stockholm, 1889. New York: Reprinted by Dover Publications, Inc., 1973.

Portugal/Brazil: The Age of Atlantic Discoveries." From book accompanying exhibition of same name, New York City Public Library. New York: Brazilian Cultural Foundation, 1990.

Powys, Llewelyn. *Henry Hudson*, The Golden Hind Series. New York: Harper & Brothers Publishers, 1928.

Purchas, Samuel. *Purchas His Pilgrimes — in Five Books, The Third Part, Voyages and Discoveries of the North Parts of the World, by land and Sea, in Asia, Europe, the Polare Regions, and in the North-west of America*. London: 1625.

Quinn, David Beers. *England and the Discovery of America, 1481–1620 — From the Bristol Voyages of the 15th Century to the Pilgrim Settlement at Plymouth: The Exploration, Exploitation, and Trial-and-Error Colonization of North America by the English*. New York: Alfred A. Knopf, 1974.

Read, John Meredith, Jr. "A Historical Inquiry Concerning Henry Hudson, his Friends, Relatives and Early Life, his Connection with the Muscovy Company and Discovery of Delaware Bay." Delivered at Wilmington, Delaware, before the Historical Society of Delaware on its first anniversary. Albany, New York: 1866.

Singer, Dorothea Waley. *Giordano Bruno — His Life and Thought: With Annotated*

Translation of His Work On the Infinite Universe and Worlds. New York: Henry Schuman, 1950.

Smith, John. *Description of New England: or The Observations, and Discoveries of Captain John Smith (Admirall of that Country) in the North of America, in the year of our Lord 1614: with the success of sixe ships, that went the next yeare 1615; and the accidents befell him among the French men of warre: With the proofe of the present benefit this Countrey affoords: whither this present yeare, 1616, eight voluntary Ships are gone to make further tryall*. London: Humfrey Lownes, 1616. Reprinted (with a facsimile of the Original Map) Boston: William Veazie, 1865.

Smith, John. *The generall Historie of Virginia, New England, & the Summer Isles — The Third Book. In Travels and Works of Captain John Smith, President of Virginia, and Admiral of New England, 1580–1631*; Edward Arber, editor. Edinburgh: Oliver & Boyd Printers, 1910.

Smith, John. *A Sea Grammar*. London: John Haviland Press, 1627. Reproduction copy published in Amsterdam: Theatrum Orbis Terrarum, Ltd., 1968.

Stevenson, Edward Luther. *Terrestrial and Celestial Globes: Their History and Construction, Including a Consideration of their Value as Aids in the Study of Geography and Astronomy*. New Haven: Yale University Press, 1921.

Taylor, E.G.R. *Tudor Geography — 1485–1583*. London: Methuen & Co., Ltd., 1930.

The Three Voyages of Martin Frobisher — in Search of a Passage to Cathia and India by the North-west, A.D. 1576–78. Reprinted from the 1578 first edition of Hakluyt's Voyages, with selections from manuscript documents in the British Museum and State Paper Office. London: Printed by H. Bynnyman, 1867.

Waters, D.W. *The Art of Navigation in England in Elizabethan and Early Stuart Times*. New Haven: Yale University Press, 1958.

Winsor, Justin. *Narrative and Critical History of America*, Vol. I. Boston: Houghton, Mifflin and Company — The Riverside Press, 1889.

Index

Motter, Adrian, 153, 171, 175, 176, 183, 184, 185, 191, 197,198
Mount Hekla, 157
Mount of God's Mercy, 26, 28, 44
Muscovy Company, 21, 24, 44, 46, 48, 51, 73, 77, 85
Mutiny, 55, 128–129, 152, 173–200

Nantucket, 107, 143, 144
Netherlands. *See* Holland
Newfoundland, 13, 16, 46, 96, 97, 142, 209
Newland. *See* Spitzbergen
New Netherland, 144, 213
New York Bay, 14, 88, 117
New York Historical Society, xiv
Nicholas V, pope, 9
North Bluff, 163
North Cape, Norway, 48, 57, 72, 90
Northeast Passage, search for, 87, 129, 137, 138, 147, 211
  Barents's voyages, 47–48, 76, 77, 79, 80
  Hudson's 1608 voyage, 51–73
  maps of, 74–81
  rumors and fables in, 51–52
North Pole, 20, 24, 138
Northwest Passage, search for, 1
  coastline explorations in, 12–17
  Davis's voyages, 18, 75–76, 205–210
  Frobisher's voyages, 18, 75–76, 202–205
  Hudson's 1607 voyage, 22, 23, 24–46
  Hudson's 1609 voyage, 87–148
  Hudson's 1610 voyage, 149–202
  maps of, 133–138, 203, 204–205, 207–210
  overland routes, 145–146
  polar routes, 17–21, 22, 23, 24–26, 149–210
  Weymouth's voyages, 140–142, 210–211
Norumbega, 134
Nova Scotia, 101, 142
Nova Zembla, 48, 51, 53–54, 63, 66–67, 69, 74, 77, 79, 87

Orkney Islands, 154, 157
Ortelius, Abraham, 49, 52, 75

Peekskill, 125
Penobscot Bay, 141
Perse, Michael, 153, 171, 175, 179, 183, 184, 185, 198
Philip II, king of Spain, 82, 84
Piracy, xvi
Plancius, Peter, 20, 48, 52, 75, 130, 135–137, 147, 191, 211

Plato, 1–2
Playse, John, 25, 34
Pliny, 4
Pontanus, 77
Popham, George, 132
Portugal, 1, 84, 139, 140
  decline of, 82
  division of New World, 9–12
  explorations of African coast, 8
Poughkeepsie, 124–125
Powys, Llewelyn, xv, 193, 201
Prickett, Abacuk, 152, 153, 157, 191, 192, 195–196, 197, 198–199, 200, 201
Prince Henry's Cape, 162
Principal Navigations, The (Hakluyt), xiii
Privateering, xvi
Ptolemy, Claudius, 3, 5
Purchas His Pilgrimes (Purchas), xiii, xvii, 24, 55, 89, 153
Purchas, Samuel, xiii, xvii, 24, 34, 55, 89, 143, 153, 194, 211
Pythagoras, 3–4

Queen Elizabeth's Foreland, 134, 203, 209

Raleigh, Walter, 145
Raynor, Robert, 55, 60
Red Hook, 124
Regiment for the Sea, A (Bourne), 16, 17
Resolution, 201
Resolution Island, 155, 159, 203
Ribero, Juan, 12
River Ob, 51, 80
Roanoke colony, 145
Romanus pontifex (papal bull), 9
Rosier, James, 141, 142, 211
Russia, 21
Ruysch, Johannes, 5, 75, 76

Sable Bank, 99
Sagadahoc River, 132
Saguanay, 134
St. George River, 101, 141
St. Lawrence Gulf, 16–17, 209
St. Lawrence River, 17, 134, 209
Salisbury Island, 156, 163
Sanderson, William, 137, 207
Sandy Hook, 115
Senjen Island, 91
Siberia, 80
Silk trade, 7
Simmes, Nicholas, 153, 173, 176, 197